HV 551.2 .A68 1994

Aptekar, Lewis.

Environmental disasters in
global perspective.

DATE DUE

NOV 0 6 1997		
DEC 0 9 1997		
FEB 1 0 1998		

DEMCO 38-297

ENVIRONMENTAL DISASTERS IN GLOBAL PERSPECTIVE

SOCIAL ISSUES IN GLOBAL PERSPECTIVE

David Levinson
Melvin Ember
General Editors

The Social Issues in Global Perspective series is prepared under the auspices and with the support of the Human Relations Area Files at Yale University. HRAF, the foremost international research organization in the field of cultural anthropology, is a not-for-profit consortium of twenty-two sponsoring members and 300 participating member institutions in twenty-five countries. The HRAF archive, established in 1949, contains nearly one million pages of information on the cultures of the world.

Environmental Disasters in Global Perspective

Lewis Aptekar

G.K. HALL & CO.
An Imprint of Macmillan Publishing Company
NEW YORK

Maxwell Macmillan Canada
TORONTO

Maxwell Macmillan International
NEW YORK   OXFORD   SINGAPORE   SYDNEY

G.K. Hall & Co.
An Imprint of Macmillan Publishing Company
866 Third Avenue
New York, NY 10022

Maxwell Macmillan Canada, Inc.
1200 Eglinton Avenue East
Suite 200
Don Mills, Ontario M3C 3N1

Macmillan Publishing Company is part of the Maxwell Communication Group of Companies

Library of Congress Catalog Card Number 93-12836

Printed in the United States of America

Printing Number
1   2   3   4   5   6   7   8   9   10

Library of Congress Cataloging-in-Publication Data
Aptekar, Lewis.
    Environmental disasters in global perspective / Lewis Aptekar.
       p. cm. — (Social issues in global perspective)
    Includes bibliographical references and index.
    ISBN 0-8161-7381-8 (hc : acid-free paper). — ISBN 0-8161-1608-3
    (pb : acid-free paper)
    1. Emergency management. 2. Disasters—Psychological aspects.
    3. Disaster relief. 4. Disaster victims—Psychology. I. Title.
    II. Series.
    HV551.2.A68 1994
    363.3'4—dc20   93-12836
                                                                                CIP

The paper used in this publication meets the minimum requirements of American National Standard for Information Sciences—Permanence of Paper for Printed Library Materials. ANSI Z39.48-1984 ⊚ ™

I dedicate this book to my daughter, Rachel Tenney, who came into this world during my travails of writing the manuscript, and who in her wisdom crumpled, scribbled, and threw the papers that later became the pages of this book. I thank her for editing and for the smiles she brings me.

Contents

Acknowledgments

I began to study disasters somewhat late in my professional life. I had already spent a decade studying street children in Latin America. As a result of this work I was awarded a Kellogg Fellowship in International Development by Partners of the Americas. As part of this fellowship I had the opportunity to "learn something new" in my field. I chose to learn about people's reactions to disasters. I attended the annual conference of the Natural Hazards Research and Information Center at the University of Colorado. I was encouraged to continue my studies and, with the Partner's help and some assistance from the National Science Foundation, to work with the victims of Hurricane Hugo. The day before I was to leave on this project, an earthquake occurred in California. The epicenter could be seen from the front porch of my house. Again I found myself helping other victims, this time in my own backyard.

During this period a long-time friend and mentor, Marshall Segall, gave me the opportunity to study in Geneva. I spent considerable time in the Institut Henry Dunant, the research center of the International Red Cross, where I was given great help and treated with much affability by the director, Dr. Jeri Toman. I also owe a great deal to Ingrid Nillson, director of library services at the United Nations Disaster Relief Organization (UNDRO).

As my work in disaster studies widened I became more interested in cross-cultural differences and similarities in people's response to disasters. I want to thank Mel Ember, president of the Human Relations

Area Files, who has continually encouraged me to think of disasters as a world problem and to study the effects of culture on disaster victims.

While writing this book, I was helped considerably by Susan McArthur and Alan Boye who read, suggested changes, reread, and suggested yet more changes in the multitude of drafts I gave them to review.

In addition, I also want to thank many others whom I have not mentioned simply because of space, for their encouragement, insight, and support.

Introduction

Throughout the day of September 22, 1989, televised weather reports showed Hurricane Hugo steadily approaching the coast of South Carolina. As the storm drew closer, almost a fifth of the 5,000 residents of McClellanville, South Carolina, went to Lincoln High School, the town's designated shelter. The school was a mile and a half from the sea, but only twenty and one-half feet above sea level.

As night fell, the school principal directed the 1,125 townspeople who had sought shelter into three areas of the school building: the cafeteria, the gymnasium, and the home economics room. The cafeteria was soon filled with 200 families, more than 500 individuals in all. Concerned that people would continue to stream into the cafeteria, the principal ordered the doors to that room locked, ensuring that no one could enter but inadvertently making those inside virtual prisoners in protective custody.

As they waited for the tidal surge to hit, the power went out, leaving them without light (Aptekar, 1991). The winds, reaching nearly 140 miles per hour, were so fierce they broke loblolly pine trees in half and uprooted two-century-old live oaks. Trees in nearby 250,000-acre Marion National Forest were flattened, leaving a billion board feet of lumber on the ground (Graham, 1990).

At 11:50 that night the tidal surge of approximately eighteen feet began to overtake the school. The huge surge of water burst the air conditioning units at the base of the cafeteria walls, and water began pouring into the building. Within minutes it was knee-high and rising. When the water came up to their waists, the storm refugees knew they would have to find a way to get above it or drown. Desperately, work-

1

ing in absolute darkness, they were able to maneuver tables onto the cafeteria stage, constructing their own high ground.

But the water continued to rise, forcing the people on the stage to put chairs on top of the tables in their last-ditch effort to escape the flood. Still the water rose. Thirty minutes after the air-conditioning units had broken and the water had begun pouring in, it had reached chest level, even for those who had climbed as high as they possibly could.

There was nowhere left to go. Standing on chairs, atop the tables on the cafeteria stage, parents lifted their children over their heads in an effort to keep them above the steadily advancing water. Paula, a young thirty-three-year-old mother, said, "I gave my daughter a last goodbye, never expecting to see her again."

Then, miraculously, forty-five minutes after the tidal surge began, the water stopped rising. Stacked together like the fish they packed in the local fisheries, water up to their chests and without light, these two hundred families had withstood the flood. The water rose to the height of their chests, peaked, and receded slowly throughout the night. By morning, people were still knee-deep in water.

There are lessons to be learned from these and other victims of disasters. In spite of myths to the contrary, disaster victims rarely display panic, mass hysteria, or antisocial behavior such as looting (Drabek & Quarantelli, 1967; Fritz 1957, 1961; Quarantelli 1954, 1957, 1977). Although people are frightened, they seldom act selfishly (Quarantelli, 1988). Often their behavior is quite rational. An example is the McClellanville woman who became separated from her husband in the Lincoln High School during Hurricane Hugo. She had the medicine he needed for his heart condition but she could not see him in the pitch-black darkness of the building. By calling her husband's name and hearing his response, she was able to locate him by the sound of his voice, and with the help of people standing between them, she passed him the prescription bottle.

Myths about Disaster Victims

Stories of this type notwithstanding, there is a common misconception that disaster victims act irrationally. Evidence does not support this perception, however, even for one of the most terrifying of environmental disasters, earthquakes. Earthquakes are particularly distressing; not only do they come without warning, but because of the after-shocks, victims never know when they will end. This uncertainty causes earthquake victims to remain under stress for long periods of time. In spite of the trauma caused by this type of disaster, study results confirm that even in earthquakes people act rationally, and these results hold across many different countries: Italy (Mileti & Nigg, 1984), the United States (Aptekar, 1990, 1991; Stein, 1974), Nicaragua (Kates et al., 1973), Guatemala (Olson & Olson, 1977), and Japan (Takuma, 1972).

Generally, the behavior of victims in any emergency is quite similar, whether these are environmental or other types of situations. Several studies of victims caught in a fire showed that they, too, responded in a rational manner (Weisaeth, 1983). They went to the exits if they knew where they were; and if they did not, they followed others. They did not stampede or run over each other; in fact, they did much to help each other. Similar findings have been obtained in other disasters of close quarters such as airplane crashes (Butcher, 1980) and movie theater fires (Silber, Perry, & Bloch, 1957). This behavior is cross-cultural, as found in studies in Japan (Yamamoto & Quarantelli, 1982) and in France (Chandessais, 1980). Similar cross-cultural examples of rational behavior following disasters can be found in the work of Mileti, Drabek, and Haas (1975), who have reviewed the literature concerning behavior of disaster victims.

Of course, there will be panic in some situations, but Fritz (1957) postulated that this would occur only in certain circumstances. If victims felt immediate and severe danger, found there were few if any escape routes, perceived that these were quickly becoming closed, and had no idea of what else to do to save their lives, then circumstances would be ripe for panic. Yet, even in the most dire emergencies, panic does not necessarily occur. The McClellanville residents trapped in Lincoln High School did not lose their heads. These victims displayed behavior that had a clear sense of purpose and was directed toward the common good.

Rational behavior in desperate circumstances is also not limited to adults, as shown by the American story of twenty-six elementary school children who were kidnaped from their school bus (Terr, 1981a, 1981b). Their ordeal began when three men wearing ski masks held their bus driver at gun point and transferred the children into two vans—one for the older children, the other for the younger. The windows in the vans were painted, and the children were driven around for eleven hours in total darkness without food, water, or an opportunity to go to the bathroom. Their kidnappers eventually buried the bus with the children in it; they remained underground for sixteen hours. At the end of this time they escaped by the efforts of two children, aged fourteen and ten, who worked together in very cramped quarters to dig their way out. A third child held a flashlight for them while a few others looked after the youngest children. As frightened as they all were, they did not panic (Terr, 1990).

Another myth is that people will loot during a disaster, particularly if homes are destroyed, the agencies in charge of public order are spread thin, and merchandise in stores is exposed. Contrary to that concept, large-scale looting is rare after any disaster (Kasperson & Pijawka, 1985; Quarantelli & Dynes, 1972, 1976, 1977). In fact, the presence or lack of looting has been used to distinguish between environmental disasters and civil disturbances. After disasters, communities forego, at least for a short time, the notion of private property when they seek to restore the community. Thus, if it is in the common good, some private property might be used publicly if the owner agrees (such as large homes given over to housing people whom the owner !oes not know) and some public property might be used privately (victims being housed temporarily in public buildings). These changes are often done with goodwill, which when coupled with other examples of altruism such as feeding victims and offering them transportation or money to buy necessities, helps to explain why looting is uncommon after disasters.

Even when looting does follow a disaster, it is different from what occurs in a civil disturbance. Looting after disasters is done by individuals acting privately and without political reasons. In civil disturbances it is done by groups, acting publicly, often giving political justifications for their actions (Quarantelli & Dynes, 1976). In these disturbances private property norms are upended. Those without private property claim that racial prejudice or class bias has unjustly meant that they have been discriminated against. As a result they claim the right to take over the land of others who they feel got the land because of these or other injustices and thus looting is much more common (Drabek, 1986).

Some observers hypothesize that looting in response to environmental disasters occurs when there are severe differences in economic status within the society and there is an authoritarian government. This is how Drabek (1987) and Kates et al. (1973) explain the rioting that followed the 1972 Managua earthquake and the lack of rioting following all environmental disasters in the United States.

When people do fear looting, however, they are far less likely to evacuate their homes (Dynes & Quarantelli, 1976a; Perry, Lindell, & Greene, 1981). This conclusion is not isolated to the United States. After the 1976 Guatemalan earthquake many people refused to leave their animals and homes because of the fear of being robbed if they left their possessions unguarded (Bates & Killian, 1982).

Another myth is that disasters are followed by epidemics. After the Guatemalan earthquake, rumors spread that there were outbreaks of hepatitis, measles, dysentery, and typhus (Spencer et al., 1977). In fact, there were no epidemics. In Southeast Asia such rumors led to the influx of large amounts of aid for diseases that were not a threat (Shaw, 1979). Because of this misconception, generating appropriate aid sometimes becomes a problem (Drabek, 1986).

For an epidemic to occur, either the disaster must introduce a disease into the community where there is no immunity to it, or the population must become more susceptible to diseases due to malnutrition. The major reason epidemics are associated with disasters is not because of the disasters per se, but because of the poor health that accompanies poor nutrition (Paulozzi, 1980). Nutrition can be a problem if the disaster is great enough to disrupt food distribution for an extended period of time.

An additional myth is that people will flee from the disaster site. In fact, the opposite is the case. Rather than fleeing, victims are likely not to want to leave. Many more people actually come into the disaster area than leave it. People who are not victims come into the area to see the damage or to offer help. This widespread convergence of people to disaster areas is known as the "convergence phenomenon" and has been reported in the United States (Fritz, 1957), in Italy (Boilcau et al., 1978), in Canada (Scanlon, 1980), and in Australia (Wettenhall, 1979a, 1979b).

In the aftermath of a disaster, communication needs are very high, in great part because people want to get in touch with their families to share information about the extent of damage. Thus, instead of fleeing, many victims remain, deciding that this is the best way to keep their families intact. Such behavior has been seen in a comparative study between the United States and Italy (Mileti & Nigg, 1984) and following the Managua, Nicaragua, earthquake (Kates et al., 1973).

Immediately after a disaster, there is certainly great disruption and misery. Some victims are in a state of temporary shock, manifested by their mental confusion, increased non-goal–oriented behavior, withdrawal, or some combination of these. But another phenomenon is often also evident: helpfulness. Cross-cultural evidence suggests that immediately after a disaster the desire to help other people is very strong. Disaster studies in Australia (Leivesley, 1977), France (Chandessais, 1980), Belgium (Lechat, 1976), Cyprus (Loizos, 1977), Italy (Boileau et al., 1978), and Japan (Nakamura, 1981) all have reported a strong desire among people to help each other in extraordinary ways at these times.

The degree to which a community believes the myths of how people will respond to disasters (that individuals will loot, panic, and become hysterical; that communities will fall apart or become hostile) is particularly important because it often determines the reaction of officials. People in charge of warning systems who believe that panic and looting are associated with the first response to disasters often delay warning the community. A comparative study of two border towns along the Rio Grande river suffering from the same flood showed that Mexican authorities did not issue a warning because they believed that doing so would produce panic, making the flood itself more difficult to deal with (Clifford, 1956). Similar behavior was found among officials in Italy when Florence was facing flooding (Quarantelli, 1977), and in Japan after a volcano erupted (Hirose, 1979). Fortunately, authorities in some communities with disaster experience are less likely to believe these myths; on the other hand, many continue to maintain their belief in spite of their experience to the contrary (Wenger, Thomas, & Faupel, 1985).

Disasters in the Developing World

Regardless of how a community reacts to them, environmental disasters, with their attendant human suffering, are a global phenomenon occurring with great frequency. It is expected that in the 1990s the planet will experience a million thunderstorms, 100,000 floods, tens of thousands of earthquakes, wildfires, landslides and tornadoes, and several hundred to a few thousand hurricanes, some as powerful as the one that hit McClellanville (Hays, 1990).

While the citizens of McClellanville endured a frightening ordeal, had they been living in the developing world, their fate would almost certainly have been worse. For each disaster-related death in places such as South Carolina, there are fifteen such deaths in the developing world (Kent, 1987; Tiranti, 1977). Ninety-five percent of human loss from environmental disasters occurs in the less developed countries (Ball, 1979; Kent, 1987). The number of disasters that affect large parts of the earth's population is increasing, and those that have long-term ecological effects and cause deaths are also becoming more frequent (Dworkin, 1974). In 1965, 15 percent of all disasters affected 100,000 or more people; in 1985 the figure rose to 45 percent because more people became vulnerable to environmental hazards (Kent 1987).

More and more, the developing nations must bear the brunt of environmental disasters (Shah, 1983; Taylor, 1979; Wisner, O'Keefe, & Westgate, 1977). The heavy burden does not fall on the developing world because the physical events that cause environmental disasters have changed; for the most part, they have maintained a regularity for millennia. The massive toll is because people in the developing world are becoming more vulnerable to environmental events. This is a tangential but important contributing factor to the increasing gap between rich and poor nations.

One reason for their heightened vulnerability is that more people in developing countries, particularly the poor of these countries, live on land that is increasingly susceptible to damage from climatic events. This phenomenon can be seen by any visitor to Rio de Janeiro who looks at the surrounding steep hillside slopes crowded with slum dwellings. Every rainy season, these huts are in danger of being lost in a landslide. Another example of vulnerability can been seen in the Bay of Bengal, where migrant farmers work the "chars," fertile flat lands of silt left by the floods. By living and working in areas certain to be flooded again, the Bengalis are gambling everything—their homes, their livelihood, and all their worldly possessions—in an effort to reap the economic rewards that farming this rich land provides.

It is estimated that in Guayaquil, Ecuador, 60 percent of the city's population of over a million live in the Guasmo, a shantytown built directly over tidal swampland. The bamboo houses are placed on stilts. To go between homes, people must walk over floating timber catwalks. When the seasonal rains come, the toilets and sinks back up, oozing waste into people's homes. The inhabitants of Guasmo are extremely vulnerable to floods and storms.

A typical example of low economic status and natural events combining for a disastrous situation in the developing world was demonstrated in Honduras in 1974 when Hurricane Fifi hit. In the decade prior to 1974, large foreign interests had bought up the fertile bottom land in Honduras to grow bananas for export. The rural poor were forced to live on the steep surrounding hillsides. To build their homes they cut down trees, leaving the slopes even less capable of holding water. For these peasants, "development" meant a change from raising their own subsistence crops to growing cash crops. It also meant they joined the money economy, and eventually that they lost their jobs as agricultural workers for cash crop farmers. They were also forced by economic necessity to live on land that was environmentaly hazardous. When Hurricane Fifi came, 5,000 Honduran peasants perished when they were swept off the slopes by the mudslides. Those who did not lose their lives were soon starving; they could not grow their own food because they no longer had the fertile land to grow it on, nor could they buy their food because they no longer had the jobs that earned them the cash to buy it. Thus, their economic vulnerability directly exacerbated their physical situation (Snarr & Brown, 1984).

The strength of Hurricane Fifi was almost identical to that of Cyclone Tracy, which hit Darwin, Australia, in the same year. Only forty-nine people were killed in Australia, however. The difference was the Australians' better economic base, which allowed them to build less vulnerable houses, place the houses in less hazardous locations, and develop adequate warning systems (Susman, O'Keefe, & Wisner, 1983).

Not only do the poor in the developing world live in vulnerable areas but they also live in homes that are prone to environmental disasters. A 1976 earthquake in Tangsham, China, killed 250,000 people, in large part because they lived in top-heavy adobe homes; in comparison, the 1989 Loma Prieta, California, earthquake of comparable intensity killed only sixty-five (Comfort, 1990).

A comparison between Tokyo, Japan, and Managua, Nicaragua, two cities that are prone to earthquakes, is illustrative of relative vulnerability to natural disasters. Tokyo has a strict building code. In Managua many people, particularly the poor, live on hillsides in dangerous adobe homes. Between 1960 and 1980 Japan suffered forty-three disasters, losing, on average, sixty-three people per disaster; in Nicaragua there were seventeen disasters, with an average loss of 6,235 people per disaster (Hagman, 1984). Nicaragua's average death rate is even more striking compared with that of the United States. Records from the American Red Cross indicate that between 1960 and 1976 the average American disaster caused the death of a single person, injured a dozen, and caused the destruction of fewer than five buildings (Rossi, J. Wright, S. Wright, & Weber-Burdin, 1983).

Evidence that the effects of environmental disasters are disproportionately borne by the world's poor shows that there is more to the severity of environmental disasters than the random chance of extreme climatic events. The physical event is only the trigger that might or might not unleash a disaster. It is the phenomena of vulnerability, as the preceding examples illustrate, that determine the extent of a disaster. To understand disasters one must study the interaction between human behavior and nature, the relationship between people and their environment, and the ways the physical event interacts with social, political, and economic factors.

In short, the study of environmental disasters goes beyond the parameters of the natural science of earthquakes, floods, hurricanes, tsunamis, drought, and so on to the larger field of human environmental interactions. The largest concern of disaster research, from the global perspective, is not how to deal more effectively with each isolated disaster, no matter how severe it might be, but rather to understand and interpret the interconnectedness of disasters with other social problems. Environmental disasters are linked to political factors, and almost any environmental disaster in the developing world can mean the end of the social order in the society where it occurs.

To understand fully the cause of the disasters in the Bay of Bengal, for example, one must take into account the deforestation that makes each of the five river basins draining into the bay more susceptible to flooding. The economic reasons for this deforestation must also be weighed, and we must consider the cultures of the Muslim and Hindu peoples living along these rivers as well as their long-standing political conflicts. Without knowledge of these multiple factors, the cause of the disasters in the Bay of Bengal cannot be fully understood.

In the following chapters, several factors that increase people's vulnerability to natural disasters will be illustrated. First, in a global perspective, environmental disasters are very much a part of everyday life. They occur frequently and people have changed their lives to cope with them. Additionally, the way people in the developing world interact with their governments may increase their susceptibility to environmental disasters. Additionally, because many people in the developing world do not have the ability to influence decisions made by their governments, many of the poor have become poorer and more vulnerable to natural disasters. For example, in many cases governments choose to develop land for industrialization, a decision that forces the poor to move onto land that is so poor it will not support crops, making these people very susceptible to environmental disasters

A second factor is that as people engage in everyday acts, such as farming, cutting wood for fire and heat, and selecting materials and sites for building homes, they radically change their vulnerability to environmental disasters. Certain farming techniques lead to erosion of top soil, which increases droughts and flooding; adobe homes are much more susceptible to earthquakes than other types of construction; and building on flood plains or near volcanoes invariably increases vulnerability. This behavior is often dictated by economic reasons and people's struggle for survival.

A third factor is the nature of disaster relief, which can increase a community's vulnerability in two ways. First, it focuses on providing immediate help to victims and communities, not to remediating the causes of disasters. Second, aid often makes people less able to cope on their own and more dependent on outside help. This dependency often causes them to become isolated from their traditional way of life and their accustomed community.

Finally, a community's level of economic development is tied closely to people's vulnerability to disasters. The poorest people are the most vulnerable. To make them less so they need more than disaster aid; they need a broader type of assistance that enables them to become less impoverished.

Traditionally, disasters have been seen as the cause of other problems. For example, homelessness was considered the result of an earthquake or flood. More recently, disasters have been viewed as the result of social problems that first set the stage for a violently disruptive event. Lack of funds or the misappropriation of public funds can increase poverty. Poor people, in turn, cannot afford to build houses of disaster-resistant material; often the only building sites available to them are vulnerable locations.

This set of all too common circumstances in the developing world actually increases an area's susceptibility to disasters. It is this vulnerability caused by political, economic, and social factors that transforms a normal, recurring climatic event into a human disaster.

1

Defining Environmental Disasters

Quick Onset Disasters

The interaction between human factors and physical triggers (environmental events that may or may not trigger an actual disaster) is the perspective from which environmental disaster is defined here, a task that is more difficult than it appears. Historically, environmental disasters have included earthquakes, tsunamis, volcanic eruptions, floods, and storms.

In some ways, earthquakes are the prototypical disaster. One of the first recorded earthquakes is in the Bible. Psalm 114 says the "mountains skipped like rams, and the little hills like lambs." For as long as there have been earthquakes, human beings have tried to predict them in order to lessen their impact, but no system has proved reliable. From the high technology of the developed world to the ancient practice of watching nature for signs (chickens roosting in trees, farm animals showing distress), still used in places such as China, earthquakes have defied prediction.

In 1935 Charles Richter devised a scale to measure the energy of earthquakes. The scale is logarithmic; each increase of a full number is equal to ten times the energy of the lower number. An earthquake that measures 7.8 on the Richter scale is ten times as strong as a 6.8 earthquake, and a hundred times stronger than one that measures 5.8 (Verney, 1979). On average, somewhere in the world each year two earthquakes occur that register over 8 on the Richter scale (Wijkman & Timberlake, 1988).

Historically, the most devastating earthquakes, those accounting for more than 100,000 dead, have occurred in Asia, most notably in China. In 1976 the Tangshan earthquake killed nearly a quarter of a million people, injured 160,000 more, and destroyed 98 percent of the city's residences (Maybury, 1986). The earthquake measured 7.8 on the Richter scale.

The number on the Richter scale does not measure the amount of damage. This depends on the density of the population where the earthquake strikes as well as other factors. Differences in population density explain why the Tangshan earthquake was so deadly, while the more powerful 9.1 Alaskan earthquake of 1964 killed only about 100 people. The degree of damage is also affected by the soil and rock conditions under buildings and the types of buildings in which people live. Wood houses withstand earthquakes better than those built of adobe or masonry, which are the two predominant building types in the developing world. Houses built on bedrock do better than those on sedimentary soil.

Earthquakes, as well as under-ocean volcanic eruptions, can cause tsunamis, ocean waves of great size. Possibly the first recorded tsunami was in 1500 B.C.E. and completely annihilated the Minoan civilization.

Any earthquake-prone location that is next to the sea is particularly vulnerable to tsunamis. More than sixty-five tsunamis have been recorded in Japan, one of which, in 1896, killed 25,000 people (Maybury, 1986). Hilo, Hawaii, was completely destroyed by a tsunami in 1946.

Many tsunamis begin with a gentle swelling of the sea above its normal high tide. The tide increases so that when the sea retreats, the force takes the water farther out than normal. This process continues, growing in strength, until eventually a wave comes ashore at a speed of more than 100 miles per hour. The water stays on land far longer than normal waves do. When it withdraws it creates an enormous vacuum, making a huge sound as if a gigantic plunger were being pulled, and sucks everything in its wake out to sea. Fishermen who are at sea sometimes are not even aware of the waves building beneath them. Historic accounts tell of them returning to shore to find that their villages have been completely destroyed by a tsunami (Pararas-Carayannis, 1986).

An equally destructive force is the eruption of volcanoes. Two-thirds of the world's people live in a volcanic area referred to as the "ring of fire." This area surrounds the Pacific Ocean and includes Japan, the west coast of the Americas from Alaska to Chile, the islands in the Pacific including Hawaii, and the east coast of China (Wijkman & Timberlake, 1988).

Volcanic eruptions are difficult to predict, as demonstrated by the recent explosions of Mount St. Helens and the volcano in Armero, Colombia. People could avoid the threat by not living near volcanoes, but the land surrounding them is highly fertile and populations concentrate on such soils. In many tropical parts of the earth, volcanic areas may be the only places where there is rich soil. That is why, for example, the majority of people in Indonesia live in these vulnerable areas (Wijkman & Timberlake, 1988).

Volcanic eruptions can also cause other extreme environmental events such as avalanches. A volcanic eruption in Huascaran, Peru, in 1970 caused an avalanche of nearly 80 million tons of snow and ice, which came roaring down the valley at a rate of nearly seventy miles per hour. This avalanche has been described as the greatest geological phenomenon in recorded history (Ebert, 1986).

A third great destroyer is flooding. In the last century nine million people have died in floods (Maybury, 1986). A single flood in 1931 along the Yellow River in China killed almost four million people, the deadliest single environmental disaster in history (Ebert, 1986). In fact, China's Yellow River has caused the death of more people than any single geographical feature on the earth's surface (Wijkman & Timberlake, 1988).

The destructive power of floods is increased by deforestation. When the trees have been stripped from the watershed of rivers such as the Yellow River, rain water flows off the hills rather than soaking into the soil, carrying topsoil and swelling the river beyond its banks. The prevalence of deforestation in the developing world helps to explain why flooding is particularly dangerous there. The Yellow River flows for 2,500 miles through central China. People have harvested the trees near its source for millennia, but for most of this time the rate of tree cutting and the rate of replacement by natural growth were roughly equal. During Mao's Great Leap Forward, however, many forests were clear-cut to provide fuel for steel production and to open fields for planting. Now, because there are no trees to help the soil absorb the water, the rains wash the topsoil into the river. Each year, as more silt is deposited on the riverbed, the water level rises. In attempts to control flooding, the people have built dikes, but these must be continually rebuilt and raised higher to combat the ever-rising riverbed. The result is an ever-increasing strain on existing dams.

By the time the river reaches the Yellow Plain where the majority of the people live, it is almost 45 percent silt. In 1980, for much of the river's course, its level was twenty-five or more feet *above* the level of the fields through which it flowed. Each year over 3,000 square miles are flooded. Any unusual degree of rain can cause severe flooding (Wijkman & Timberlake, 1988).

When the floods recede, they leave behind the rich topsoil brought down by the river as silt. These flood plains are particularly attractive to human settlements because of their fertile lands. Indeed, the great populations of history have lived along such flood plains as those of the Nile, the Ganges, and the Yellow itself. Fifteen percent of the people of Bangladesh live less than ten feet above sea level, many of them on the Brahmaputra-Padma flood plain.

Despite the destructive potential of floods, they are not the most lethal disasters. More devastating than floods, earthquakes, volcanoes, or tsunamis are storms. Called hurricanes in the Atlantic, typhoons in the Pacific, and cyclones in the Indian Ocean, storms are the most lethal of disasters in terms of loss of life. The single cyclone of 1970 that struck Bangladesh killed between 200,000 and 400,000 people (Maybury, 1986).

In addition to high winds, storms also bring rain; because they are accompanied by such a severe reduction of atmospheric pressure, storms cause the seas to rise, producing what is called a storm surge. These surges have been reported to be as high as forty-six feet and they are responsible for many of the deaths. Not only do storms cause fatalities but they can also completely wipe out the economic growth of a developing country for several years (Maybury, 1986).

Storms most often strike in predictable places. In 1737 there was a cyclone and storm surge in the Bay of Bengal that killed 300,000 people. In 1876, in the same spot, 215,000 people were killed by a storm. Again, in 1970, a storm surge killed between 200,000 and 400,000 people there, and in 1991 a storm in that bay killed more than 60,000. After the last two storms people began to resettle the flood plain before the debris was cleared off.

Although this rush to resettle such a disaster-prone area seems suicidal, there are two reasons people in less-developed countries continue to live on the flood plains. First, this land is very fertile, and second people have few alternative places to live (White, 1974). Because of the danger, living on a flood plain is often free; one needs only to "squat." Ironically, there is another enticement: since the land floods regularly, the people who live there are also likely to receive periodic financial assistance, which to the very poor can make the difference between going hungry and having something to eat.

Chronic Disasters

When environmental disasters are considered, often they are thought of singly, and, like the ones discussed thus far, characterized as arriving with little or no warning. This categorization tends to oversimplify what is really a complex interrelation. First, it isolates events that in fact are often combined. Storms and floods often go together, as do earthquakes and avalanches, or volcanoes and mudslides, and earthquakes and tsunamis. The Great Kanto earthquake of 1923 in Japan occurred in the late morning on a clear September day. About 143,000 people were reported to have died in this quake; another 100,000 were injured. The high toll of injured and dead was not directly from the earthquake but from the fires that broke out about an hour after the earthquake, raging for forty hours and destroying almost half of Tokyo. Three hundred seventy thousand houses were lost. The fires caused tornadoes, which were strong enough to carry people off their feet and throw them into buildings. But this was not the end. The earthquake also stirred up the ocean, causing huge tsunami waves that washed away thousands of homes and killed more people (Nakano & Matsuda, 1984).

The second and more severe problem with the traditional categorization of disasters is that it ignores as causes of them chronic situations such as droughts, which are not of rapid onset. This is a serious exclusion because droughts affect more people in the world than any other environmental disaster. In the 1970s more than 24 million people were affected by droughts, compared to about one million from earthquakes (Wijkman & Timberlake, 1988).

Droughts also bring to the forefront the human factor that interacts with the natural events to cause a real disaster. Because poor people in the developing nations are forced to overcultivate, to overgraze, and to deforest, their land becomes more susceptible to droughts. Without trees and other plants to help absorb the water, the rain washes off the topsoil, filling the rivers with silt and making them more likely to flood. With the topsoil washed away, the land is less productive, making famines more likely. Without trees to provide windbreaks, winds also remove the topsoil, drying the land, contributing to its susceptibility to drought.

Lack of trees also increases an area's vulnerability to storms. Over the twenty-year period between 1960 and 1981, the Philippines, a country of middle to high-middle income, suffered thirty-nine violent storms causing about 5,000 deaths. During the same period Bangladesh had thirty-seven cyclones in which nearly 400,000 people died. The difference principally was the deforestation in Bangladesh (Wijkman & Timberlake, 1988). The denuding of the forests in the Himalayas had left that country little windbreak for storms, while the forests in the Philippines protected that nation's citizens.

The highly precipitous slopes of the windward islands in the Caribbean (Dominica, St. Lucia, Grenada, St. Vincent) also have problems with drought. Bananas are cultivated on these steep slopes, which fall abruptly to the sea. Because the woodlands above the slopes have been deforested by the poor of the islands, who need the wood of the trees they cut for fuel for cooking, the rain washes the topsoil into the sea. Only a small amount of good soil is left to nurture the bananas and to hold the moisture they must have to survive. Lack of trees and topsoil has considerably diminished the time period during which the banana crop can survive between rains. If the rains do not come every day, the bananas will dry up. Thus, a drought can come during the rainy season if only a day goes by without rain.

Bananas account for 70 percent of St. Lucia's exports. From 1970 to 1975 over 20 million dollars in the banana crop were lost due to drought. The drought often occurred in the middle of the rainy season (Wijkman & Timberlake, 1988).

The Indian subcontinent, though generally known for its floods, actually has severe problems with drought. Eighty percent of the continent is drought prone. Weather records indicate that until 1983 India had more drought victims (120 million were forced off their land) than any other continent. This was due in large part because of the deforestation of the Himalayas (Wijkman & Timberlake, 1988).

The extensive droughts of the African continent drew little public attention until the early 1980s when British and American television began to show images of people starving. It was at this point that the United Nations Disaster Relief Organization (UNDRO) and the International Red Cross began including droughts on their list of environmental disasters.

Unlike other natural disasters, droughts come about slowly, often over a period of years. Over this extended period of time communities in danger of drought change their way of life to adapt. This can be seen among the Enga who live in the central highlands of New Guinea. During the drought of the 1960s this tribe experienced several years of unusual but not unheard of shortages of rainfall. By oral history each generation informed their children about ways to cope with the lack of rainfall. Thus the Enga developed several strategies for coping. These included planting crops at different times of the year, placing gardens in more drought-resistant places—most commonly by moving them to the areas with more daily dew—planting crops closer together to reduce the need for water, and increasing the tribe's foraging and hunting activities.

When British agricultural experts in the capital labeled the lack of rain a drought, the Enga became eligible for aid. Even though they did not request it, they received foreign assistance. As the relief arrived, the Enga began to abandon their age-old coping skills and soon began preferring foreign goods to what they raised on their own. Waddell (1975, 1983) charted their increasing dependence on aid and on the state, and their reduction of home-grown products in favor of imported consumption patterns. He found that being drought "victims" changed their lives, even more than did the physical event.

Nomadic peoples of Africa, whether in East Africa, the Sahel, or the Kalahari, have traditionally adjusted to periods of sparse rainfall by decreasing their herds. They would either lend their cattle, change to more drought-resistant animals like goats, or trade the cattle for grain. They became drought victims more because of man-made problems than from a simple decrease in rainfall. For example, when political strife makes it impossible for a nomadic people to leave an area that is drought stricken and move to land where there is a more abundant water supply, they become victims. In this case lack of rain coupled with political factors brings drought. Such a scenario would adequately describe the plight of the people of Ethiopia and Eritrea who were more capable of dealing with the lack of rain than they were with the political maze they faced, a dilemma resulting largely from their condition being given the status of an "official drought" by the international organization (Hewitt, 1983b). Once people are included in this category they become eligible for assistance; however, they often find themselves confronted with problems beyond their control but which must be solved before they can get relief. For example, because the international organizations recognized Ethiopia but not Eritrea, only Ethiopians were drought victims. Drought funds were funneled only to Ethiopia. Eritreans did not receive help and they viewed the decision as aiding the enemy. Likewise, Ethiopians had no desire to share the aid they received with their enemies, the Eritreans. By including droughts in the list of disasters, the international organizations brought in several human factors that actually contribute to disasters.

Human-Induced Disasters

Another step away from defining disasters only by physical events (earthquake, tsunami, flood) is to classify them by the way they affect the environment. This approach allows for the inclusion of other physical events such as technological accidents, oil spills, chemical leaks, or nuclear accidents, all of which can have severe effects on nature. In these cases the triggers are not natural phenomena but events induced by humans. It is the results that are destructive to the environment.

Human-induced disasters can be divided into those caused by acts of omission and those brought about by acts of commission (Berren, Beigel, & Ghertner, 1980). In those deliberately committed, there is a willful spoiling of the environment such as done by ecoterrorists or in civil strife. An example occurred during the 1991 Gulf War when Iraq purposely set afire Kuwait's oil wells. Some predict that in the future the worst environmental disasters are more likely to come from ecoterrorists than from climatic events (Quarantelli, 1990).

The Chernobyl accident of 1986 was an example of a human-induced disaster caused by an act of omission. The plant was poorly constructed and had potential for a major accident. Given time, particularly without any human interference to stop what appeared to be problematic, such an accident was increasingly possible. No one acted to prevent the disaster for several reasons: there were insufficient national funds to make the plant secure, the facility was perceived to be in better condition than it was, and the nation's funding priorities were elsewhere (Mark & Carver, 1987).

There are clear differences in how people react to natural versus human-caused disasters (Kasperson & Pijawka, 1985). In human-induced environmental disasters there is rarely a "low point," a time when victims realize the worst is over. Recognition of when the low point is past is important in victims' recovery. Once the low point has passed the victim's psychology shifts from whether he or she is going to survive to estimating the losses and planning recuperation (Frederick, 1980). For example, when the tidal surge peaked, the people trapped in the high school at McClellanville knew that the worst was over—the strongest winds had passed and the water was going to recede. The following morning they were able to leave the shelter, go home, and see what needed to be done to rebuild.

In contrast, at Chernobyl it was unclear from the start just how much damage had been done. There were no photographs of fallen trees, no images of high water marks, no pictures of collapsed buildings. Despite the huge potential for damage, victims of Chernobyl were not able to perceive what had happened to them through their senses. Unlike the victims of the hurricane, whose experiemce was extremely physical, victims of Chernobyl had to rely on highly complicated and technological equipment to gauge the degree to which they were victimized, or trust what they were told by the press.

Unfortunately, the press was less than forthright. People were never really given adequate information about Chernobyl (Rubin, 1987). Some authors believe a meltdown did occur at that facility. This opinion is based on the amount of radiation released into the environment, which was about 80 million times larger than what was released in the Three Mile Island leak, and comparable to the fallout from the bomb dropped on Hiroshima (Mark & Carver, 1987).

About 100 million people in the vicinity of Chernobyl were exposed to levels of radiation much higher than normal. Scientists expect about 10,000 cases of cancer caused by the radiation to appear in the exposed population over the next fifty years. The damage goes even further. For example. Ingvar Carlesson, the Swedish prime minister at the time, said that 100,000 reindeer in Lapland would have to be destroyed because the deer would be eating radioactive lichen. The death of so many reindeer will threaten the Laplanders, whose way of life is so dependent on the reindeer herds (Mark & Carver, 1987).

Chernobyl victims were kept in ignorance by their government; only a few were aware of the extent of the radioactivity. Like other victims of human-induced disasters, they could not know how long their victimization would last (Baum, Fleming, & Davidson, 1983). In the case of severe radiation, because people do not know how badly they have been victimized, the psychological effects can last for a long time. They might suspect, for example, that they have undergone genetic changes and consequently suffer the tension of not really knowing whether their future is in jeopardy (Lifton, 1967).

Victims of human-induced disasters often have a good deal of diffused anger, made stronger by the difficulty of knowing who to blame or the inability of finding someone or some agency to take responsibility. In their desire to learn who caused their problems and how severe their problems are, victims of human-induced disasters are often themselves blamed for causing trouble (Cuthbertson & Nigg, 1987).

In natural disasters people receive sympathy; they are comforted by their communities, their suffering is acknowledged. Victims of human-induced disasters, on the other hand, are often not given the same consideration because in these disasters there is a need to find the institution (or persons) that can be held responsible (Baum, 1985; Cuthbertson & Nigg, 1987). In natural disasters, conversely, no one can be blamed. Because of the difference in their treatment, victims of human-induced disasters experience more stress than do victims of natural ones (Baum, Fleming, & Davidson, 1983; Erikson, 1976b; Gleser, Green, & Winget, 1981; Levine, 1982).

In actuality, the distinction between natural and human-induced disasters is rarely clear-cut. Take the example of the victims in the McClellanville shelter. It was human error that picked a shelter so close to the ocean and only twenty feet above sea level. In the case of Hurricane Fifi, was it natural phenomena that caused the deaths or the human element that had begun a series of events years before that caused the victims to be more susceptible to the flooding? Researchers of the 1985 earthquake in Mexico City, for example, claimed that one reason there were so many dead and injured and such widespread destruction was that building contractors had used inferior materials and had built the structures in clear violation of the specifications in the government contracts they had received (Berren, Santiago, Beigel, & Timmons, 1989).

Complex Disasters

The United Nations General Assembly has designated the 1990s the International Decade for Natural Disaster Reduction. Through the experience and advice of its United Nations Disaster Relief Organization (UNDRO), the United Nations has acknowledged that disasters are caused by a combination of human and physical phenomena and has adopted the term *complex disasters* to describe them. This term encompasses the role of technology in creating disasters as well as the impact of civil strife and political factors in exacerbating the effects of disasters.

Complex disasters are more germane to the developing world where economic and political factors compound the effect of physical events. As the physical events become disasters they also generate economic and political phenomena that make people even more vulnerable to the next physical event. An example of this chain of events are the Karamoja, who are seminomadic cattle herders of Uganda. Like most people from traditional societies, the Karamoja had developed coping mechanisms (most commonly the selling of their cattle in exchange for grain to eat) when the periodic lack of rainfall would occur. With the onset of limited rainfall in 1977, the Karamoja, as they had in the past, responded by selling cattle. However, by 1979 Uganda's economy had collapsed, and the Karamoja found it all but impossible to sell their cattle. At the same time the country was beginning a civil war. Because of the war, the Karamoja were further hindered from selling their cattle by the Idi Amin government. As a result they began to suffer from hunger (D'Souza, 1984).

When Idi Amin left the country his armory was looted by the traditional enemies of the Karamoja. Disputes became more severe because of the lack of water. Problems that had been settled in the past with spears were being resolved now with automatic rifles. Increased deaths among the men made it even more difficult for the tribe to cope with the lack of rain because there were fewer people to work the fields. With fewer Karamoja men, it was easier for the enemies of the

Karamoja to force them to settle in what amounted to refugee camps where, after a time, a cholera epidemic broke out.

It was at this time the UN relief agencies became involved. They were forced to consider whether they were dealing with a civil war, an issue of refugees, a famine, a drought, or an epidemic. This experience, and other similar ones, led UN officials to understand that environmental disasters were increasingly becoming "complex disasters" (Wells, 1984).

Differentiating between Accidents, Emergencies, and Disasters

The international relief agencies (United Nations Disaster Relief Organization, League of Red Cross Societies, World Health Organization, World Food Program, Oxford Committee for Famine Relief [OXFAM], United States Agency for International Development) are responsible for providing aid and on any given day they are faced with responding to many incidents. As a result, they have developed their own system of definition by separating accidents, emergencies, and disasters. Although all three come without much warning, one distinguishing characteristic between them is the difference in magnitude. By definition, accidents are situations in which fewer than one thousand people die; in disasters, more than a thousand but fewer than a million people are dead or in imminent danger of dying. If more than a million people are dead or in danger, the situation is referred to as a catastrophe (Ebert, 1986).

If there is any doubt about the realism of catastrophes, particularly in light of complex disasters, we need only remember the Black Death of 1337 to 1351. Caused by a combination of bubonic, pneumonic, and septicaemic plagues, it killed nearly 75 million people. In the more recent epidemic of 1918, over 20 million people died of influenza (Ebert, 1986).

Accidents are localized events; only a small group of people and their immediate families are affected. Most people in the community are not even aware that an accident has happened. Emergencies are less localized and they involve more people. Victims share a sense of community. A greater number of people who are not directly involved with the trauma are affected by it. Because there is some damage to the community's infrastructure, many people know of the emergency. Emergencies, unlike accidents, are not resolved quickly or easily. Disasters damage large segments of the community's infrastructure and they affect the community's social systems. Not only is there a community of victims, but there are large numbers of secondary victims (relatives and friends of victims) who are indirectly affected by the event.

With a disaster, the proportion of victims to nonvictims is considerably higher than in emergencies. As a result the mental health problems are much larger. Survivors of Buffalo Creek, a mining community in West Virginia that was completely destroyed by a flood in 1972, suffered both individual and "collective trauma" (Erikson, 1976a, 1976b). Four years after the flood a full 30 percent of the people still had symptoms of mental illness. Their dreams were haunted with images of water and death. The incidence of sleep disturbance was triple that of the comparable nondisaster population (Gleser, Green, & Winget, 1981).

Disaster victims experience more than psychological problems. Their notion of justice and order and many of their basic meanings about life are challenged. What was normal has been disrupted to the extent that their basic values are called into question. This phenomenon extends beyond the victims to the secondary victims and the entire community. Thus, disasters are more than physical acts. They are a combination of the physical events and the social changes that result from them (Barkun, 1974).

In disasters social organizations are forced to develop new alliances to meet unexpected, intense, and large problems. Often the normal boundaries between public and private sectors become blurred. The citizenry is forced to give up certain private rights. For example, after the 1989 Loma Prieta earthquake in California many private business owners were forced by the state for reasons of safety to abandon their shops or were given only fifteen minutes to gather and carry out of their stores as much of their inventory as possible.

After the 1972 earthquake in Managua, Nicaragua, the Somoza government, also to protect public safety, ordered the central city to be cordoned off and all the buildings in the area destroyed. The owners of these homes and businesses were not consulted about the decision nor were they reimbursed for their losses. However, the government then gave private construction companies contracts to rebuild on the abandoned sites. If people wanted to live where they had been living before the earthquake they were forced to buy back what they had never sold. Studies of this earthquake have suggested that the manner in which the Somoza government responded to the earthquake was a significant factor in that government's demise (Black, 1981; Bommer, 1985; Green, 1977; Haas & Drabek, 1973).

Cultural Factors in Defining Disasters

By using the magnitude of social crises to ascertain the degree to which the physical event has impacted people, the international organizations responsible for helping victims are able to acquire some guiding focus for delivering their aid. However, as cross-cultural examples illustrate, not all extreme physical events cause social crises. In fact, in some cases even dramatic physical events are taken as part of the normal course of human life.

An illustration is the typhoons on the Island of Yap, which is located in the Micronesian archipelago. Typhoons on Yap are recurrent. Although they do not produce many deaths, they do considerable damage to property. Yapians themselves classify typhoons as catastrophes (Schneider, 1957). According to Yapian tradition, at least until 1957 when the Yapians were studied by Schneider, typhoons have in part a supernatural origin. Chiefs have the power to order magicians to bring typhoons to the island. However, chiefs cannot order typhoons willy-nilly; they are able to call them only when the people, in their lack of wisdom, are not following the chief's directives. Even so, the chief has only limited power, as it is rare for a chief to be allowed more than two typhoon orders in a lifetime, and never more than three. Thus, while the people of Yap believe that typhoons are caused by supernatural forces, they also believe there are considerable human factors that control and limit their occurrence.

Yapians do not see typhoons as problems of nature nor as coming from the supernatural alone; they view them as symbolic representations of interpersonal problems. Therefore, according to their belief, if people got along better, typhoons could be controlled. After a typhoon, Yapians make amends to people with whom they are at odds. Thus the storm brings about an increase in social solidarity rather than social disintegration.

The Yapian example shows that what constitutes a disaster is not the statistics of death and destruction, nor the degree of social crisis, but the perception of the event as shocking beyond one's experience. Victims must have the feeling of being out of control and in a situation seemingly beyond their capacity to adapt.

As stress mounts beyond what is socially and culturally understandable, people have to cope not only with the physical event but also with the unfamiliar. Because there is no cultural understanding for the unfamiliar, the past is not effective in defining the present situation. From this perspective, the dazed and disoriented mental state commonly experienced by victims immediately after a disastrous event can be seen less as the reaction to the physical event per se than as a response to the unknown. The same can be said of the social crisis, which is not only a reaction to the physical events but also a reaction to the fear that comes from facing an occurrence far beyond one's expectations. In this view disasters are mental constructs; consequently, for an event to be considered a disaster there must be a perception of an uncontrollable crisis, a sense of being made vulnerable beyond one's experience, and a feeling of being unable to find an adequate explanation for what has occurred.

Disasters have a very personal component; they force people to find meaning and come to terms with what has happened. Likewise, disasters have a cultural component. The array of meanings at the disposal of victims is within the context of what is available in the culture. Looking at two different cultural points of view about disasters will make this point clear. The dominant Islamic view, similar to that of Old Testament prophets, is that calamities come to people who are immoral, idolatrous, or vain. Victims blame themselves for their problems. To people in power, disaster helps to explain their superior status and the low condition of the powerless and disenfranchised (Scott, 1968).

Westerners' attitudes toward disasters have changed significantly over time. Up until the 1755 Lisbon earthquake, disasters were viewed as being caused by God, and their meaning was explained as some form of divine retribution. What made the Lisbon earthquake important was that not all victims saw the earthquake in a religious context; many defined it, for the first time, in scientific terms (Barkun, 1974).

With the growing industrial revolution, the importance of secular thought increased. At the same time there was a decline in religious explanations for extreme natural events. As a result, people no longer had the same fear of them. This was because they were no longer viewed as a sign of a vengeful, omnipotent God who must be feared but were seen as scientifically understandable events.

The perception of disasters as fearful events produced by the unknown and having unknown consequences has undergone considerable cultural change throughout Western history. By the twentieth century the great fear had shifted to human-induced disasters, a phenomenon that was peculiar to the advanced industrial nations. People from these nations are not as frightened by earthquakes or storms as by disasters resulting from human errors, either from technological accidents or from mismanagement of human affairs. Their focus has shifted from fearing God to blaming people.

The fear of natural disasters has been removed in the developed nations largely because of the relative affluence of these countries; they have reliable warning systems, good evacuation plans, well-enforced building codes, and insurance to help with rebuilding. In a natural disaster both property damage and loss of life is far lower in the industrialized nations than in the emerging world. The developing nations, however, continue to suffer great losses—of both property and life—when a disaster strikes. The severity of their suffering often has man-made causes that exacerbate the destructiveness of natural elements.

In spite of the vast differences in the developed and developing worlds, victims in both need assistance when a disaster strikes. If agencies are to provide effective aid, they need to learn from past disasters. By examining the behavior of victims, learning the importance of cultural differences, and observing the effect of aid that has been given in other circumstances, agencies can improve the appropriateness of the assistance they offer.

2

Why Study Disasters?

Disasters are interesting to people because they allow us to wonder what we might be like under extreme stress. Would it bring out the best or the worst? Would we be the heroic person we dream of, or the needy victim we fear? Disasters demonstrate people's breaking points and their resilience. Resilience of those who have experienced a disaster gives those who fear catastrophe a vision of what people are capable of enduring.

There is more than the potential for personal discovery to the study of disasters. For the social science researcher disasters provide a laboratory for testing several important theoretical questions about human behavior. These include questions about basic human suffering, about people's relationship to their environment, and about the connection between human behavior, economics, and political science.

The field is open to cross-disciplinary research, inviting not only the collaboration of different social sciences but also of social and natural scientists. Because disasters are global phenomena, comparing people's reaction to them helps us to learn how culture influences all these issues.

Disasters cause people and organizations to change. Changes that come slowly are manageable, but quick and intense changes force an emergency response. In the moments of crisis individuals will have to learn a new set of skills. In addition, they will be faced with moral choices—having to decide if, or who, they should help. The quick acquisition of new skills and the fast moral choices to be made are not only necessary for individuals; they also are the burdens of institutions, from small groups to the largest and most influential organizations in a society. Information about how these processes occur can best be understood through cross-cultural research. The data are important for adding to social science theory, but they also serve disaster planners by helping them plan appropriate programs.

Practical Applications

The study of disaster itself has many practical values. It can teach us how people respond to warnings, when and under what conditions people will panic, and whether the media are effective in changing people's behavior. Orson Welles's infamous radio program simulating an invasion from Mars is a good example of people's reactions. On hearing Welles announce the landing of the Martians, some people looked out the window and were reassured when they saw a normal amount of traffic; others who saw the same amount of traffic were convinced that people were fleeing the city. People's interpretation of the same information caused some to panic and others to feel reassured (Cantril, 1940).

Relief agencies must know how to transfer their methods and skills from one society to another; cross-cultural disaster research can help them avoid insensitive and counterproductive actions. Accounts of aid agencies delivering inappropriate materials to disaster sites include the shipping of pork to Muslim countries where eating pork is forbidden, of sending emergency equipment that runs on electricity to places without electrical power, of building igloo-shaped houses in tropical societies where they are unacceptable culturally, and of sending canned foods to cultures that believe such foods should be used only for domestic animals (Bolduc, 1987). People who are involved with disaster management study disasters to learn how to plan search and rescue operations and how to give guidelines to social agencies such as police and fire departments, mental health facilities, and hospitals. Issues of public policy, such as how to prepare building codes or provide educational programs to mitigate for disasters, are also highly reliant on disaster research. Much of this research should also have a comparative and cultural component for effective results.

Disaster research helps reduce the probability that people will be injured in future disasters. Research has shown that teaching people in advance what to expect and what to do is the best way to help them avoid being victimized (Tierney, 1989). Many disaster preparedness programs do this; but to be most effective they must take into account different cultural factors. Most people in the developed world believe that disasters are a product of understandable extremes of nature that can be dealt with by the scientific application of technology. But this is not the case all over the world. In order for disaster preparedness to be effective in a global context it must take into account the differences in cultural beliefs in various societies. This knowledge comes from cross-cultural disaster studies.

By studying the same type of disaster in different cultures, researchers can determine whether there is a pan-human reaction to a particular disaster or whether disaster responses are the product of cultural differences. Clifford's (1956) study of the same flood on either side of the Rio Grande showed that Mexicans and Americans responded much differently to the same disaster. In Mexico people reacted to the flood in the context of their extended families. They received information about the danger from their families. They believed the warnings when they came from their families, but they ignored information from the government because they had little trust that the information would be neutral or accurate. In contrast, Americans ignored information about the impending flood when it came from people they knew because they thought it would be lacking in sophisticated knowledge and would be too subjective. For these reasons they accepted information when it came from government authorities.

One cross-national study of flooding collected data in the United States, India, Panama, Turkey, and the Philippines to illustrate how cultural factors influence disaster relief (Dynes, 1988). In all these places people were forced to make choices about what to give up and how to proceed, but these choices were greatly affected by cultural beliefs. There are studies of behavior during hurricanes (Firth, 1959; Lessa, 1964; Marshall, 1979; Schneider, 1957), tornadoes (Wallace, 1956), and volcanic eruptions (Belshaw, 1951; Keesing, 1952) that illustrate the same phenomena.

As information is collected about the factors that inhibit or help people cope with disasters, decisions can be made about which people are at greatest risk and appropriate plans can be made to help them. Barton (1969), for example, predicted that women with children would be under extreme stress, a finding that was corroborated in the Three Mile Island nuclear scare where mothers were the first to flee from their homes (Bromet & Dunn, 1981). The women also showed the most anxiety in being separated from their families and were the most prone to acute and chronic impairment of their mental health. Special plans, which are best developed from disaster research, need to be prepared to respond to those most at risk.

Effective disaster programs, such as developing warning systems to alert people to potential disasters and hazards, can also be helpful in dealing with other social policy questions. Disasters are excellent laboratories in which to learn what skills are needed to adopt a new behavior, who is motivated to change, and what motivates them to change. The answers to these questions can then be applied to other social problems such as smoking and drug abuse.

Value to Social Science Theory

Disaster research provides a good deal of information about individual and community stress (Baker & Chapman, 1962; Baum, 1985; Horowitz, 1986b, 1990; Lazarus & Cohen, 1977). Based on differences in the impact that disasters have on people and communities, it is possible to ascertain the relationship between the amount of stress and the manner and degree to which people can cope.

The people who experience the highest degree of impact have the worst reactions. A study of victims of the Mount St. Helens volcano sorted people into groups based on the extent of their losses. Those who had experienced the highest impact—that is, had suffered the greatest loss—had more incidences of mental disorders (Shore, Tatum, & Vollmer, 1986a). Shore postulates a dose-related pattern of mental disorders: the higher the dose, the greater the amount of mental disorder (Shore, Tatum, & Volmer, 1986b). However, the correlation is not always so simple. Prior psychological functioning affects people's response (Horowitz, 1990), and their reactions to stress are frequently difficult to ascertain because people often deny their symptoms to themselves and the public display of symptoms might not begin for some time. When the symptoms do manifest themselves, they suggest a pattern of waxing and waning (Horowitz, 1986a). There is much to be learned about stress from the study of disasters.

Stress shows itself in different forms. Whereas most people demonstrate anxiety, community norms against complaining about emotional symptoms and favoring self-reliance force many victims to convert their symptoms to physical problems (Moore, 1958; Penick, Powell, & Sieck, 1976). Comparative disaster research can add to the study of how social norms change the patterns of coping with stress.

Disasters can help psychologists understand how people's cognitive processes function. In general, people prefer to be cognitively consistent and would rather reorganize their perceptions of the environment than reorganize their thinking. It is not surprising that disaster victims also avoid cognitive ambiguity. They deny new information that might be contrary to their attitudes by either discrediting the source of the information or rejecting the manner in which the information is obtained. This factor can influence not only how disaster victims act or fail to act but also the success or failure of disaster relief. A disaster relief officer in the U.S. Aid for International Development (AID) Office for Foreign Assistance received an electronic communication describing a hurricane in a developing country asking for aid. Because the officer felt this particular developing country was exaggerating the severity of the crisis in order to obtain aid, he made the determination that the account of the damage was inflated. As a result the aid for a real disaster was delayed (Kent, 1987).

In the absence of sufficient information, people tend to fill in the gaps by categorizing and labeling, a process identified as *schema theory*, which is a part of the attribution literature (Kelly, 1976). When the Save the Children Fund (SCF) first reported that children were dying in Ethiopia, the relief officer at the British embassy did not believe them. The embassy staff's attitude was based on their belief that SCF was overly committed to helping and therefore they considered the agency untrustworthy as a source of information. In this case schema theory, as an example of social psychological theory, explains how the gaps were filled in by the relief officer.

Disasters also can shed light on the process of loss and grieving. Common sense indicates that the greater one's loss, the more bereft the victim will be; disaster research, however, has shown that people's sense of loss is more complex (Barton, 1969). Disaster researchers found that victims with very serious losses in one disaster felt less bereaved than people with less serious losses in another disaster. In the most devastated area of a serious disaster where people suffer the highest impact, there are always people to be found who see others worse off than themselves. Instead of grieving at what they have lost, these people rejoice in what they have left. In McClellanville, South

Carolina, a woman who had just seen the roof of her house being blown off was surprisingly happy. As she looked at the totally destroyed house of her neighbor, she thanked God for what she had left (Aptekar, 1990).

Disasters have also been studied in the context of role theory. Disaster victims must often take multiple and competing roles (Killian, 1952). In Watsonville, California, after the Loma Prieta earthquake, the school principal at Watsonville High School struggled with the need to stay at school to protect the children there and the equally strong desire to go home and be with his family (Aptekar, 1990). People's allegiances to their family, their work place, their personal friendships, and their social responsibilities, which normally operate efficiently and effectively, are greatly disrupted during disasters.

People's ability to maintain mutual role membership in their important groups is difficult in normal times and often a major cause of stress. However, during disasters taking care of all one's roles becomes exceedingly stressful. Usually role preference is accomplished in private but after disasters, role preference, because it is so difficult, is more open to public scrutiny. Disaster research can therefore help explain how people like the Watsonville High School principal disengage from accepted role responsibilities and how they handle the overload of social demands caused by acting in many roles at the same time.

Disaster research also relates to other areas of social psychology. *Interactional theory*, a model developed from the sociology of Merton (1969), claims that people define themselves or assume roles based on the mutual expectations of people interacting with one another. In this context people become victims only when there are others to help them to define *victim*. Likewise, victims define for helpers what it means to be a helper. The key aspect of the victim's role is dependence on the aid of helpers, and the central fact of the helper's role is the feeling of goodwill that comes from aiding the needy (Taylor, Zurcher, & Key, 1970).

After the Loma Prieta earthquake the media were filled with stories about the great problems victims faced. Information from people in the schools, community organizations, and shelters suggested that in the first few days after the earthquake people were in great need of help. Volunteers came from every walk of life offering their goodwill. However, by the time they arrived, the victims had already begun to deny the stress they felt. The volunteers had no victims upon whom to shower their goodwill. Some volunteers were still needed for direct service, but others were shifted to jobs removed from the victims, such as sorting food and clothing, assignments that did not meet their own expectations of being heroic helpers. Volunteers in the more favored positions began to protect their territory and became defensive or even argumentative when they perceived that someone might come into their domain. Tensions between volunteers became commonplace as they vied for victims, who, in turn, made it more difficult for the volunteers by denying their problems (Aptekar, 1991).

Because disaster victims are in situations that they never expected to be in, they do not know how to respond. Their uncertainty leads them to look at others to see how they behave. By comparing themselves with other victims they learn the norms, and they learn how they are faring by comparison with others. This process is quite similar to what Festinger (1954) described in his work on social comparison theory.

Attribution theory is another social-psychological model that is appropriate for the study of disasters (Kelly, 1967). This theory attempts to show how people make sense of their social world. People can attribute behavior to either situational or personal factors. As a rule, people explain their own behavior as being situationally motivated and the behavior of others as being personally controlled. Victims see themselves as victims of fate but see other victims as masters of their fate. A case in point would be Margaret, a survivor of Hurricane Hugo. Margaret sat on a folded wooden chair by the South Carolina sea marsh among the six pillars of her former house. This was all that was left of her 150-year-old colonial home after the hurricane struck. She explained that her great-grandparents had built the home before the civil war. She said, "It's God's will that destroyed what the Civil War didn't." It was no fault of her own, but she "couldn't understand why the black folks built their houses so close to the sea and with such flimsy material. No wonder they lost everything. That's their problem, don't you think?" (Aptekar, 1990)

The study of disaster victims has also been seen in the context of locus of control (Silver & Wortman, 1980). People with an internal locus of control base their worldview on their own beliefs rather than the beliefs of others (external locus of control). One expects that all victims will find meaning from the disaster by comparing themselves with others, but victims with an external locus of control feel that their disaster-related problems stem from their prior personal inadequacies. They are more likely to seek mental health services than victims with an internal locus of control who see disasters as stressful external events and view their reactions to them as appropriate responses to the events (Taylor, Wood, & Lichtman, 1983).

The early sociological disaster researchers illustrated the close connections between disasters and general sociological theory (Barton, 1969; Fritz, 1961; Prince, 1920; Sorokin, 1942). In particular, they saw disasters as belonging to a larger set of collective stress situations. Disaster research, by comparing how communities respond to disasters and civil conflicts, has helped scientists understand collective behavior of emergent groups, social crowds, and social movements.

After disasters there is typically an emergence of altruism and from it an increased positive identification with one's community; however, this is not always the case (Dynes & Quarantelli, 1971, 1976b). Some communities support their victims while others do not. One of the first community disaster studies showed that the people of Halifax, Canada, supported the victims and their families after an ammunition truck exploded (Prince, 1920). Neighbors took in homeless people, restaurants gave food to victims and their families, and donations were made in the names of victims. The same type of behavior occurred in Mexico City after the 1985 earthquake (Andrade, 1988).

On the other hand, civil disturbances erupt after some disasters. The Nicaraguan earthquake planted the seeds of anger in the wake of the government's disposition of private property with no regard for prior ownership. After Hurricane Hugo people on the island of St. Vincent roamed the streets gathering whatever they wanted from stores and burning buildings. People's attentions were riveted on past problems. Social class differences were highlighted and provided people with a rationale to loot.

Surprisingly, after the same storm, social altruism was seen on most of the other Caribbean islands, in spite of their having similar social problems. On St. Lucia, Martinique, Dominica, and Barbados, victims, often with great heroism, walked into flooded areas to help others who could not help themselves. Only comparative research can help explain why such differences exist.

Disaster study can also provide information about change in formal organizations (schools, police and fire departments, and church groups, among others). Disaster studies have shown that organizations rarely change after the immediate impact of the disaster (Anderson 1969;

Stallings 1978), but these studies have not been confined to the developed countries.

Many sociologists have studied community reactions to disasters, effectively disproving the myth that collective behavior reduces people to their lowest level of functioning. Collective response is often altruistic and therapeutic (Rosengren, Arvisson, & Sturesson, 1979; Wenger, 1980). Citizen participation is expanded, and people engage in activities such as search and rescue, and law enforcement, in which they would not normally participate. Immediately following the Loma Prieta earthquake, for example, two men entered the rubble of the collapsed Oakland freeway viaduct to extract trapped motorists. The structure was far from stable, yet the men looked for victims in it with little regard for their own safety.

In almost all cases disasters reduce social differences. People work together across social class boundaries. There is an orientation to the present with a commitment to putting aside past problems. Prior to the Mexico City earthquake of 1985 it was very rare for people of the high and low social classes to intermingle in that city. Immediately after the earthquake, social class boundaries temporarily disappeared; people united in helping each other under their common interests as humans in distress.

Francisco de la Torre, a middle-class engineer, helped retrieve some of the bodies of the six hundred seamstresses who died in the rubble of a building that collapsed on them. He told a reporter that the earthquake made him a humble man. He recalled that he had been able to go to the university and become an engineer only because of the goodwill of his country. He said, "My way of paying my country back is to help the people here while they wait for their dead; rescuing them is also my homage to the dead" (Poniatowska, 1988, p. 18).

Contributions to Cross-Cultural Research

Cross-cultural researchers have studied disasters to understand changes in relationships between social classes (Oliver-Smith 1979a, 1979b), to understand how international aid changes a community (Dudasik, 1978, 1982), and to examine the diffusion of cultural values brought with an influx of disaster refugees (Colton, 1932; Mackie, 1961). Disasters have also been viewed in the context of events that overburden social institutions (Quarantelli, 1979). By studying the disaster recovery process in different societies it is possible to compare the reaction of different societies to change (Bolin & Bolton, 1983; Dynes, 1972, 1974, 1975; Sjoberg, 1962).

The field of ecological anthropology—which classifies environmental problems into those that are recurring, like droughts, and those that are acute, like earthquakes—has shown through cross-cultural studies that in many societies family and kin are dramatically changed by environmental circumstances (Vayda & McCay, 1975). The size and constellation of grouping among the !Kung bushmen depends in great part on the amount of rain that falls where they live (Lee, 1972). A similar phenomenon was seen among the Navajo, whose family constellations changed from large and extended to small and nuclear as a response to persistent droughts (Downs, 1965). Rules concerning where and with whom people live, alliances between kin and ethnic groups, and rules for traveling outside of one's boundaries are all changed by environmental events. These events also change systems of agriculture, including which animals are raised, how they are fed and slaughtered, which crops are planted, and how they are tended.

From the outset of disaster research, ethnographic studies have shown the impact that environmental disasters can have on societies. In 1952 Spillius (1957) conducted an ethnographic study of social change on the South Pacific island of Tikopia. Unexpectedly during his stay, the islanders encountered two hurricanes that were followed by a drought. They made considerable adjustments to these disasters, which Spillius recorded. The islanders created and enforced laws against stealing from people's gardens, a practice that had been widely accepted in the past. They began catching and eating birds that until then were not considered sources of food. Initiation rites were postponed to save food, which meant that adolescence was prolonged. Important new moral questions had to be answered. If there was a food shortage in a family, who was to go without: the mother, the father, the aged grandparents, or the growing children? Should traditional hospitality rules, which were tied to status and self-esteem, continue? If so, to what degree? Through this ethnographic study it was possible to ascertain how the many changes caused by environmental disasters were carried out and at what cost to those who were forced to make them.

Thus, disasters are worthy of study, not only to answer our own psychological questions of how we might react and behave in extreme situations but also because disasters provide a good deal of information about human behavior in more commonly occurring times. For those who are involved with disaster management, the study of people's reaction to disasters helps them do their job better, which includes being more attuned to cross-cultural differences and similarities. As the numbers of disasters increase and the numbers of injured and dead rise, the importance of disaster research will become known to a wider audience, bringing greater resources and talent to the study of disasters.

3

Research Issues

Because of the different approaches to defining disasters, identifying a research agenda has been very difficult. The last thirty years have seen considerable changes in definitions. In 1961, Fritz conceptualized disasters as events that made an impact on a social unit: an independent variable acting upon a dependent variable. By the late 1980s, Hewitt (1983b) emphasized the social unit prior to the impact as the independent variable, using the physical event as the dependent variable. The difference between these two approaches remains, but there has been considerable work on defining the important factors that contribute to our understanding of human behavior in disasters. Barton (1969) found that if four factors were known—the scope of the disaster, the speed of its onset, the duration of its impact, and the preparedness of the community—it would be possible to predict how a community would respond to the disaster. From these factors he constructed several hypotheses that affected much of the disaster research in the 1970s.

In the 1980s other important research variables emerged. These include the type of the disaster (natural versus human-induced), the degree of personal impact (from no involvement to the death of a significant other), the scope of the disaster (including the amount of geographical space and the duration of time), and whether there was a "low point" (a time when victims of a disaster realize that the worst is over) (Berren, Beigel, & Ghertner, 1980).

The Development of a Research Schema

A sociological theorist, Quarantelli (1979), developed a schema that divided disaster variables into time periods and units of analysis. The time periods were separated into five phases: predisaster, warning or threat, immediate response, organized response, and long-term post-disaster. The units of analysis were individuals, small groups, formal organizations, community systems, and states, regions and nations. Because many disasters affect more than one community—indeed, these disasters are often causes of or caused by international disputes—one more unit of analysis could be added: the international unit.

The unit of analysis is quite important and not always simple to distinguish. A drought, for example, cannot simply be understood at the level on which the community experiences it. To study only the peasants who are suffering from the Sudanese drought, for example, would miss the fact that these peasants are affected not only by the national agricultural agenda but are susceptible to the international agricultural market as well. The drought exists at four levels: local, regional, national, and international. At the local level, drought can be controlled by giving peasants the same access to water and food as the wealthy have. As the unit of analysis expands toward the international, the drought becomes more a function of large-scale international agricultural factors, such as the need for capital for machinery, seed, fertilizer, and pesticides. Unless this need is met, marginal farmers are forced off their land and into urban areas. All the levels identified by Quarantelli must be merged to understand fully the peasants' local problems with drought (Jeffery, 1980).

Quarantelli and his colleagues at the Delaware Disaster Center (Quarantelli, 1979) have changed the schema somewhat by adding a greater human dimension to the time sequence so that there are now eight categories that include various human factors. These include (1) warnings, (2) pre-impact preparations, (3) search and rescue operations, (4) care of the injured and dead, (5) welfare needs of victims, (6) restoration of necessary community services, (7) protection against continuing threats, and (8) community order. Using this model Quarantelli (1988) and his colleagues have found that in all cultures several responses to a variety of environmental disasters are similar. For example, in almost all cultures the less seriously injured are treated first.

Another cross-cultural similarity that has been widely corroborated is that citizens who are not trained in emergency relief are the first to offer help to victims. This was the case in the Mexico City earthquake of 1985 (Comfort, 1990), in the Armenian earthquake of 1988 (Mileti, 1989), in the Loma Prieta earthquake of 1989 (Aptekar, 1990), and after

Hurricane Hugo in South Carolina in 1989 (Aptekar, 1991). Quarantelli (1984) also argued that at the level of individuals there are few cross-cultural differences, but as the perspective moves toward the level of societies these variations become more significant.

Similar findings were reported by Drabek (1986), who later developed his own schema. Drabek views disasters as having a life history. His schema also has a time phasic classification that uses many of the human factors associated with disaster aid. The first phase is *preparedness*, or the process of education and practice drills. An example would be the American school children in the 1950s who practiced ducking under their desks readying themselves for a nuclear attack. Similar drills are currently being carried out in California for earthquakes. Drabek's second phase is the *response* period, the short time after the disaster strikes when services are still widely disrupted and before the relief agencies have arrived. The third phase is *recovery*, the longer period during which aid helps to restore the community, plans for rebuilding occur, and people resume a sense of normal life. Finally, there is *mitigation*, the formation of regulations and laws intended to reduce both individual and community vulnerability to the next disaster. Examples of mitigation would be the passage of state regulations setting standards for building materials and delineating specifically where buildings can or cannot be constructed.

Drabek contended that several levels of variables could be studied during these different phases. The levels closely correspond to Quarantelli's units of analysis and include individual, group, organizational, community, society, and international variables. This approach is well suited to cross-cultural study. Mileti, Drabek, and Haas (1975) analyzed the similarities and differences of such research by reviewing previous studies of disasters and codifying the results among the different social levels and by different types of disasters. Their work is very helpful in explaining why the results of studies often seem contradictory.

Taking a slightly different point of view that emphasizes the human factor in disaster, Kreps (1985, 1989) noted that phenomenologically, in spite of the variety of definitions of disasters, everyone seems to agree on the point when an extreme event becomes a disaster. The 1970 East Pakistan cyclone that killed 200,000 people is classified as a disaster because of the extent of suffering it caused. Not only did it kill an incredible number of people, it also set off a widespread famine, which caused another 100,000 to 200,000 deaths. The ultimate result was the considerable political strife that eventually led to the formation of a new country, Bangladesh. Although, no social science studies examined how individuals responded to the disaster and the series of events that followed, other studies reported the great degree of suffering they endured.

The classification of disasters by phenomenological reality can be further analyzed by the components people use to decide which events are indeed disastrous. Essentially, a disaster includes events that are nonroutine, that cause physical and social harm to the family or to the entire planet, and that are experienced as acute by the victim. The definition differs from one person to another and it is likely that within the same event, say an earthquake, one person who was greatly affected will call the event a disaster, while another person not affected at all would have a more benign view of the event. Nevertheless, the phenomenological point of view is helpful because it begins with the individual's perception of the events and keeps the focus on the person's experience.

Kreps (1989) developed a taxonomy of disasters that he considered better than a simple categorization because taxonomies yield both conception and measurement. From his taxonomy Kreps has produced a sixty-four-cell table that has reference points showing where disaster variables can be studied. The reference points explain disasters by their physical, temporal, and social impacts and responses. For example, disasters can be characterized by their energy release, such as a number on the Richter scale (physical), the regularity of their occurrence or the suddenness of their onset (temporal), and the way the events formally become disasters (social).

The impacts of disasters can also be considered in terms of their physical damage, how long the disasters last or if they recur, and the degree of social disruption they cause. Responses to disasters can be seen in terms of engineering problems that they activate (physical), the timing of these problems, which might stem from situations before, during, or after the event (temporal), and by the solutions to the problems or the failure to reach solutions (social).

Kreps has proposed cataloging all the archival information that exists on disasters in order to further develop his proposed taxonomy. Some preliminary data exist at the Disaster Research Center at the University of Delaware, but these are insufficient to satisfy Kreps's ambitious proposal. Essentially, he desires to construct a codified sample of disasters (similar to the Human Relations Area Files), in a global context, that would yield a wealth of information about the cross-cultural aspects of disasters.

Research Problems

Disaster research presents a variety of problems. Some of these relate to the lack of communication between academic disciplines; others stem from the difficulty of putting research results into the hands of practitioners. There are also research design problems, such as the lack of experimental control groups, difficulties with instrumentation, and intrusion of cultural bias.

According to Torry (1979a), in several cross-cultural disaster studies (see Burton, Kates, & White, 1978; Haas, Kates, & Bowden, 1977; White, 1974) the researchers did not ascertain how social and cultural factors influenced the data, making it difficult to know the extent to which the results are due to cultural or individual differences. In one major sociological review (see Mileti, Drabek, & Haas, 1975) with nearly 200 citations, only six are from anthropologists, even though many anthropologists have conducted disaster research.

Torry criticizes conclusions stating that people do not know how to cope with the hazards that affect their communities. From the North American perspective, for example, it might seem that the people of the Sahel do not know how to cope with drought, but anthropological evidence clearly shows that they have made numerous adaptations in their daily lives to adjust to a lack of water. They have changed the type of animals they raise to those that need less water, they have regrouped their clans to put less strain on what water there is, and they have begun to interact with other tribes to open up trading for needed items (Colson, 1979; Spitz, 1977). Torry also criticized sociologists who have inferred that in developing countries there is more damage to people than property (see Fritz, 1968), that it is easy for a community to reach postdisaster consensus (Dynes & Quarantelli, 1976b), and that theft is rare in disaster communities (Quarantelli & Dynes, 1972)—conclusions that he believes are not supported.

Whatever the pitfalls of the research itself, an additional problem arises when the research results come into the hands of the practitioners. One comparative study of different disasters was carried out to determine how the research results were employed by people working in disaster recovery operations (Yin & Moore, 1985). The study suggests that research results be used only if they meet these three criteria: they must come from studies that have been sanctioned by official recovery organizations, the studies must be aimed directly at recovery personnel, and the studies must directly address policies or practical problems faced by recovery personnel. One problem with these suggestions is that using only sanctioned studies limits the degree to which critical material will be used.

Some research problems are inherent in the study of disasters, particularly the study of quick onset disasters where it is very difficult to do anything but ex post facto research. Conducting studies with pretests is impractical because it is nearly impossible to predict where a disaster will strike and equally as hard to know which people will be affected. It would simply not be cost effective to set aside a vulnerable area and collect predisaster data on a sample of people. Experiments on interventions are less difficult to do since they occur after the disaster; therefore, interpreting comparisons is easier. Yet the problem of comparing samples on predisaster factors still remains difficult.

As long as there is a lack of true experimental design it is difficult to know why differences occur or indeed just what the differences are. But it is possible, even without true experimental conditions, to study the processes of organizational adaptation and of how those adjustments are made. It might be that the same is true for the study of individual adaptations to disaster.

Disaster studies can provide an excellent opportunity to see the inner workings of organizations and individuals. After disasters, organizations are working full tilt. They are without their commonly occurring bureaucratic mechanisms, and because they are functioning in a less-than-routine manner, they are open to view as they rarely are in more normal times.

The most common way to overcome the problem of not having predisaster information from people is to interview them after the disaster and ask for their recollections. This is problematic because people's memories are commonly distorted. Interviewing disaster victims has other methodological problems. Often victims do not have a wide view of what happened. What they tell about their ordeal has the air of a fishing or a war story. Although such stories are valuable interpretations of an individual's experience they do not necessarily reflect the actual events that transpired.

Interviewing potential disaster victims about evacuations has clearly shown the fallacy of predicting behavior by what people say they will do. Almost all say they will evacuate in the case of nuclear threat, for example, but in fact, most did not do so after the Three Mile Island event (Mileti, 1983). Another problem is the tendency of interviewers to enter the field immediately after the disaster to interview victims, but not to remain there. Reactions to stress are cyclical; they appear, disappear, and resurface again. Without multiple time samplings it is possible to miss them (Horowitz, 1990; Horowitz, Wilner, Kaltreider, & Alvarez, 1980).

Two new methods of cross-cultural disaster research have been devised to eliminate some of the biases associated with interviewing. One is a standardized cross-cultural interview that is being developed by Bates (cited in Mileti, 1987); designed specifically to reduce some of the interview bias, it has already had some use in several countries. The second method to reduce the bias is by using multiple regression techniques (Carter, Kendall, & Clark, 1983).

Some researchers have used archival data as predisaster information, but it is difficult to obtain the precise data that are most useful for disaster research. This is particularly true in developing countries where there is often no archival data base at all. The use of questionnaires is also problematic, but it should be noted that the percentage of returned questionnaires is much higher in disaster research than in almost any other field—about 80 percent versus 50 percent for sociological research (Mileti, 1987). One suggestion to solve the data dilemma has been to use the Epidemiological Catchment Area findings from the National Institute of Mental Health (Soloman, 1989). These findings, which are collected from many studies, could be used as a way to match samples and thus give a researcher data that could approximate an actual predisaster sample. This is similar to the process employed by cross-cultural researchers who use the Human Relations Area Files.

The inability to use true experimental design studies in disaster research is not the only methodological barrier. There are also problems with the use of instruments. Perhaps two researchers are interested in ascertaining how an impact affects a person's mental functioning. They may both agree on a system of classifying impact—from no involvement, to house damage, to injuries to neighbors, to death of an important friend—but the first researcher measures mental functioning by instrument X, a standardized projective test, while the second researcher uses an open-ended interview, or a nonstandardized structured interview.

The two researchers may be studying two different disasters. The first could be working on a storm that the victims know will not return in the immediate future; the second researcher could be gathering data on an earthquake while the aftershocks are still strong, making it seem quite possible to the victims that a larger earthquake is imminent. Comparing results from these two studies would be very difficult. They use different instrumentation, and they are dealing with disasters that have different psychological meaning for victims.

Seeking a better way to compare responses of people across disasters, two researchers have developed the Diagnostic Interview Schedule Disaster Supplement (DIS/DS) (Robins & Smith, 1983). Their idea was to have a standardized instrument that could be used for a wide variety of disasters. The questionnaire categorizes the type of disaster, the extent of loss, the family risk factors, and the degree of support systems; it then provides information for several diagnostic mental disorders (American Psychiatric Association, 1987).

The DIS/DS has already been used in several cross-disaster studies (Robins et al., 1986; Smith, 1984). In one case it was used to obtain psychiatric evaluations of a community before two different types of disasters struck: a chemical spill and a tornado (Smith, Robins, Przybeck, Goldring, & Soloman, 1986). Using postdisaster evaluations and control groups, the researchers were able to conclude that for adults, disasters "contribute to the persistence or recurrence of previously existing disorders, but are not responsible for the genesis of new psychiatric symptoms or disorders" (p. 75).

Several problems in disaster research can be related to cultural bias. Nearly 90 percent of the studies on disasters have been carried out in the United States, and more than 90 percent of the researchers in studies around the world have been American (Quarantelli, 1979). Thus, the findings may not be applicable globally.

In the United States and most developed countries there is a rush to report, as this is the first step in securing government aid. In contrast, the developing nations may be slow to report events as disasters. An admitted disaster could reduce tourist income or add fuel to certain internal political problems (Green, 1977). The more ethnically diverse the developing countries are, the higher is the chance of their underreporting because it increases the possibility of trouble between ethnic groups and the central government (Seitz & Davis, 1984). In other cases the governments of developing countries are too eager to report. Overreporting is most common in countries that desire international aid and the hard currency associated with it. This phenomenon is not unique to disasters; it also occurs with other socially sensitive data, such as crime figures or numbers of victims of acquired immune deficiency syndrome (AIDS), which are typically underreported. In each case, overreporting or underreporting can wreak havoc with research results.

Perhaps the major problem in cross-cultural disaster research is the difficulty of classifying events in different cultures. Most work on impact has come from American samples or samples from other developed countries (Drabek, 1986). One study, however, used a comparative approach in the same culture (Geipel, 1982). Holding impact constant, the researcher compared reactions of the same victims to the two 1976 Friuli, Italy, earthquakes. He found that it was impossible to use absolute damage as a measure of impact; more important was relative damage. The impact a person felt was related not to the amount of damage he or she received but to the relative amount of that damage in comparison with what was experienced by others. Thus, in categorizing the impact of a disaster, the author devised a system that used the percentage of the dead, the homeless, and the evacuated compared to the total population.

One way to measure the size of impact across cultures is to add the loss of life and the amount of damage to the infrastructure and divide it by the capacity of the community/society to respond to the loss (Bates & Peacock, 1987). The magnitude of the community loss can be seen as the dollar value of the destroyed property, divided by the gross domestic product (GDP). The GDP reflects the community's productive capacity for a year. Thus, by using the quotient of the property loss it is possible to ascertain the number of years it would take for a given community to recover its losses.

To demonstrate how this formula can work toward making cross-cultural comparisons, imagine a developing nation of 10,000 people whose GDP is $1,000 per person. Assume the infrastructure is valued at twenty years of GDP. This society might suffer three different disasters: one that destroys 100 percent of the infrastructure, one that destroys half, and another that destroys one quarter. In all three cases the value of the GDP is 10,000,000 (10,000 x 1,000), and the value of the infrastructure is 20,000,000 (20 x 1,000 x 10,000). The magnitude of the disaster where 100 percent of the infrastructure is destroyed is 2 (20,000,000 divided by 10,000, divided by 1,000), and the magnitude for the disaster that destroyed 50 percent of the infrastructure is 1, (10,000,000 divided by 10,000, divided by 1,000). The magnitude is .5 for the disaster that destroyed 25 percent of the infrastructure.

Certainly, it is impossible to compare the extent of damages from different disasters in different countries without taking into account the value of lives lost. On one level, this is impossible to calculate; but in economic terms the value of human life can be calculated by the person's life expectancy and yearly income. This is accomplished by using the following formula: the value of lives lost equals the number of lives lost times the life expectancy, divided by two times the per capita GDP. The product of lives lost and life expectancy is divided by two in order to estimate the average amount of productive years lost, bearing in mind that deaths are most likely to occur in older people, that people working for money are mostly male, and other factors.

In this fictitious example, the developing country has a life expectancy of sixty years, the GDP per capita is $1,000, and the disaster has killed 100 people. The formula would be 100 (the number of lives lost) times 60 (life expectancy), divided by 2 (the estimate of the average amount of productive years lost), times $1,000, which is the per capita GDP. The value of the 100 lives lost in this country is therefore $3,000,000.

By using an expanded formula that adds the value of lost lives to the value of lost property and dividing by the community's GDP, it is possible to estimate the number of years it would take to rebuild the economy to the level it was before the disaster. The value of using this method is that it allows cross-cultural researchers to measure how serious each disaster is in local (relative) terms and thus make comparisons between disasters across cultures.

Another way to make cross-cultural comparisons between disasters is exemplified in a study of postdisaster housing patterns after the Guatemalan earthquake (Bates & Killian, 1982). In this case the authors used the Belcher scale, a cross-cultural living scale that takes what is common about homes across cultures—they provide shelter, they use water, they are places in which to store and prepare food, and so on—and placed these into a schema that allows for cross-cultural comparisons. Belcher constructed a five-level scale for each function (for example, from storage of food in a clay jar to storage in electric freezers). The fourteen different functions identified by Belcher result in a level of living scale.

The Belcher scale has been used in the Guatemalan earthquake study (Bates & Killian, 1982) as well as in a comparative earthquake study in California, Turkey, Peru, Mexico, and Yugoslavia (Dynes, 1988). It has cross-cultural value not only to researchers but also to aid agencies because they seek to restore the comparable economic well-being of a household to its predisaster level. The scale, however, could be viewed as ethnocentric because of its reliance on material things and because the value of these things to people in different cultures is not equal.

Another cultural bias in disaster research comes from the problem in measuring differences between ethnic groups, particularly when the distinctions between them are more subtle than overt. To understand how the two main ethnic groups in Guatemala (Indian and Latino, of Spanish descent) were affected by the earthquake, several researchers constructed a relative ethnicity scale (Peacock & Bates, 1982). The scale was necessary because of the difficulty of defining who was Indian and who was Latino, since there had been so much intermarriage between them. The authors examined particular behavior patterns such as language, religion, dress, housing, cooking, and occupation. Language was given particular stress in their scale, which ranged from monolingual Mayan to Mayan-dominant bilingual Spanish, to Spanish-dominant Mayan bilingual, to monolingual Spanish. Footwear was classified from barefoot to primitive sandals to shoes. The authors conducted their relative ethnicity scale by using this type of method.

The study results showed that the more Indian and less Latino the people were, the greater was their relative economic loss as a result of the earthquake. Over the four years following the earthquake when aid was forthcoming, the degree of relative economic differences between the Indians and Latinos actually widened: the Latino got wealthier and the Indian poorer. In fact, the more Indian a person was on the relative scale of ethnicity, the worse the situation was; those Indians who had some Latino characteristics (acculturated) did relatively better than those who had none.

There is a good source of data for cross-cultural disaster researchers that is not being widely utilized. This is the Disaster History Update Program in the U.S. Office of Foreign Disaster Assistance. This is a comprehensive list of disasters, containing information about more than 1,000 disasters, all of which occurred outside the United States. The majority of these cases happened after 1964 when the agency was organized. Using factor analysis on this data base, Davis and Seitz (1982) showed that there was much less difference in the severity of impact of disasters in developed and developing countries than is commonly reported. Whether the results depended on what had been entered into the data base has not been studied.

Another potential solution to research problems related to cultural factors is having researchers of different nationalities study the same disaster. Such joint study has been suggested by the Disaster Research Center at the University of Delaware (Quarantelli, 1979). The procedure adopted there was to have both researchers use similar research protocols and then come together to discuss their results; however, they normally published their results separately.

A different comparative approach is to take one aspect of a disaster and study it from several different disciplines. Quarantelli (1979) suggested studying evacuation by police, and looking at the psychology of evacuees and evacuators, the sociological factors that come into play by the organizations involved in the evacuation, the legal factors involved in displacing people, the economic factors associated with the plan, and the way the plan affects subsequent economic development at the household and community levels.

As the field of disaster research matures, several attempts have been made to overcome the traditional weaknesses of ethnocentrism. These include the use of the Bates cross-cultural interview, the adaptation of the Belcher scale, the incorporation of the method of measuring loss across cultures, and the effort to include researchers from other cultures. Nevertheless, researchers whose main focus is social science cross-cultural investigation continue to show little interest in disaster research.

4
Reactions to Disasters in a Global Perspective

Two key characteristics of disasters is that they are embedded in people's fear of being subjected to unknown forces beyond their control and that they produce social crises. The fear of the unknown and uncontrollable forces is discussed farther in the next chapter, which examines the psychological reactions to disasters.

The difference between emergencies and disasters is determined by the degree to which each influences the social and physical infrastructure of their communities. Disasters have a substantial impact on their societies. There are many different types of societies, however, and not all disasters alter each of them in the same way. One value of cross-cultural research is that it provides information on the ways acute or chronic collective stress, brought about by disasters, is manifested in different cultural circumstances.

Only a few cross-cultural studies have purposely tried to ascertain how cultural differences affect people's responses to disasters. The first, and probably the most often quoted, was carried out on the American and Mexican border where flood victims of two communities, one on each side of the border, were interviewed (Clifford, 1956). The premise of the study was that predisaster cultural conditions would influence community response. The researcher predicted that the Mexican culture was more oriented to helping through kin groups and less connected to formal institutions. As a result he expected Mexicans to be less likely to adhere to predisaster governmental warnings or to accept postdisaster governmental relief. The results supported his hypotheses.

Many of the ideas of the research built on the pioneer work of Prince (1920), who studied people after a large ammunition explosion aboard a ship in the harbor of Halifax, Canada. Prince was convinced that after a disaster social change was inevitable. He reached this conclusion by observing the responses of the victims, the aid that the local community offered them, and the help the community received from outside relief agencies. As the physical infrastructure in Halifax was repaired and replaced, the community was exposed to many outside influences. Local people met many foreigners for the first time and those outsiders brought in new ideas. They showed the local artisans new methods of construction and how to use new materials. They gave suggestions about how to organize relief efforts, and they helped to modernize the social infrastructure. The disaster caused a change of technology and culture in the community. As the recovery process continued in Halifax, new groups came into existence and interacted with each other, creating new situations of conflict and cooperation. These factors also contributed to the postdisaster social change.

Prince also noted that there was a different rate of destruction among the social classes. Poor people's homes suffered greater damage. Later, he also observed an unequal rate of assistance. Poor people received less. Similar conclusions about the different rates of destruction and repair were reached in Italy (Geipel, 1982), in Nigeria (Watts, 1979), and in Bangladesh (Feldman & McCarthy, 1983). Likewise, studies of African droughts in the Sudan (Holy, 1980), in Kenya (O'Leary, 1980), and in Senegal (Copans, 1979) produced similar results. In light of the unequal rate of destruction and assistance in Halifax as well as changes to the infastructure and the arguments over scarce resources, Prince hypothesized that after disasters, differences between social classes increase. He also hypothesized a distinct possibility for political change.

Several other cross-cultural studies have shown that social change does not necessarily come to postdisaster communities, either with respect to the power structure and the redistribution of wealth or through changes of social institutions (Bates, Fogleman, Parenton, Pittman, & Tracy, 1963; Friesema, Caporaso, Goldstein, Lineberry, & McCleary, 1977; Haas, Kates, & Bowden, 1977; Oliver-Smith, 1977). A series of studies about human behavior in disasters across cultures was also conducted by Fritz (1961), who confirmed that natural disasters often unify communities. Similar results were found in Detroit after a toxic chemical spill where the community used the problem to solve some of its long-range problems rather than to succumb to intra-community bickering (Aronoff & Gunter, 1992).

It is possible that disasters contribute to both change *and* stability, because *both* consensus and conflicts emerge. People come together to make decisions where only conflict had existed, and where where there had been tensions between groups, new alliances emerge. One example happened on the last day of May, 1834, when a sizable earthquake struck Safad in what is now Israel. The quake killed many people and destroyed not only numerous homes but also many religious buildings important to the Arabs. The Arabs blamed the Jews for the earthquake and the misfortune they suffered. Thus, they began to massacre Jews and destroy their religious symbols. At first the Turks allowed the Arabs to destroy the Jews, thus staying on the side of their old allies. But after time the balance of power between Jew and Arab, which had supported the power of Turkish rule, tilted away from the Turks. So they interceded, and Turks and Jews found themselves allied for the first time, while Turks and Arabs, who had been allies until the earthquake, were enemies.

The apparent conflict between such results comes from the tendency to overgeneralize societal variables when examining community behavior after disasters. Even within a society, different groups of people are affected differently. For example, while the floods in the Bay of Bengal are frequently fatal to the migrant farmers who work the chars on the flood plains, they provide an opportunity for many wealthy people who use the disaster to buy more fertile land cheaply (White, 1974). A similar situation occurred when unexpected heavy frosts came to the central valley in California in the winter of 1990–91. Many migrant farm workers lost their jobs and were forced to return to Mexico, while the land-owning growers who were able to save their crops profited from the higher than normal prices.

Given the caveat of societal variables, using a classification system similar to the one employed by Dynes (1975) will allow researchers to examine more closely Prince's hypothesis: that changes are inevitable after disasters. This system divided the world's societies into three categories: traditional societies, nations of the developing world, and countries of the developed world.

Disasters in Traditional Societies

Traditional societies have a relatively small population. Their economy depends on hunting, gathering, or simple agriculture. Their social structure, centered around family and kin, is closely connected to their environment and their economic base. When an environmental disaster strikes a traditional society, people are forced to leave their land and migrate, usually to an urban area. In the cities, victims are obliged to work for wages and join the market economy. Many are not able to make these adjustments, and even those who can find little opportunity. One reason is that the economy, which may have been marginal, is placed under further stress after a disaster. As a result, many victims from traditional societies lose their way of life and their independence; often they are reduced to dependence on state assistance.

Changes do not come just to individuals; there are also changes to social structures. Before a disaster, traditional local leaders are important; but as the society adopts to the changes brought about by a disaster, new leadership skills are needed. Leaders are no longer chosen in the traditional way. They are selected because they are capable of functioning in the new order. These leaders are picked because they can lead society to its new reality. In many cases the new leaders are the very people who, prior to the disaster, were in conflict with the traditional leaders.

On the last day of November, 1960, Typhoon Ophelia struck the island of Ulithi in the southwest Pacific (Lessa, 1964). Ulithi is one of the thirty Caroline Islands of Micronesia. Each island is small; the whole archipelago is only about nineteen miles long and ten miles wide. Given Ulithi's small size and isolation, there was little opportunity for its inhabitants to escape Ophelia. The islanders dug in and withstood the winds, which exceeded 100 miles per hour. When the winds subsided and the people emerged from their huts, they saw the destruction of their food resources and the loss of their fishing canoes. With nothing to eat and limited possibility of getting food, they realized that they would need outside assistance or they would perish.

Aid was provided largely by American assistance. As a result, the islanders underwent significant acculturation of American values and way of life. At the time of the storm, men and women were forbidden to cover their upper bodies with clothes; within six weeks after the typhoon, everyone was vying for American-style shirts. Because the houses were destroyed in the storm, new homes had to built. Traditional materials, such as grass, were replaced with cement, which had to be imported onto the island. C rations were used as emergency food, and this led to changes in dietary habits. People became accustomed to canned food, sugar, meat stews, coffee, chocolate, condensed milk, and rice. To obtain these commodities they had to abandon their system of exchanging goods for services. In its place they adopted a market economy that would allow them to buy the items they desired.

Changes in the islanders' work habits and gender roles altered their kinship patterns. Sexual taboos were eliminated that had formerly forbidden menstruating women from participating in cultural activities or husbands/fathers from seeing their pregnant wives and newborn infants. For the first time women began working in cash-producing activities. By working harder some families were able to earn more than others. Several young men migrated to Guam in order to earn higher wages and buy more goods, therefore receiving higher status. Kin groups were now experiencing large differences in wealth, disparities that resulted in new tensions. The typhoon also greatly reduced the power of the old king. Because he was not able to communicate with the people giving aid and because he knew little of their culture, he was in large part unable to carry on with his role of leader. Younger people, more knowledgeable of the foreigners and able to speak their language, replaced him.

Ulithi is an example of a traditional society greatly changed as a result of experiencing an environmental disaster. Three other studies of Pacific island cultures affected by such natural disasters illustrate a similar process of social change (Firth, 1959; Schneider, 1957; Spillius, 1957). These studies point out that the progression of societies from traditional ways to those of the developing world is greatly speeded up by environmental disasters. The research has, in essence, confirmed Prince's hypothesis.

Modernizing changes brought about by disasters in other traditional societies also confirm Prince's hypothesis. After the area surrounding Huaraz, Peru, suffered a major earthquake, traditional farmers abandoned their exchange of services for a market economy (Dudasik, 1982). A similar shift occurred after volcanic eruptions among farmers in El Salvador (Sheets, 1979) and peasants in Mexico (Nolan 1979), and among herders in the outback of Australia following a tornado (Butler, 1976).

When pastoral Somali nomads were forced by drought to move into a Kenyan refugee camp and assume a sedentary agricultural way of life, they sustained a series of social and personal changes that inexorably modified them. Their diet, which had been milk and meat, became rice and maize; their social relations moved from totally within kin groups to almost totally outside of family; their once pastoral democracy was converted to a severe hierarchy of social status; cooperative leadership changed to leadership by domination; and in their formerly stateless society, the state now controlled all resources and many important life decisions, such as access to medical care and food stuffs and the terms of life in the refugee camp (Merryman, 1982).

In spite of these gloomy examples, all changes toward modernization are not necessarily evil. For one thing, a research study is more likely to report negative than positive changes. One study that is in accordance with Prince's theory of social change was done after a volcanic eruption in Yungay, Peru. According to the author, greater economic and social equality than had existed previously came about as a direct result of the disaster and the international aid that it brought (Oliver-Smith, 1979b). The disaster occurred in May of 1970 with the eruption of the largest mountain in Peru, Mt. Huascaran, which spewed out more than 50 million cubic yards of ice and rock. This volcanic matter began to career down the valley at about 270 miles per hour, directly toward the town of Yungay with some 4,500 inhabitants. Within minutes the entire town, with the exception of four palm trees in the main plaza, was buried.

As evening descended on Yungay, the region's capital city, the few survivors huddled in a cornfield under makeshift cornstalk shelters against the cold Andean night. Indian peasants from other areas of the mountains soon arrived to give victims food from their small harvests. Within a day, food, water, and shelter committees were organized by survivors. The community worked for over two months to bury the thousands of dead. Citizens had to form teams to patrol every night, shooting the dogs that wanted to scavenge the bodies. After time, official aid organizations arrived. They offered to build a new town nearby, but the survivors insisted on staying close to their old site. Citizens of all social classes and of different ethnic backgrounds worked together to thwart the government's plans for their relocation. They began to work together to meet the long-term demands of rebuilding their town.

Oliver-Smith's study of the survivors of Yungay and other small towns near the Mt. Huascaran avalanche points out the many difficulties the people endured, including the long task of burying the dead. However, the way the survivors faced their recovery contributed to their postdisaster well-being. The government insisted that the survivors rebuild their town in another locale. At first the townspeople agreed, but after a short time they realized that they wanted to return to their original site. In resisting the resettlement plans of the government, the survivors were able to show that they still had the power to direct their own lives. This resistance not only helped them affirm themselves but it also prevented the collapse of their social system, which surely would have occurred had they left their valley for another place (Oliver-Smith & Hansen, 1982).

After examining many disasters in traditional societies in India, Fernandez (1979) noted several ways that Indian society was improved following disasters. According to him, people who had not had any political skills prior to the disaster became knowledgeable of the political process for the first time. In many communities local leadership emerged and there was an increase of cooperation by citizens of different castes and gender far in excess of what had occurred prior to the disasters.

A comparative study of several of the least developed countries showed that people in traditional societies have indeed learned to cope with recurrent environmental hazards. They have learned to depend less on one crop. They have found better ways of storing food and have discovered new ways to store nonfood stuffs that can be traded in times of need for food. They also widened their social encounters to expand their trading partners and established better systems of communication between themselves and other communities (Colson, 1979).

In studying the Zapotec Indians in Oaxaca, Mexico, Kirby (1974) found that after droughts and flooding, people developed new rituals and ceremonies that centered around sharing what wealth was left. A comparative study of several African societies' reactions to drought showed that they had all changed their lives in order to cope; contrary to popular opinion, none of these societies relied on mystical intervention to see them through the drought (Torry, 1978b). In several societies people adapted their religious ceremonies to use less food in times of famine.

The Fulanai of Niger exemplify an African society that actively altered their lives to cope with drought. Normally they planted crops each year and after the harvest would move to the pastures in the Sahel when the rains arrived. Faced with a lack of rainfall, they began to live in smaller groups so they did not overburden what water supplies there were. Because the water was more widely dispersed than the people, the Fulanai divided up into smaller living groups to live closer to the water sources and thus to conserve the calories that would have been expended in walking greater distances to water.

The Fulanai also diversified their herds, reducing the numbers of animals such as cows and sheep that were heavy water users, replacing them with goats. They traded more items than usual, exchanging milk and leather for staples that they could no longer produce on their own. They developed a system of sharing animals between their own and other tribes. Not until all these coping devices failed did they begin to work for wages in town or on large farms.

The evidence suggests that people in traditional societies do as much as they can to avoid becoming victimized by environmental disasters. One author claimed that traditional societies were better able than developed ones to cope with disasters because they were more accustomed to reacting to terrifying circumstances (Sjoberg, 1962). After comparing reviews of global reactions to disasters, Torry (1978a, 1978b) corroborated the ability of traditional societies to adapt to disasters more readily than developed countries.

The people of traditional societies relate to one another differently from the ways of people in the developed world, and this affects the way they cope with disasters. Because people in the poorest societies have little basic security in normal times, they are more likely to share what they have with each other in times of disaster. In a study that compared the impoverished English in the eighteenth century with Hausa of Nigeria of the current century, Thompson (1971) found that the Hausa, like the poor English of the eighteenth century, supported their neighbors in what he referred to as a "moral" rather than a pecuniary economy. In a moral economy people help each other even if their immediate financial interests suffer.

Several cross-cultural studies have found "moral economies" among people in traditional societies who have faced disasters and who have learned to adapt to them by intrasocietal and interpersonal arrangements (McLuckie, 1970; Schneider, 1957; Sjoberg, 1962). The "moral economy," however, is not likely to last indefinitely nor are the coping strategies.

Because the Muslim Hausa of northern Nigeria live within the Sahel, they have long been accustomed to a recurrent lack of rainfall (Spitz, 1977). Indeed, they have a variety of religious rituals, folktales, fables, and other cultural manifestations demonstrating that drought and famine are part of their collective consciousness. When the Hausa were living in their traditional style, they dealt with drought by sharing among themselves. They had little expectation that the state would help them; indeed, they had no concept of the modern state at all. At first they changed their foods, switching to less healthy, drought-resistant foods. Some people tried farming in places where irrigation was not possible. They had to plant where they thought the natural supplies of water would be sufficient. As a result they planted in several places, often far from each other. They had to move between fields and thus leave their families behind. Others sold whatever they owned and then began to borrow food or money.

As Nigeria became more economically developed, the Hausa, most of whom did not have title to their land, were compelled to leave their traditional life-style, forced either to rent land to grow staples or to buy food. Those who did rent found that they had little time to cultivate their own food because they had to work for wages to pay the rent. They began buying food with the cash they earned from wages. Eventually, they started working for wages on large agricultural farms producing cash crops. This made them more vulnerable to the inevitable shortage of rainfall. With less rain, the cash crops they were hired to raise were not growing, which meant they lost their jobs. Without money, they could not buy food, and they had raised none of their own.

Since the turn of the twentieth century, as Nigeria has been "developing," the Hausa have starved as a result of droughts while the townspeople, who have traditionally been the consumers of the food the Hausa grew, have experienced no famine. When the Hausa moved to town they were unable to find work. As a result, when the drought came they had no money to buy food. This is the lot of many poor peasant farmers who leave their traditional way of life to join the developing world. They encounter development policies that favor urban industry over rural agriculture. Modernization for the Hausa, and others like them, has made them particularly vulnerable to environmental disasters.

People in some traditional societies, instead of moving into town to work for wages, or working for wages on a cash crop farm, move into other rural places where people in other traditional societies live. As they do so, they create extra demands on the new area's resources. This causes friction between the original residents and the newcomers, often leading to conflict.

The Embers (1992a, 1992b) have pointed out that the unpredictability of natural disasters is strongly correlated with societies going to war. The authors used the Human Relations Area Files (HRAF) to examine the ethnographic findings of 186 mostly preindustrial societies.

It was not the actual scarcity produced by the disaster as much as it was the fear of the unpredictable scarcity of food that lay behind the aggression. Societies invaded other groups, not because they were fearful of having no food as a result of a predictable disaster, but because they were afraid that at some unknown time they might not have food. Therefore they attacked other groups to gather enough food to store for possible scarcity. The possibility of being invaded increased people's fear of each other.

Although the HRAF files do not contain information on developed countries, the authors suggest that war among developed countries might be explained the same way. For example, industrialized nations go to war because they fear the unpredictable possibility of not having basic resources such as oil (Ember & Ember, 1992a, 1992b).

Cross-cultural data illustrate how nomadic and pastoral peoples in large part are forced by environmental disasters to leave their traditional way of life and homelands. Eventually they are forced to live in cities working for wages, or become dependent on welfare, or move into other rural areas that do not have sufficient resources for them. Depending on one's point of view, environmental disasters can be looked on as either modernizing or destroying traditional societies, an observation originally made by Prince (1920) and later confirmed by Dynes (1972), who contributed the system of demarcating societies.

Disasters in Developing Nations

Developing nations, the second type of society, are also changed by environmental disasters. In these countries the populations are large and their economic bases are a combination of agriculture and emerging industry. Almost always they have a history of colonial exploitation. Their social structures are centered around the family and the local community or village. The population's sense of belonging to the national state varies directly with social class and the degree of urbanization. People who are rural and poor are much less likely to be committed to or aware of their national states than are urbanites and people of higher social class.

In traditional societies, coping with an environmental disaster is beyond the country's economic means; in developing nations it is difficult but possible to meet the economic problems caused by a large disaster. To help the citizenry the government either calls for outside help or attempts to manage the crisis on its own. In either case, a large-scale environmental disaster in a developing country places a significant burden on the social and political order.

Most commonly, in a developing nation local government officials representing the interests of the power structure make the important postdisaster decisions. If the developing nation is economically and politically strong enough, and the disaster is not too large, the local power brokers, with the aid of their allies in the nation's capital, will likely handle the disaster. The people in power usually come out of such an experience with equal or more power than they had prior to the event. A case study carried out following freezes of Brazilian coffee crops determined that after the freezes the small coffee growers were eliminated and the larger power brokers gained even more control over the market than they had had previously (Margolis, 1979).

If, however, local authority is not able to control the situation—often the case with large disasters—the military frequently takes over (Anderson, 1970; Anderson & Dynes, 1976). The way victims are handled by the military, or by local government officials, is often what determines the social change to follow. At some point the country is forced to make a decision about whether to accept foreign assistance. Not all developing countries ask for international aid. Ethiopian officials would not acknowledge a cholera outbreak following the drought in 1973 because they feared that other countries would stop buying their export crops, thus putting the nation deeper into debt (Green, 1977). The fear of frightening away tourists is another reason some developing nations fail to ask for outside assistance. Others do not want international aid because of the exposure that would accompany it. When aid comes to the developing country, the world watches. The country's shortcomings—its inefficiency, corruption, and incompetence—all are exposed to world scrutiny (Glantz, 1976).

Political parties out of power use the treatment of victims as well as the distribution of money for rebuilding the infrastructure as part of their political rationale for running against their opponents. Haile Selassie tried his best to ignore the drought in Ethiopia in the early 1970s. It was the images of starving children on television that brought the Sahelian drought to the attention of the world community. When aid finally arrived the government was accused of misappropriating it. As a result, Selassie was deposed (Mayer, 1974). Similarly, the cyclone of 1970 in the Bay of Bengal which gave rise to the secession of Bangladesh from Pakistan (Green, 1977). After a large earthquake in Iran in 1978, the Shah handed out tents and blankets to victims, but neglected to provide any further aid. The fundamentalist Muslims donated food and helped the Iranian people to rebuild. The fall of the Shah was, in part, attributed to his indifference to his people's needs (Wijkman & Timberlake, 1988).

A few days before Christmas of 1972, Managua, Nicaragua, was struck by an earthquake that measured 6.1 on the Richter scale. Three-quarters of the city's housing was destroyed, 200,000 people were homeless, and nearly 20,000 died (Bommer, 1985). For forty-eight hours there was no assistance until President Somoza ordered the National Guard to patrol the city, effectively placing it under martial law. The government ordered the evacuation of the city but failed to protect the property left behind. Reports said that members of the National Guard were among the first looters (Bommer, 1985).

The people whose property was destroyed were never consulted. They were charged for the costs of demolishing their buildings, and for the costs associated with keeping their land patrolled by the police to prevent their belongings from being looted. But the sad fact was that the police were widely accused of stealing what the poor had left behind (Bommer, 1985). When international aid did arive, the National Guard was accused of hoarding the materials and then using them to develop a thriving black market (Black, 1981). Other members of the administration were reported to have earned huge profits from reconstruction (Green, 1977). When these abuses (and others) came under public scrutiny the Somoza power base was quickly eroded. Incensed by the government's callous disregard, the people of Nicaragua ousted their leaders. Many observers believe that the post-earthquake behavior of the Somoza regime contributed to its demise (Haas & Drabek, 1973).

Four years later, on February 4, 1976, Guatemala was struck by another earthquake—7.5 on the Richter scale. This one killed 25,000 people, severely injured 75,000, and left more than one million homeless (Bates, 1982; Dynes, de Marchi, & Pelanda, 1987). Entire towns and villages needed rebuilding, and the capital, Guatemala City, was also in severe need of repair. Eighty percent of the city's health infrastructure was destroyed. The homes of the wealthy were built to earthquake specifications; the homes of the poor were constructed of adobe, which is highly susceptible to earthquake damage. Thus, the earthquake inflicted much worse damage on the poor, increasing the already existing disparity between the well-to-do and the less well-off (Bates & Killian, 1982). At the outset, two factors controlled the reconstruction effort. First, because the rainy season was only 100 days away, homes had to be built quickly; without shelter in the constant rains to come, many people would become ill. Second, people remembered the 1972 Nicaraguan earthquake and its aftermath. The government believed that the fall of the Somoza regime was directly related to its corrupt handling of the post-earthquake reconstruction—and the widespread knowledge of this corruption (Green, 1977).

Several decisions had to be made about housing the homeless. Each of these had economic and political repercussions. Prior to the earthquake, as is true for most developing nations, there was no program for supplying housing for the poor. The government was forced to adopt a housing program. The pressing question was who would pay for it. Some of the international relief agencies proposed free housing—that is, housing paid for by the government—but the government opposed this idea, saying it would increase the economic dependence of the citizenry and retard the country's economic development.

Another issue was the degree to which victims would be involved in the rebuilding. The business community wanted to share in the profits that would come from construction contracts. Most international relief agencies proposed competitive bidding for supplies so that local vendors in favor with government contractors would not make exorbitant profits. This view put the international agencies at odds with local business interests.

In large part because of fear of what happened in Nicaragua after the 1972 earthquake, the Guatemalan government allowed victims to participate in the reconstruction efforts. An ad hoc reconstruction committee was formed, with the support of several nongovernmental Guatemalan organizations (NGOs) and many international governmental organizations (IGOs). They worked for the first two years by coupling earthquake reconstruction with broader development issues. Victims, for example, were encouraged to join together to buy materials, to draw up their own architectural plans, to decide on the subcontractors, and so on.

Because of the responsibilities lodged in the local communities, victims became more adept at making decisions. They felt more empowered. Local leadership developed. In short, the citizenry increased their democratic skills, gaining more control over their destiny than they had had prior to the earthquake.

To the extent that the nonprofit organizations and the victims themselves were doing the work, they were depriving the private sector of a great deal of potential income. This was not received well among the business community who felt they should be getting the contracts for cement, lumber, plumbing, electrical equipment, and so forth. They complained to the government, saying it was they who had the know-how and experience to accomplish reconstruction. They pressured the government to give them the rebuilding contracts.

In 1978, two years after the reconstruction process began, the issues of the presidential campaign centered around the earthquake. The liberal candidate, who came from the reconstruction committee, challenged the conservative candidate, who held power with the private sector and the military. The liberals lost the election, which many people felt was fraudulent. The re-elected conservative government, fearing the emerging political consciousness of the lower social classes, changed its course on reconstruction. They ended the programs that had contributed to democratizing peasant villages and poor communities in the capital. The people, however, had already developed local leadership and political skills and so they fought back. It became necessary for the government to put down their opposition with force, a move that led to more opposition, and then to more force. "Ultimately, the formal reconstruction process in Guatemala came to an end in the midst of what must be regarded as a civil war" (Bates & Peacock, 1987, p. 320). The disaster and its aftermath contributed to the repressive Guatemalan government of the 1980s with its large number of human rights abuses.

In each case mentioned above, outside aid helped the segments in society that were powerful before the earthquake, at the expense of the poor and powerless. In several developing countries, economic development has led to the enrichment of one segment of the society at the expense of marginalizing others. This widening of the gap between rich and poor has increased the vulnerability of the poor to disasters.

In many countries of the developing world the move toward economic development often means that the poor of those countries are particularly susceptible to environmental disasters. The history of Belize's response to hurricanes and droughts reveals that small farmers have been forced to leave their land because they never receive enough aid after disasters to rebuild (Hall, 1983). When they leave their own land, they begin working for wages on large, cash crop farms, living in such places as steep hillsides, which are vulnerable to environmental hazards. Similar circumstances were found in Honduras after Hurricane Fifi (Susman, O'Keefe, & Wisner, 1983). A cross-cultural study of aid from international agencies in different African countries in the Sahel showed that in each nation, aid heightened the conflict between factions vying for power (Glantz, 1976).

To understand the relationship between the physical event that leads to the disaster and the political fallout that disasters bring to developing countries, imagine a fictitious country, a typical nation in the developing world. It is threatened by flooding, cyclones, earthquakes, and dangerous chemical spills. In any given year, it is possible that this country will have a catastrophic disaster. It is also likely to have several regional disasters as well as a dozen or more local emergencies or accidents.

In the northern part of the country are highlands where trees have been cut for heating, cooking, and to build homes. As the forests are stripped, the hills hold less water; when the rains come the water rapidly washes the topsoil into the drainages. As a result of the added silt in the rivers, the rivers rise more and more quickly, increasing the possibility of flooding along their paths. Ten years ago the country had a large flood that forced 50,000 people into the capital city. These victims, having no money, began living on the steep hills surrounding the city where they could "squat" on free land.

Last year the region flooded, largely because the river had no dam. The plans for the dam were stalled by local politics, the national debt, and international aid negotiations. Because the land of nearly 10,000 people was under water, these farmers could not plant and harvest a crop. Being homeless, many of the farmers were forced to migrate to the capital city, where the only housing they could find was on a flood plain on the outskirts of the capital. Like their neighbors who had arrived from past environmental disasters, they were able to appropriate land by squatting on it.

In order to satisfy the needs of the increasing numbers of urban poor, the government has been subsidizing food. This competition makes farming even more economically difficult for all but the large landowners. As a result, more small farmers come to the city, increasing the burden on the government and fueling inflation. The inflation makes seeds and fertilizer prohibitively expensive, forcing more farmers to the city.

In the last census of this mythical country, 40 percent of the population lived in urban areas. The majority of them are squatting on land where anyone with more resources would not chose to live. The squatters build their homes on steep slopes and on flood plains, both of which are vulnerable to environmental disasters. They have little access to potable water and less to sewage facilities, making them vulnerable to sickness and disease.

Other factors in the country have also contributed to the rural-to-urban migration. In the whole nation there are only two cash crops for export and these account for a great deal of the nation's foreign exchange. Two different ethnic groups, with a long history of hostility between them, each control one of the crops. The ruling party of the state is in the hands of a third ethnic group, which has a history of hostilities with the other two.

After several years of inflation, rural-to-urban migration, and a decreasing number of small farmers, there are a few years when the rainfall is below average. The people left on the farms begin to hoard their food as they cannot afford to buy any. Meanwhile food in the city has increased in price beyond the means of the poor. Without food, people begin demanding that the government help them. However, because of increased needs and expenditures to meet these needs over the last several years, government resources are depleted. Attempting to prevent large civil disturbances, the government shows its force by using the military to enforce a curfew, which only exacerbates the existing ethnic feuds. People realize that the escalation in force can only lead to more problems, both economic and civil. They flee to a safe haven, creating a refugee problem in the neighboring country. These neighbors, in the meantime, have been waiting for generations to retrieve land that they feel has been stolen by the refugees' country.

This fictitious scenario is not greatly unlike the actual events after the 1976 earthquake in Guatemala, after the 1972 earthquake in Nicaragua, after the Ethiopian drought and famine in the 1970s, and after the 1970 flood in the Bay of Bengal. In the first two cases the government was forced out of power. In the Ethiopian case, the disasters not only led to the fall of Selassie but to a civil war and ultimately to the formation of a new country, Eritrea. The 1970 flood in the Bay of Bengal also led to a civil war and to the formation of a new country, Bangladesh. There are many more examples in the developing world that illustrate the reciprocal relationship between environmental hazards and complex social and political realities. As Prince predicted, both traditional societies and the nations of the developing world undergo social changes after disasters. It is difficult, however, to know how large the influence of the disaster is among the other factors that also contribute to change.

Disasters in Developed Countries

In the developed world there are large populations living in urban industrial centers. The state is elaborately organized and has reduced many of the functions of family, kin, and village found in traditional societies and developing countries. A specialized social infrastructure—schools, hospitals, police and fire departments, and so on—replace many family and village functions.

In times of disaster many parts of the social structure are involved with disaster relief and reconstruction. However, there are problems with coordinating each particular part with the overall reconstruction efforts. Priorities are difficult to set. A bureaucratic structure emerges to take central authority. This bureaucracy is often slow to respond for several reasons. Those in charge of relief must exert control over several specialized agencies. To be effective they must form political alliances with private and public agencies, some of which are local while others are national. In the alliance each agency must function in a fashion different from what it is accustomed to, depending on the uniqueness of the particular disaster. These problems of adjustment contribute to the difficulty of coordinating efforts, as does the continual change that is forced onto all the people involved, especially those in the several agencies who must learn new ways of acting during the disaster.

Because developed societies have a great reliance on technology, and people in developed countries live in large population centers, there is a possibility of their being vulnerable to catastrophic disasters. Cities with high-rise buildings, underground transportation and high-speed highways are particularly susceptible. This susceptibility, however, is manifested primarily in loss of property rather than loss of life. In a comparison of many disasters from 1970 to 1980 in the United States, Rossi and others discovered that the main loss due to disasters was in destroyed property (Rossi, Wright, Weber-Burdin, & Pereira, 1983). There were very few disaster deaths. The Red Cross claims that it has never found a true food shortage after a disaster in the United States (Dacy & Kunreuther, 1969).

In contrast to traditional societies and developing nations, developed countries do not undergo social change in the society as a whole as a result of disasters (Friesema et al., 1979; Rossi, J. Wright, S. Wright, & Weber-Burdin, 1978a, 1978b; J. Wright, Rossi, S. Wright, & Weber-Burdin, 1979).

Developed countries do have problems in the aftermath of disasters, however. Victims often complain about being victimized twice—once by the disaster and a second time by the highly technological and bureaucratic system designed to serve them. Their sense of impotence sometimes kindles old social and political differences. The newly opened conflict may contribute to local political or economic changes, but there is little likelihood that it will alter the political process in any significant manner. This observation was corroborated in a cross-national study of North American and Latin American disaster victims (Bolin & Bolton, 1983).

A comparative study of two ethnic minority communities suffering from two different disasters showed that while old social issues contributed to the formation of recovery groups, which altered the course of recovery, neither community experienced any long-lasting social changes (Aptekar, 1990). This study examined the two costliest environmental disasters in the history of the United States: Hurricane Hugo and the Loma Prieta earthquake. Hugo's costs were estimated at more than five billion dollars (Federal Emergency Management Association,

1990) and those of the earthquake at more than six billion (Dames & Moore, 1989; Plafker & Galloway, 1990; Ward & Page, 1990). In each case the data came from small agricultural towns (Watsonville, California, and McClellanville, South Carolina) that were severely impacted by the disasters.

The two towns had similar histories. Both began as agricultural communities based on cheap labor—from slaves in the case of McClellanville, and from foreign migrant workers in the case of Watsonville. Both towns had similar ethnic/racial proportions of non-whites. In Watsonville more than half the adult population was Mexican or Mexican-American. In McClellanville, African-Americans represented about eighty percent of the population.

Each disaster also had very painful events. In McClellanville there were cases such as the people who were trapped inside Lincoln High School. In Watsonville, buildings collapsed in full view of citizens. The fright this engendered was so substantial that many people preferred to live in tents for weeks rather than return to their houses. These catastrophic occurrences contributed to the people's widespread feeling of vulnerability to events that were powerful beyond their experience and outside of anyone's control.

Findings from Aptekar's study showed that in both the hurricane and the earthquake, predisposing issues related to the ethnic minority communities contributed to how people recovered from the disasters. African-Americans in McClellanville, South Carolina, and Mexican-Americans in Watsonville, California, had historically experienced unequal access and opportunity. They had been unable to change their low status, and each time a community issue surfaced they felt vulnerable at the prospect of losing more status. Once recovery efforts began, they feared and expected to get the smaller piece of the pie.

On the other hand, the groups in power were accustomed to having power. They came out of the disasters expecting to regain their high status. Although everyone was humbled by the disasters, the prior status of each group in the community influenced how they perceived and reacted to disaster relief.

In a developed country, the private insurance companies and the governmental agencies are the main organizations involved with long-term recovery. As they try to work with the ad hoc recovery groups and the Red Cross, many difficulties develop. Research with the Red Cross has shown that it has trouble when national staff members must be mixed with local volunteers (Adams, 1970), a situation intensified in this case by the two disasters occurring within weeks of each other.

The government's power to exert its will in the moment of crisis and the victims' need to accept the government's will was most apparent in the "fifteen minute rule" after the earthquake. This rule allowed people at the earthquake site fifteen minutes, but no more, to retrieve their belongings or business stock from condemned buildings. Peter had operated the Hallmark Shop in Watsonville for sixteen years. It was located in a shopping center that was badly damaged. The buildings were scheduled for demolition and the store owners were given fifteen minutes to get their business stock. Peter received a call at 10:30 P.M. Friday, October 27, and was put on stand-by for Saturday when he would be given fifteen minutes to retrieve his business stock. He rented a truck and brought five friends to help him. When they arrived at the shop, an engineer was standing by with a stopwatch.

The six of them, acting like they were grocery store prize winners given a certain amount of time to fill their grocery baskets, rushed into Peter's store and went to work filling boxes with his merchandise. The stress that Peter was under was magnified by the knowledge that his house had also been damaged. In addition to the $100,000 of lost stock in his store, he had already calculated an equal loss to his house. He could not understand why he was not allowed an hour in the store—the amount of time he calculated he would need to get his merchandise out. He was willing to take the risk of being hurt, especially since his part of the building was not very badly damaged. "What's so magic about fifteen minutes?" he kept on asking (Aptekar, 1990).

John, the engineer who condemned the buildings and was responsible for the fifteen minute rule, said, "At first I was going to allow only ten minutes, but then I thought that people might rush too much and hurt themselves. On the other hand, if I had allowed a half hour, they would start bringing out items that were unimportant and easily replaced" (Trabing, 1989).

The Federal Emergency Management Agency (FEMA) is the principal U.S. governmental agency for administering disaster relief. FEMA's first task after a disaster is to determine whether the local and state governments can handle the damage. If they cannot, these governments must ask the president of the United States to declare the region an official disaster area, making it eligible for federal assistance. FEMA is then allowed to supply loans, technical assistance, and temporary shelter in the region for up to eighteen months. In both disasters FEMA received much criticism for having too much paperwork and too many regulations, for its inability to respond in a timely fashion, and for being insensitive to ethnic and racial groups (Cockburn, 1989). Within a month or so of each disaster, people had had plenty of time to assess the damage to their property. They had talked with friends and had learned which government programs were set up to assist them.

Bob had married a local woman a dozen years before and had settled into life in McClellanville, raising three boys and working as a carpenter. He had built a house on the salt marshes less than a mile from the Atlantic Ocean. In spite of having talked over his distress with his family and friends, he was unable to find a satisfactory answer to why his house had been destroyed. Bob was neither religious nor a believer in fate. Because he was the kind of person to take action, he was one of the first people to enter the FEMA office.

Instead of being personally greeted, he received a number. He then waited for thirty minutes until he was asked to enter a room to receive an application. After filling out the application he went to see the map reader who determined whether his property fell within the designated area. Since there was only one map reader for the 104 people who filled out applications that day, Bob spent several hours waiting to learn whether his property qualified, even though his house had been nearly completely destroyed. After receiving a positive determination from the map reader, he waited to see the single small business loan representative, who also had the power either to approve or refuse him a loan on his carpentry tools that were destroyed.

At each step of being accepted or rejected for aid, Bob was required to fill out government forms without much help. Even when all the forms were completed, he was never sure whether he was even eligible for aid. This uncertainty increased his sense of helplessness. Because he could not understand (and was given little help in understanding) the complex rules and regulations that were so important to his welfare, he was cautious about how decisions concerning him were being made and was anxious to ask questions. He was not in the best of mental health since he had just been through the hurricane and had lost his house. All these factors led to an accumulation of frustration.

The next day he was to see his private insurance agent. The agent's company had reserved several motel rooms in a town a forty-five-minute drive away for these interviews. Because the storm had also damaged his car, Bob and his sons had to catch a ride in the back of a truck with a couple of friends. When they arrived, they had to wait in the motel lobby for two hours. When he finally was able to see the agent, Bob was shown several long forms and told that his insurance covered part but not all of the damage to his home. He was given the choice of signing a short form immediately, which would enable him to receive a check for about $4,500 in a week, or taking home all the forms and waiting to see how much of his damage was covered. Realizing how inadequate the offered amount was for repairing his home, Bob took the longer forms and returned home. There he found that his wife had returned from rummaging through a clothes shelter where she had found used clothing for all of them.

The next day Bob went to get food, to check on his FEMA application, and to talk with his friends about the insurance forms. He learned from them that almost no one had fared any better than he had. At about this time he began drinking. He began to express his anger with his friends, with God who had brought the disaster, with the government who refused to treat him decently, let alone give him what he was due, with the insurance companies that refused to honor his claim, and finally with himself for being reduced, for the first time, to the status of welfare client (Aptekar, 1990).

Like Bob, almost all the people in both disasters were dissatisfied with the treatment they received from their insurance agents (Smith, 1989). Private insurance companies are the other major players, along with FEMA, in handling disasters in the United States. From them, most homeowners in the hurricane area learned after the fact that they would have needed at least three types of insurance for their houses to be covered: homeowner; wind, storm, and hail; and flood. Even this combination would not fully replace all that was damaged.

A similar pattern held for victims in the earthquake area. In order to get insurance benefits from private companies, people had to obtain itemized estimates of the damage to their homes. This proved to be difficult, however, because contractors generally do not calculate expenses by itemization. Instead, they estimate by square footage or by an ongoing "time and materials" arrangement. When Jaime, a Watsonville contractor, began receiving calls from his neighbors for estimates on individual items, he had to expend a tremendous amount of time, effort, and cost to make the calculations. He was concerned because he was not really sure what the actual cost would be. To protect himself he tried to avoid his neighbors' requests. They interpreted his behavior as a personal affront to them because they assumed that making an estimate was a simple task, which normally it was.

In short, victims faced a complexity of rules, regulations, bureaucracies, and bureaucrats. Each of these occupied a particular niche in relief or recovery, but none of them was much aware or very concerned about the others' roles, functions, and most important, the impact they had on victims. The tremendous sense of impotence the physical event created in the victims was greatly intensified by the indifference of the bureaucratic "helpers" who were assigned to aid them.

The various segments in each community had had different experiences with governmental agencies before the disasters; after them, they had different degrees of luck getting help. Many African-Americans victims in the small community of McClellanville had passed down stories of slave days and being helpless and dependent on white plantation masters. Mexican Americans in Watsonville recalled their families' stories of being deprived of their land, of being punished for speaking Spanish, and of being threatened with deportation. In short, the collective memories of each of the communities contributed to keeping many people dependent and frustrated. The postdisaster mitigation efforts had a way of reactivating these feelings. Social class, which mirrored ethnic boundaries in these communities, played a significant role in people's reactions and in their treatment.

Two years after the disasters the social class disparities that had existed prior to the earthquake and hurricane were as apparent as they had been before (Rubin & Popkin, 1991). The same strains between social classes and between ethnic or racial groups existed. The aftermath of the disasters had brought no changes in the political process (Aptekar, 1991; Philips, 1991). Prince's hypothesis of inevitable social changes after a disaster appears not to be as valid in developed countries as it is in the less developed world.

Political Ideology and Disaster Relief

This chapter began by drawing a distinction among traditional societies, developing nations, and developed countries in order to ascertain whether Prince's hypothesis—that social change is inevitable after disasters—has cross-cultural validity. There are other ways to divide the world's societies in order to explore Prince's hypothesis. One classification schema was developed by Seitz and Davis (1984), who studied a number of environmental disasters that struck Latin America and Africa between 1964 and 1973. They reasoned that since these two continents account for nearly three-fourths of the world's developing nations, and that almost every one of those nations lacked resources to manage disaster relief, each government would have to decide how to use what resources it had. Each one would also have to decide whether to ask for foreign assistance. Because the governments would have to make decisions concerning economic choices and outside resources, the authors felt that by studying this process they could ascertain the relationship between type of government and disaster relief.

The researchers coded each government with respect to its ideology concerning allocation of its resources after a disaster. The categories were ethnic pluralism, corporatism, and equalitarianism. Ethnically pluralistic governments had difficulty adopting central planning as they had to respond to so many competing ethnic groups. Corporate governments had central planning, but they stressed development of infrastructure, even at the cost of social equality. Equalitarian government had central planning and gave resources equally to all citizens.

Seitz and Morris (1984) examined the differences between the types of governments, the numbers of people killed, the amount of damage to buildings and the infrastructure, and the number of victims. They discovered that in all three types of governments, political choices determined how resources were allocated. If the ethos of the government's allocation was defined by restoration of damaged property (corporate), there were higher incidents of tragedy, death, and victimization than if the government were oriented more toward people (equalitarian). In this case, Prince's hypothesis of social change following a disaster was further refined in relation to governmental ideology.

Another researcher, Wisner (1978), suggested comparing countries' responses to disaster by their mode of production. He divided countries into feudal, capitalist, and socialist. He then compared two countries, Bangladesh (capitalist) and Vietnam (socialist), both of which are prone to flooding. Both countries were colonized by European powers, both are densely populated with over a thousand people per square mile, and both have low-lying areas susceptible to storms and floods. In order to prevent flooding both countries have built a system of dikes to protect themselves.

The 1970 cyclone in the Bay of Bengal killed nearly a quarter of million people. In 1971, three typhoons submerged the Red River delta in Vietnam. The dikes were broken, but there were no deaths despite the American military's prediction that destruction of the dikes would kill more than a million people. Both countries had access to meteorological warnings, but the warning system broke down in Bangladesh. Bangladesh relied on satellite communications systems that did seem to function, but the information was not translated into the dialects of the poor migrants who lived on the flood plain. Therefore, for all practical purposes, the people who lived in the most vulnerable places were not warned. One explanation for this failure was that most people in the West Bengali villages, which were in greatest danger, were from a different and competing political party from those in power (Schware, 1982; Schware & Lippoldt, 1982).

Even though the Bangladesh flood plains are frequently inundated, no advanced community organization had been developed to help potential victims, nor was there a means of evacuating people from the affected area. In Vietnam the method of warning was less technologically sophisticated but far more effective because of advance planning. The warning system relied on human brigades that had been organized before the floods came. Members of these groups were able to warn, remove, and house a half-million homeless people.

Another comparison between two countries of different political systems points out considerable differences in how each was reconstructed (Ebert, 1986). The countries studied, socialist Romania and capitalist Nicaragua, suffered from earthquakes in 1977 and 1972, respectively. In Rumania the strong central socialist government acted swiftly after the 1977 earthquake. Within forty-eight hours food was delivered, small cash grants for rebuilding homes were given out, and within a year the total reconstruction effort was completed. In Nicaragua, with a capitalist government (in 1972 the Somoza government was in power), the poor urbanites were left to fend for themselves. There was no governmental housing program. Looting took place and fires were rampant. Eventually international forces had to quell the rioting. Members of the government, including the Somoza family, allegedly made millions of dollars in the reconstruction effort, while very little government money went to the poor (Bommer, 1985).

The notion that a country's political ideology influences the way it responds to disasters has also been illustrated by a description of

Mozambique's (socialist) response to flooding (Wisner, 1979). Since gaining its independence from Portugal in 1975, Mozambique has sustained an average of over 40 million dollars a year in flood damage—about 12 percent of its annual budget. The country has greatly organized its citizenry through preventive measures that include resettlement of people from hazardous into more benign areas. The author suggested that Mozambique was able to perform so well because of its political ideology. In comparing other countries, Wisner found that the best predictor of human tragedy following a disastrous event is the country's political ideology.

These studies have examined Prince's hypothesis in relation to a society's political system. Another type of comparison concerning political differences is the degree of a country's political centralization (McLuckie, 1977). McLuckie's study sampled three countries, Japan, Italy, and the United States. Japan was the most centralized, the United States the least, and Italy was in between. McLuckie found that warnings of impending disasters and evacuation procedures were delayed in relation to the degree of centralized political decision making in the country. The reasoning was that because the citizenry were accustomed to waiting for centralized directives in more normal times, they were less capable of acting on their own in times of stress.

A similar schema was used in a study that compared Guatemala and Nicaragua; close in proximity and culture, both had suffered earthquakes (Kreimer, 1978). The two countries differed in the degree to which their governments were centralized. At the time, Nicaragua was considerably more centralized than Guatemala. Kreimer concluded that the more centralized a government was, the less efficient it would be in the recovery process. Her reasoning was that people in centralized governments would wait to get information from their capital, whereas people in decentralized governments would be more independent and thus used to acting on their own without waiting for direction from central authorities.

Other Factors That Influence Reactions

In addition to governmental centralization, McLuckie (1977) also identified other factors that could be used to compare a society's response to disasters. These included the dominance of the family unit in the society. The more powerful the family was, the less likely the society would be to accept governmental or official warnings. This finding was similar to the conclusion drawn in the bi-national study of a flood along the Mexican American border (Clifford, 1956).

McLuckie also hypothesized that the higher the society's level of technological development was, the more vulnerable it would be. In part he based this idea on one of the first ethnograhpic studies of disasters, Schneider's study (1957) of a typhoon on the island of Yap in Micronesia. Schneider compared Yapians to people who live in more developed societies, hypothesizing that the more dependent a society is on material goods and technological sophistication, the more social problems would emerge following a disaster. Cross-cultural research is needed to test this hypothesis.

These studies did not factor in the history of most developing nations—one of colonial control over their natural resources. Their past experience leaves most indigenous people unlikely to believe that warnings of environmental disasters by former colonial powers will be value-free. Riddington (1982) reported on an indigenous community listening to expert witnesses telling them of the hazards of a small well in their community. The villagers did not believe the experts and continued to use the water in spite of the fact that it was making them sick. In this case it was not the power of family life in a society that determined whether the people heeded cautions but the degree to which they trusted the people giving the warnings.

A thorough cross-cultural comparison, using some of the variables mentioned, was conducted in fourteen nations responding to different disasters (Burton, Kates, & White, 1978). The researchers found that the preexisting economic level of a country, defined in terms of wealth, technology, and social organization, determined disaster response. Although this study did include level of technology as an indicator of economic development, it did not look at technology in more sociological terms—that is, how it affects groups of people and institutions. The study did find that victims in the least economically developed societies adapted by using different farming techniques and by finding different ways to live more cooperatively with one another; but it also found that they took few proactive measures to control potential hazards.

Other research has confirmed that in developing countries the level of technology increases as a result of the postdisaster rebuilding (Ciborowski, 1967; Hogg, 1980). In industrial societies, victims relied less on their families and kin groups than they did on collective plans such as insurance and other relief efforts funded by tax money. Because these nations had more sophisticated technology, they attempted to control potential environmental hazards through planning and national policy. Thus, the Prince hypothesis that disasters inevitably bring social change appears less valid as the socioeconomic level of the country rises. In developed countries there appears to be little change following a disaster.

In many ways environmental disasters run courses like physical illnesses. The event brings with it a loss of well-being, which is followed by a treatment or a series of treatments aimed at eliminating the consequences of the event and bringing about recovery. Even if a country can return to its original level of health, it will emerge changed by having had the experience of being victimized and of going through "treatment." The collective memory of the experience prevents the citizenry from returning to their preimpact feeling of being invulnerable. It appears that vulnerability, however, is not evenly distributed over the globe. Traditional societies and developing nations are much more likely to be changed by disasters, as are the poor in every society.

5

The Psychology of Disaster Victims

Common sense as well as decades of research in the field has shown that disasters absorb people's emotional lives. Since the pioneering study of Lindemann in the 1940s, psychologists have been exploring the ways in which disasters consume a person's psyche, how they worsen some emotional problems while dissipating others, how they feed and fester on victims' spirits, how they stand in comparison with other emotional traumas, and how they challenge people's ability to cope, to maintain their faith in God, and to continue their belief in justice and fairness. Even after years spent researching these phenomena, however, the conclusions to be drawn are still unclear, particularly when the problems are considered in a global context.

Lindemann (1944) described victims' emotional reactions to the Coconut Grove nightclub fire in Boston, in which nearly 500 people died. His description later became known as the *disaster syndrome*—a process of grieving that includes flashbacks, preoccupation with feelings of distress toward those who died, guilt about surviving or not taking care of other victims, anger at what happened, and hostility toward those who tried to offer aid. Victims also had a compulsive need to talk about the trauma, and many developed obsessive thoughts and compulsive behaviors. Lindemann concluded that these symptoms were part of the process of healing, and that after time in most cases they would abate.

In the next decade other writers wrote about symptoms that were similar to those of the disaster syndrome. Menninger (1952) described victims as dazed and apathetic, often wandering around aimlessly. These reactions were followed by a period of goodwill in which victims became suggestible, felt gratitude, acted altruistically toward others, and became enthusiastic about their community.

After his study of Hiroshima, Lifton (1967) described the *survivor syndrome*, which included a death imprint—an inability to escape the images and thoughts of death. Victims had difficulty coming to terms with why the event happened at all and particularly to them. This inner turmoil manifested itself in many debilitating symptoms. Victims developed survivor guilt, a sense of guilt because they but not others—particularly their loved ones—survived. Psychic numbing was another symptom—a feeling that all of one's emotions were spent and no new stimuli, no matter how intense they might be, were capable of producing an emotional response. Victims also were in conflict over their nurturing needs, wanting to be independent but needing to be cared for.

Conflicting Points of View

Lifton's work was the first of this type that examined subjects outside the United States in such detail. In fact, one shortcoming with the literature on psychological reactions to disasters is the scarcity of evidence from developing nations. Another problem is that not all researchers have found the same reactions.

One of the first statistical estimates of the degree to which victims were affected by disasters predicted that 75 percent of the population would become stunned, but only about 10 to 25 percent would show lasting impairment (Tyhurst, 1951). The validity of these statistics was not widely supported as many people felt that a much larger percentage would suffer lasting problems.

By 1970 an important theoretical work on disaster psychology was published (Barton, 1969). Barton offered seventy-one hypotheses concerning victim reactions that could be tested. Some of these took into account various cultural factors while others were formulated to test the discrepancies found in the earlier literature. Much of the psychological research since that time has involved testing these hypotheses.

Almost all researchers agree that immediately after a disaster people demonstrate dazed behavior with a sense of generalized anxiety, often marked by docility and obedience. However, there is little agreement about the long-term psychological impact, including the extent to which the disaster syndrome turns into longer-term emotional problems (Perry & Lindell, 1978).

There are two current and opposing positions with regard to the lasting psychological reactions to disasters. One is that natural disasters produce catastrophic psychological reactions that may endure for some time (Erikson, 1976a, 1976b; Gleser, Green, & Winget, 1981; Lifton & Olson, 1976; Menninger, 1952; Moore, 1958; Titchener & Kapp, 1976; Tyhurst, 1957). The other is that psychological adversity following a disaster is relatively minor and almost always short-lived (Bates et al., 1963; Drabek & Key, 1976; Fritz, 1957, 1961; Quarantelli & Dynes, 1977). Two excellent reviews describing the issues and the conflicting findings were done by Smith et al. (1986) and Rubonis and Bickman (1986).

The following sections examine the ways that disasters do and do not produce long-lasting psychosocial problems. Reasons for the conflicting findings are then hypothesized, after which the sequence in which psychological reactions occur is explored.

Disasters Produce Long-Lasting Psychological Adversity

Buffalo Creek is in a narrow winding valley in West Virginia where, in the early 1970s, 5,000 inhabitants lived in the fourteen mining towns scattered throughout the valley. Stretching across the creek was a dam, built by mine owners to contain the metallic residue from the ore refining process. In 1972, the dam broke. One hundred thirty-two million gallons of metal ore mud, filled with debris and water, poured down the valley. Bridges, cars, houses, even human bodies were carried with it. The people who were able to escape to the high ground witnessed the destruction. More than 4,000 of the valley's 5,000 houses were destroyed.

It was many weeks before the black mud and debris could be cleared away. To help those who had lost their homes, the federal government bought trailers, which they placed outside the community. These were distributed on a first-come, first-served basis. As people moved into the trailers, they left the community they knew and the neighbors who had given them support.

At about the same time, the state decided to build a road through the narrow valley. This decision made it impossible for the dispossessed to begin rebuilding their homes; they were not willing to invest in building houses on land they were afraid the state would claim for the new highway. The state did not decide exactly where the new road would be for two years, a delay that forced people also to wait for two years before they could begin rebuilding.

Insurance companies argued relentlessly about paying claims. Not knowing whether they were going to receive insurance payments or how much they would receive also slowed people's ability to rebuild. As a result of all the delays, many people decided they could no longer continue to live with relatives or friends or wait to find new jobs in the area. In order to get on with their lives, they were forced to leave their neighbors. In the end, the victims lost not only their homes but also their sense of community.

Titchener and Kapp (1976) reported that over 90 percent of the Buffalo Creek flood victims had disabling psychological symptoms that went well beyond healthy grief two years after the event. Several other studies have also shown long-lasting emotional problems among these victims (Erikson, 1976a, 1976b; Gleser, Greene, & Winget, 1981; Lifton & Olson, 1976).

In his early theoretical work, Barton (1969) wrote about the importance of the *therapeutic community*, that is, the pulling together of people after a disaster. Barton believed that the existence of such a group greatly helped the mental health of victims. In such a community, citizens support each other, giving help that ignores social class and ethnic and racial boundaries. Because of the social support it supplies, the therapeutic community has been cited as a major reason for the absence of profound or long-term emotional distress following disasters (Barton, 1969; Fritz, 1961; Tierney & Baisden, 1979). A therapeutic community failed to develop in Buffalo Creek, largely because of the immediate relocation of community members; the lack of this support system has been cited as one of the reasons these victims suffered so badly.

Long-term adverse effects were found in a study of 1,000 French miners who routinely went down a mine shaft to work. One day that shaft caved in, killing all but twelve of the miners. The survivors found themselves surrounded by numbers of dead bodies, many of which were the bodies of people they had known since childhood. Unable to escape, they had to ration water and food. The only way for them to survive was to eat everything they found in the mine—each rodent and insect, even the plants that grew on the dripping walls. They stopped short of eating the dead bodies or each other. Only after discussing this awful alternative did they decide that they preferred death to cannibalism.

Eventually they were saved. In a follow-up study of these dozen miners, all but one showed recurrent phobic responses and other severe psychological symptoms (Ploeger, 1970). These two studies illustrate that if the personal impact is extreme enough, the severity of psychological problems will rise accordingly.

In a major study of the mental health effects of the 1980 Mount St. Helens volcanic eruption, the researchers noted persistent elevated levels of pathological reactions among the victims, including a tenfold increase in depression, anxiety, and post-traumatic stress disorder (PTSD). In this disaster the events had been substantially less horrifying than those endured by either the French miners or the victims of Buffalo Creek, yet years after the event, those who had been through the eruption of Mount St. Helens showed symptoms of depression, anxiety, and post-traumatic stress disorder (Shore, Tatum & Vollmer, 1986a, 1986b). PTSD often comes about as the result of environmental disasters and its symptoms are discussed later in this chapter.

On March 28, 1979, there was a malfunction in a unit of the Three Mile Island (TMI) nuclear reactor. In the days immediately following, the public was unsure what had actually happened—whether a meltdown had occurred or what would result from the release of radiation into the atmosphere. People knew that the governor had issued an advisory warning for pregnant women and children living within five miles of the plant to leave the area for their own safety. Almost 150,000 people actually left.

Three major studies were conducted on TMI. Two of them (B. S. Dohrenwood, B. P. Dohrenwood, Kasl, & Warheit, 1979; Houts & Goldhaber, 1981) concluded that the mental health effects, even though intense for a while, were transitory. The third study (Bromet, Parkinson, & Schulberg, 1982) was carried out by the National Institute of Mental Health (NIMH). One of the most carefully controlled disaster studies ever done, it found long-term mental health problems among victims, particularly mothers of young children who had twice the incidence of affective disorders (depression), anxiety, hostility, and somatization than the control group. Although the physical incident itself had little real impact (no nuclear leak actually occurred), the fear of being exposed to nuclear radiation was sufficient to cause prolonged distress in residents of the area surrounding the reactor.

Many other studies suggest that long-term mental health problems follow disasters (Goldstein, Schorr, & Goldstein, 1984; Houts, Miller,

Ham, & Tokuhata, 1980). Wilkenson (1985) noted that nearly every disaster victim will show some signs of PTSD. In a review of the literature, Cohen and Ahearn (1980) concluded that "there does seem to be mounting evidence that disasters produce or influence emotional problems" (p. 238).

In addition to the study of the trapped French miners, other studies from outside the United States have shown enduring emotional problems. These include the 1972 Nicaraguan earthquake (Ahearn, 1981), floods in Rumania (Grecu, Csiky, & Munteanu, 1972), and floods in Australia (Smith, Handmer, & Martin, 1980). Also in Australia, independent researchers determined that a quarter of the victims of Cyclone Tracy in 1974 developed long-term psychiatric problems (Milne, 1979; Parker, 1977). Bennet (1970) interviewed a group of flood victims in Bristol, England, and compared them with a sample who had not been adversely affected by the flood. The results indicated that one-third of the flood victims had psychological symptoms that led to a disproportionate degree of ill health and hospitalization a year after the event.

Lifton's (1967) work in Hiroshima led him to believe that the impact of disasters affects not only the victim but are also transmitted to succeeding generations. The parents pass on to their children the fears resulting from being victimized; as a result, the children become more susceptible to the disaster syndrome. A similar hypothesis was proposed by Langer (1958), who suggested that children of disasters will be conditioned to react more pathologically to the stress associated with disasters should they have to face one. From this point of view, disasters influence the normal flow of teaching about coping between generations. Disasters become carriers of culture, they foster a lack of faith in self-efficacy, and thus they serve as precursors to mental disorders.

Disasters Produce Transitory Psychological Problems

The information showing long-lasting mental health problems among disaster victims seems plausible to those who have not been victimized and can only imagine how traumatic a disaster might be. The conclusion drawn by Quarantelli and Dynes (1976), therefore, is surprising. After summarizing postdisaster research on mental health, these authors wrote that although victims show signs of anxiety such as sleeplessness or hypervigilance, the great majority are not permanently impaired. Quarantelli (1990) suggests that less than 15 percent of the victim population will have ongoing mental health problems. This view received support from Breslau and Davis. In a more recent review of the literature (1987), these authors found that "the preponderance of evidence from recent research does not support the proposition that disasters produce psychopathology in the majority of individuals" (p. 259).

Berren and his associates studied 100 junior high school students who witnessed an airplane crash in Arizona. The students, who were on a nearby playground at the time, saw the people on the plane burning to death. Contrary to what common sense might indicate, the children later showed no evidence of acute anxiety, of sleep disturbances, or of other symptoms associated with mental disorders (Berren et al., 1989).

After a tornado in Topeka, Kansas, and in one of the only disaster studies with pre-and postdisaster samples, Drabek and Key (1984) found no enduring mental health problems among victims. Some psychological changes were noted, such as victims taking the precariousness of life more seriously. They used the event as a time marker—a moment that distinguished a former life from a later one—and as part of their story of coming of age, but the victims did not have long-lasting mental health problems. Similar results were noted after the 1974 tornado in Xenia, Ohio. There were few short-term or long-term cases of severe mental illness among the victims. In fact, there were many more examples of resilience than distress (Taylor, Alexander, & Quarantelli, 1976).

Several other American studies have shown no lasting emotional effects for disaster victims. Baum (1985), comparing many natural and humanly induced disasters, noted that victims of either type of disaster rarely developed severe psychiatric disorders. Lindy, Grace, and Green (1981) interviewed survivors of the Beverly Hills Supper Club fire of 1977. They did not find any long-term mental health effects. After reviewing victims' responses to many disasters, Helzer, Robins, and McCuny (1987) noted that almost no disaster victims had signs of PTSD. Other authors have concluded that severe mental disorders are rare, but mild and ephemeral problems are not uncommon (Perry & Lindell, 1978; Tierney & Baisden, 1979).

When Baisden (1979) reviewed several American studies of the social factors affecting the mental health of disaster victims, she confirmed the temporary nature of mental health problems among them. She noted an exception with the Buffalo Creek flood, which she attributed to the large impact of the flood and to the government's housing policy that destroyed the sense of therapeutic community among the survivors.

Mileti, Hartsough, Madson, and Hufnagel (1984) examined the community's response to the Three Mile Island incident. In comparison to the NIMH study cited earlier, Mileti discovered that, given time, people's mental health recovered. There are also studies of non-American samples that illustrate no long-term mental health problems. Oliver and Reardon's study (1982) of the cyclone in Tonga, an island northeast of Australia, found almost no psychopathology. The authors visited the most severely disrupted areas and saw no people who appeared disoriented. In Rumania, only about 5 percent of the victims who were examined a few days after an earthquake demonstrated pathology (Predescu & Nica-Udangiu, 1979).

Barkun (1977) did a historical analysis of disasters in a global context and found that single disasters rarely break the existing faith of people or change society. Only a series of disasters can do this. To affect a society permanently, a disaster must be of great intensity and even then there must be more than one of great magnitude to bring about a significant change. Perhaps this is why these studies have not shown long-term mental problems for disaster victims.

Factors Contributing to the Conflicting Results

The conflicting results of these studies have forced researchers to try to determine which variables might be confounding the results. It is important not only to researchers but to anyone reading disaster studies to take into account the specific conditions under which the data were collected. Results can vary depending on many factors that are significant not only by themselves but also in interaction with one another. Phifer and Norris (1989) identified several of these variables. They noted that whether psychopathology is found will depend on the severity of the disaster, which refers not only to the degree to which individuals are affected but also the amount of destruction sustained in the community.

Some of the victims of the 1985 Mexico City earthquake had to move dead or mutilated bodies while others never saw an injured person. Some victims lost their entire families while other people who were in close proximity to these victims suffered very little personal loss and got no closer to the disaster than seeing it on television. The severity of a disaster cannot be ascertained only by a general description of the event since each person's experience is different. Most studies collect samples and analyze aggregate data instead of focusing on the individual's experience. It is difficult to predict the mental health effects of a disaster without knowing the experience of the person because disasters affect people within communities differently (Hartsough & Myers, 1985; Mitchell, 1983).

Another factor that affects disaster response is a person's prior level of mental functioning. Certain people cope easily with stress; a major stressor might not interrupt their lives for as long as a minor stressor might for another person. Thus, with the same experience in the same disaster, two people might respond quite differently, both in the short and the long term. It is also important to examine the social support a victim receives following a disaster. Some victims are given a great deal of family, religious, and community support, which might be totally absent from another victim of the same disaster (Bolin & Burton, 1986; Warheit, 1985).

In certain disasters such as airplane or train crashes, the impact is dispersed, that is, no one, or almost no one, lives in the community where the event occurs. Survivors have no community that will support them or share their experience. These victims feel isolated and alienated. In contrast, people who have been in disasters where a disaster community forms, as was the case after the 1985 Mexico City earthquake, might feel for the first time the power of an altruistic community experience, a phenomenon that often leads to an improvement in their mental health (Perry & Lindell, 1978).

The degree to which a person needs to rebuild following a disaster is also an important factor. Faced with being alone, having little social support, and finding that there is nothing left of one's former life is a considerable burden. After Hurricane Hugo, homes were literally spread among the backwaters of the salt marshes. Sitting under six cement pillars that had twenty-four hours before been the anchors of her home, a middle-aged woman recalled that her house had been her life's dream and that the possessions in it—relics from her grandparents and her parents—were her links to her ancestors. Although her insurance would help her rebuild some kind of house, it could not replace her personal belongings.

Other important and possibly confounding variables include the type of disaster that occurred (natural versus human-induced, for example). In the case of a natural disaster, victims often feel they have been victimized by fate but not by human incompetence or greed, which is often the case for human-induced disasters. With modern technological disasters (Chernobyl, Bhopal, or Three Mile Island, for example), people are not able to know exactly what has happened to them as the amount of radiation or poisonous gas they have received is difficult to ascertain. Rather than progressing through the stages of grief associated with natural disasters, victims of human-induced disasters find it difficult to reach closure; they remain in a state of anticipation, of waiting to see how bad their exposure really was. They must rely on information from official sources whom they do not trust, a dependence that increases their anxiety and anger. Closure on the situation is very difficult to achieve, and this ambivalence contributes to additional unresolved anxiety and stress. For these reasons victims of human-induced disasters are generally slower to recover than victims of natural ones (Baum & Davidson, 1985; Drabek, 1986; Frederick, 1980).

Another variable to consider is the level of the society from which the data are collected. Disaster studies have taken data from different levels of society where stress has occurred (Perry & Lindell. 1978). Some studies have looked at families (Bolin, 1982), some at organizations (Dynes, 1970a, 1970b), and others at communities (Perry, Lindell, & Greene, 1982). Because of this variety it is not surprising the results differ among studies.

Many demographic variables can confound results. In the United States, poorer people and those with larger families are more likely to report emotional problems following a disaster (Bolin & Burton, 1986). Women seem to have more problems coping with disasters than do men, a finding that was true in France (Chandessais, 1980), Australia (Raphael, 1979), and the United States (Flynn & Chalmers, 1980).

The types of instruments used to measure the reactions also can cloud the results. Instruments that seek a broad symptom complex might be less sensitive than instruments that focus on assessing single symptoms. Research that uses victim self-reports, which often have a psychodynamic point of view, illustrate more psychopathology than studies using behavioral observations, rating scales, or admissions to care facilities (Perry & Lindell, 1978). Interviews reveal more pathologies than do surveys (Green, 1980, 1982; Melick, 1985). The reasons for this are not clear. Possibly people express their feelings more openly in interviews and other forms of self-reporting.

Because the symptoms experienced by survivors wax and wane, timing in the collection of data is also a possible confounding variable. An example of time as a variable is provided by Friuli, an unfortunate community in Italy that suffered two earthquakes within a six-month period (Boileau et al., 1978). The survivors showed few mental health problems after the first earthquake but considerable emotional disturbance after the second. If the only measure taken of victims had been done after the first quake, the results would have been quite different from the combination of measures after both disasters.

Another situation in which timing affected results occurred a year after Cyclone Tracy devastated many towns in Australia. At this time many victims who had shown signs of psychopathology immediately after the storm had returned to normal functioning (Parker, 1977). The researcher explained that at first people were afraid of dying, and this fear elevated their symptoms. When that threat passed, it was replaced by the problems associated with having to leave their homes and relocate. After a time, however, victims also adjusted to this. In the end, the great majority of people returned to their predisaster level of functioning. The researcher would not have found this to be true if the data had been taken only at one of the stressful times.

Timing is also important in a community's response. As pointed out earlier, although the widespread belief is that communities dissolve after disasters, most communities unite. The unity, however, is short-lived (Drabek, 1986). This pattern was found on both American coasts after the Loma Prieta earthquake and Hurricane Hugo (Aptekar, 1990), in Italy and Peru following earthquakes (Angotti, 1977; Oliver-Smith, 1979b), and in Sweden after a landslide (Edberg & Lustig, 1983). Because the sense of communal goodwill does not last forever, sampling disaster victims too long after the event has resulted in different perceptions of how communities react.

One comparative study of volcanic eruptions in the United States and in Japan illustrated several cross-cultural differences in how people perceived their communities (Perry & Hirose, 1983). The Americans thought the volcanic eruption increased community solidarity, a belief that was in line with other American studies (Fritz, 1961; Midlarsky, 1968). Most Japanese perceived little change in the community, and those who thought there was change felt it was in the direction of decreased social solidarity. The differences might be skewed because of the timing of data collection or might reflect preexisting cultural differences in community solidarity.

Speed of onset of the disaster is a major variable in producing conflicting findings. Drought victims often are not sure when they become drought victims and almost always they do not know when the drought will cease. The psychology of drought victims is prolonged, unlike that of the victims of quick-onset disasters. Their psychology is abrupt and severe. If a disaster, such as a prolonged drought, brings deprivation for a period of years, the community does not feel that it is in a disaster. In these cases the changes associated with the stress of quick-onset disasters do not occur (Barkun, 1974). When there is no sudden or unexpected change, people accept their status since they have plenty of time to grow accustomed to it. For thousands of years people have expected the annual flooding on the Nile; they have prepared for it and changed their behavior to deal with it. It is the same with the flooding of the Bay of Bengal. As a result the psychology of these victims is different and their reactions cannot be compared to those of people who have experienced a sudden-onset disaster (R. Leik, S. Leik, Ekker, & Gifford, 1982).

Some researchers think that disasters of a sudden onset and without a certain ending are more difficult to cope with than those of slow onset (Bolin, 1985; Drabek, 1986; Leik et al., 1982). Yet, two studies that compared victims' reactions to different disasters were able to illustrate that many of the differences obtained in the research had more to do with the methods used to collect the data than with different reactions to the disasters by the victims (Green, 1982; Melick, 1985).

There is also the important point that disasters might not have the same meaning across cultures. Two factors that have been shown historically to connect disasters with social change bring this point out (Barkun, 1977). The first is the degree to which the disaster leaves a substantial proportion of the environment intact. The second is how quickly the environment can return to its predisaster state. In developed countries, even if there is a great deal of loss, the environment returns to normal quickly. This is much less true in developing nations and traditional societies. If studies do not take these factors into account, cross-cultural comparisons might be inapplicable. Many researchers have assumed that the effects associated with disaster studies in the United States can be generalized to people in less developed countries. Only cross-cultural study will tell us if this is indeed the case.

The Sequence of Psychological Reactions

In order to avoid the confusion that comes from disparate research efforts, it is valuable to look at the sequence of how disasters affect people. This approach was first tried at the end of the World War II by Tyhurst (1951) who outlined a three-part psychological reaction to disasters. The first phase he described was the impact stage, which takes place at the onset of the disaster. He believed that about three-quarters of the people during this time react with a bewildered, stunned response. The second phase, recoil, occurs after the danger has passed. During this phase Tyhurst determined that people took stock of what had happened. In the third phase, the post-traumatic period, people seek mental equilibrium. This phase was often marked by a cognitive reorganization of the trauma, which might mask the symptoms of mental stress.

The time approach, with certain modifications, is still used by disaster planners, researchers, and people responsible for disaster management. The current schema begins with predisaster preparation, which is used to reduce people's vulnerability to disasters prior to onset of the event. Legislating building codes in earthquake zones is an example. Planning can also include public education to teach people what to do should a disaster occur, or readiness training for relief personnel to increase their efficiency in dealing with the problems victims will face.

The second phase is disaster response. This refers to the help provided immediately after a disaster. The second phase includes evacuation, search and rescue efforts, care of injured persons, restoration of public order, and meeting both the physical and mental general welfare needs of the victims. The third phase, to be discussed in chapter six, is recovery, which includes the longer-term efforts to rebuild, to relocate people, and to reconstruct social institutions.

The three-phase paradigm is conducive to the study of psychological issues. There are two preimpact factors associated with disaster planning: the effectiveness of warnings and the value of predisaster training for evacuation. Phase two, disaster response, embraces the psychology of victims' first responses and how best to take care of the victims. These include many issues of individual and community psychology. Finally, in phase three, recovery, there is the psychology of recovery: the long-term mental sequel of disasters, addressing many psychological and sociological factors. Use of the three-phase schema reveals the several methodological problems surrounding the two positions regarding long-lasting psychological reactions. It also helps clarify the problems associated with the lack of cross-cultural studies.

Phase One: Predisaster Preparation

The best way to lessen the mental health problems associated with disasters is to reduce people's exposure to danger. If fewer people live on flood plains or work the fields in the paths of volcanic flow, there will be fewer deaths associated with disasters. People can be prepared by being taught what to expect should a disaster occur or being conditioned to accept warnings that a disaster is imminent and that they should evacuate or take other appropriate actions. People can also be trained so they can respond adequately should they find themselves in a disaster. In spite of the wisdom of this advice, only 3 percent of American families have plans for the possibility of being in a disaster (Petak & Atkisson, 1982; Worth & McLuckie, 1977). Similar findings come from other developed countries (Britton, 1978, 1981).

In contrast to the small degree of preparation in the developed countries are the elaborate preparation systems in traditional societies. People in these nations have made a number of everyday changes that prepare them to cope with a potential disaster. As noted in the first chapters, the Enga of New Guinea and inhabitants of many of the desert African communities have altered their patterns of crop planting, of hunting, and of ritual ceremonies to prepare themselves in advance for potential disasters (Morren, 1983; Waddell 1975, 1983). The serious attention traditional societies give to disaster preparation arises from their realization that people in these societies are quite likely to lose their lives and their way of life from a disaster if they are not prepared. In traditional societies, the environment and the hazards it poses are accorded much greater importance than they receive in developed societies, where most people live far removed from the vagaries of weather.

Between the developed countries and the traditional societies are the developing nations, which in many cases have not paid enough attention to the importance of disaster preparedness. In the earthquake-prone Fars region of Iran, engineers constructed large housing projects without sufficient thought given to the environmental hazards of the area. When the almost predictable earthquake struck, 60 percent of the people died because the houses were not earthquake resistant (U.S. Department of Commerce, 1974). Perhaps the developing nations do not have the money to deal effectively with disaster preparation, or possibly there is less than sufficient control over development projects such as the one in Iran to monitor their disaster preparation effectiveness.

Warnings

Warnings are worthwhile as preventive measures only to the extent that people believe them. A model developed in Sweden to make warnings more believable took into account the message, the communicator, and the recipient, each of which was likely to influence a person's response (Hammarstrom-Tornstram, 1977). All three factors often intermingle, and it is difficult to know which of them is the most important. A study in Hawaii, where people faced potential volcanic eruptions, found that the efficiency of warnings had less to do with the technological skill of how the warnings were delivered than with the psychological factors associated with getting people to believe the information they received (Sorenson & Gersmehl, 1980).

It is clear that the warning message interacts with the personal belief system of the person receiving it. Following the Chernobyl nuclear accident a questionnaire was sent to university students in Australia, England, France, Germany, and the Netherlands to study how people reacted to information about the disaster (Eiser et al., 1990). The study fell within the tradition of research that has examined how fearful information or warnings (for example, about developing cancer or becoming infected with the human immunovirus [HIV]) create conflicts and reduce rather than contribute to the efficacy of the warning message

(Festinger, Riecken, & Schachter, 1956; Janis & Mann, 1977). The authors hypothesized that the warning about the Chernobyl accident heightened conflict by producing dissonance in those people who viewed nuclear power as safe. Would the warnings about the dangers of nuclear power be interpreted in a way to reduce the dissonance between their beliefs about the positive value of nuclear power? The results indicated that people were not likely to change their beliefs about the advantages of nuclear power, even if the information they obtained showed how dangerous a nuclear accident could be. Similar results were found from people's reaction to oil spills. If people felt oil was an appropriate energy source, their reaction—even after a spill—was to not take the warnings as seriously as did people who wanted to reduce dependence on oil (Eiser et al., 1990).

There are also demographic differences associated with accepting or rejecting warnings (Yamamoto & Quarantelli, 1982). Across cultures, poorer people are less likely to heed and believe warnings (Baumann & Sims, 1974; Perry & Greene, 1982; Perry, Lindell, & Greene, 1982; Sims & Baumann, 1972; Turner, Nigg, Paz & Young, 1981). This was also true in the United States (Leik, Carter, & Clark, 1981; Turner, 1976) and Japan (Ohta, 1972; Ohta & Abe, 1977; Okabe, 1981). There are also gender differences, across cultures, with women being more responsive to warnings than men (Mileti, Drabek, & Haas, 1975; Yamamoto & Quarantelli, 1982).

These studies suggest that people will ignore solid information about impending disasters if the warnings run counter to their beliefs. Additionally, if there is any possible way to interpret a warning as being less than a certain prediction, people will deny that it is real or that the danger is imminent. This tendency was confirmed in the United States (Perry, Lindell, & Greene, 1982; Quarantelli, 1980), Australia (Irish & Falconer, 1979), and Japan (Okabe, 1981). In one study with data from over a dozen countries of varying degrees of development and political orientation, the results indicated that people of all cultures underestimate the degree of risk they face (Burton, Kates, & White, 1978; Drabek, 1986). Most people expect that nothing will happen to them; thus, they are not likely to heed warnings (Covello, 1983; Kunreuther, 1978; Mileti, Drabek, & Haas, 1975).

How one perceives risks also depends on personality factors. People who are more fatalistic and who have less internal locus of control (Perry, Greene, & Mushkatel, 1983) are less aware of disaster risk.

This was found in both the United States (Turner et al., 1981) and in New Zealand (Simpson-Hously & Bradshaw, 1978). When people get warnings they try to find a way to minimize the potential bad news, The classic example is the man in Kansas who, instead of seeing the torna-do in the darkened sky and great roar of wind, thought that an unex-pected, and overly loud train had arrived (Farberow & Gordon, 1981). People tend to examine their physical surroundings looking for evi-dence to discount the warnings so they do not have to respond. This behavior can be particularly problematic for many warnings such as those for nuclear leaks, chemical spills, flash floods, and other environ-mental hazards because they are not always apparent to the senses.

When people become more experienced with warnings they tend to make their own subjective judgments about the seriousness of the alarm. They act more in alignment with their own ideas than because of information they receive from authorities. This applies to both natural and humanly induced disasters (Bromet, 1989; Bromet & Dunn, 1981). One cross-cultural study of people living in flood plains and in storm locations showed how victims learn to "read" the warning signs (Burton, Kates, & White, 1978). These people look first to the physical environment, then to the behavior of their neighbors who they think have experience with similar disasters, and finally to certain particulars about the way the warning is delivered (the tone of the person deliver-ing the message, the language the person uses to tell of its seriousness, the way the material is presented, and so on). In all cases they try to find some confirmation that the warning of potential harm is in error.

When their own assessments fail, they seek out their kin, an obser-vation supported in Japanese (Okabe, 1981) and American studies (Perry, Greene, & Mushkatel, 1983). After watching Hurricane Hugo travel from the coast of west Africa to the eastern coast of the United States, Tom Huber, a sixty-year-old farmer in the lowlands of South Carolina, still felt that the storm would not be severe. It was not until his cousin came speeding up in his truck to tell him and his family to go with him to the shelter that Tom was ready to heed the advice that had been repeated on television for more than sixty hours.

People like Tom Huber who had lived in McClellanville, South Carolina, for years had heard many such warnings, but they never had experienced any serious hurricanes. Even though the media were reporting that Hugo was going to be a very bad storm, they did not take the warnings seriously. Their behavior matches that cited in the literature. Three separate studies undertaken in England, Australia, and the United States show that people who have heard warnings that were followed by disasters are more likely to take future warnings seriously (Irish & Falconer, 1979; Perry, Lindell, & Greene, 1981; Smith & Tobin, 1979).

In South Carolina, people on the coast had over the years heard many warnings of an approaching hurricane that ultimately did not make landfall where they were. Warnings that were not followed by the threatened disaster had the effect of delaying people's response to later alarms (Aptekar, 1990). Generally, people believe that past experience will repeat itself, so if dire past warnings were not followed by actual disasters people are not likely to believe future warnings. This was the case with warnings of storms in Sweden (Hultaker, 1976) and hurricanes in the United States (Baker, 1979; Quarantelli, 1980).

The community of Buffalo Creek knew that there was always a possibility that the dam could break and they obviously were aware that they lived down river from it, but they still refused to move to safer ground (Titchener & Kapp, 1976). The question is why do people fail to heed such warnings? One possibility is the "cry wolf" phenomenon. People at Buffalo Creek did not respond because they had heard a number of warnings that were not followed by a disaster. Residents of Los Angeles County received repeated "official warnings" (to be separated from warnings from soothsayers) about a predicted earthquake that never came. Turner (1983) examined this phenomenon in a potential earthquake site and concluded that after hearing repeated warnings without having an earthquake, people experienced a diminution in their sense of urgency. This might be what happened in Buffalo Creek.

Affecting people's belief that disasters are likely or not likely to occur is what has been done to prevent them. Several studies in the United States, New Zealand, England, and Australia have shown that building dams to reduce the risk of flooding creates a false sense of security that prevents people from taking other appropriate mitigating action (Ericksen, 1974; Frazier, 1979; Oliver, 1975; Parker, 1977). A similar situation might also have contributed to a false sense of security among the people in Buffalo Creek. Ironically, even though people at Buffalo Creek knew the dam could break, they never really believed it would; rather, they believed the dam made them safe from flooding. Why else would the experts have constructed it?

The lack of warning can have serious consequences as well. Indians living on the flood plains of the Bay of Bengal reported they felt safe; because there was no official warning system, they developed the idea that they had nothing to worry about (Schware, 1982). Perhaps the people of Buffalo Creek made a similar mistake.

Several studies in the United States have shown that people are willing to comply with warnings of potential disasters with which they are unfamiliar, such as chemical spills, oil fires, or a nuclear reactor leak (Perry & Mushkatel, 1984). Floods are considered familiar, not only because they are somewhat predictable but also because people know if they live in a flood plain. In a comparative study of U.S. and Japanese communities receiving warnings about volcanic eruptions, Perry and Hirose (1983) concluded that people's level of familiarity with the type of disaster was the best predictor of their compliance with warnings across cultures. Given this reasoning, it is understandable that the people of Buffalo Creek ignored the warnings: they were quite familiar with flooding.

Evacuation

One common method of disaster preparation is to inform people about evacuating their homes for safer places. This method is ineffective, however, in societies whose people believe that disasters come from some spiritual or magical entity; these people rarely evacuate (Mileti, Drabek, & Haas, 1975). In Hawaii researchers discovered that willingness to evacuate from the neighborhood of a threatening volcano was dependent upon an individual's belief about the cause of volcanic eruptions (Hodge, Sharp, & Marts, 1979). People who refused to evacuate in spite of being told that they would be in the direct path of the lava flow were those who thought that the goddess of volcanoes, Pele, did not harm anyone who had not harmed her.

Using cross-cultural evidence from people living on flood plains, White wrote in 1945 that past experience with flooding often served to reinforce the idea in people they were safe. People reasoned that such awful experiences would not be repeated, so they did not evacuate.

After the Three Mile Island incident a study determined that those who did not leave their homes feared being separated from their families. They believed that staying was the safest way to ensure remaining united (Perry, 1983). Similar findings were obtained in Japan (Ohta,

1972). In a cross-cultural study that used data from Japan, the United States, and Italy, McLuckie (1977) noted that people with the strongest family ties did not evacuate. Rural people were also less likely to evacuate than urbanites. The fear of losing one's property to thieves is another reason people do not leave their homes, as mentioned by people in the Bay of Bengal (Schware, 1982) and in Guatemala (Bolin, 1982; Bolin & Bolton, 1983).

When victims evacuate, they first seek shelter in the homes of their family, then the homes of their friends; this behavior was corroborated by studies in the United States (Perry, Lindell, & Greene, 1981), Japan (Okabe, 1981), Australia (Short, 1979), Canada (Whyte, 1980), and India (Schware, 1982). The least desirable choice is to evacuate to a shelter.

People evacuate with their families. This behavior is also cross-cultural as shown by studies in the United States (Perry, 1983), Japan (Ikeda, 1982; Okabe, 1981), Canada (Whyte, 1980), and England (Hultaker & Trost, 1976). Studies ranging from small emergencies to the atomic bombing of Hiroshima show that in the first moments of crisis people's response is to seek the comfort of family. When they cannot do this, they spend their energies trying to find them. Lifton (1967) describes hordes of victims roaming the devastated landscape of the atomic fallout wearing nothing but rags, their bodies scorched from the heat, having only one thing on their minds: reuniting with their families.

Training

A third specific aspect of preparedness is training personnel to act competently when a disaster occurs. The differences between the developed and less developed countries are once again reflected here. In an experimental simulation in France, firemen were trained to react to disasters. When they were put through a simulated exercise after the training, fewer than half of the firemen responded in the way they were trained (Py, 1978). Similarly, within ten days after completing a training program preparing them to work at the Robert Ginna nuclear facility in New York state, the new employees were faced with a crisis there. The trainees, now employed at the facility to do what they had been trained to do, were unable to carry their training into the crisis (Belardo, Pazer, Wallace, & Danko, 1983).

In the developed world training takes place as part of work life but not as part of daily life, a direct contrast to what typically happens in traditional societies. Training in traditional societies is incorporated into daily events. These societies adopt different patterns of hunting, gathering, or planting to mitigate against potential environmental hazards, and the new ways become part of the life pattern.

It appears much more likely that traditional societies will incorporate disaster preparation into their everyday life than will developed countries. People on Yap (Schneider, 1957) have prepared for typhoons by an elaborate system of beliefs and religious ceremonies that have become a part of their daily existence. In developed countries, repeated threats and occurrences of a specific disaster are required for the culture to adopt disaster planning. Even then, there is no certainty that such planning will become an automatic part of people's awareness. For two recent events in California—both the Loma Prieta earthquake and the Oakland fire—people were not prepared, even though both events had been predicted as likely to occur.

Given the apparently poor results of training for emergencies in the developed world, it would be appropriate to gather cross-cultural data on how training has benefited people in different cultures. While a careful study of the first phase of disasters—that of preparation to reduce the impact of potential events—is useful, a cross-cultural look at the psychology of disaster victims immediately after a disaster is also important.

Phase Two: Postdisaster Response—Myths and Reality

From a series of interviews immediately following the Armenian earthquake of December 1988, Mileti (1989) was able to discern the first impact on the community and individuals. There was no predisaster planning so people had not learned what they could do, nor had they been trained in any practice exercises such as evacuation procedures. Because of the extensive damage there was no communication between the victims and the outside world.

As is common, the first people to help were the victims themselves. In fact, 95 percent of the people rescued from the debris were saved by other victims and only about 5 percent were helped by national or international rescue teams. An extensive organization sprang up among the survivors. With dust still covering everything victims could not be seen but their cries could be heard. Men immediately began to dig them out. They formed lines in which rubble was passed from one set of hands to another. One man in each group emerged as a leader, offering directions and keeping the rescue operations organized. The women stood on the side, handing water or milk to the men. When the men were able to talk to a person buried in the rubble they would get his or her name. They then passed the name on to the women who immediately began searching for surviving family members. When they could not locate a family member they posted the name in a central location.

A similar response occurred after the 1985 earthquake in Mexico City. One of the hardest hit sites was Chapultepec Heights, once a comfortable upper-middle-class area in the city. Mexico's most prestigious medical center was located there until September 19 when the earthquake destroyed the *barrio* and the hospital. Nearly three thousand patients had to be evacuated.

Patients began to stumble out of the hospital, most with no shoes and wearing hospital gowns, some with intravenous units still attached to their arms. On the streets, they joined victims from Chapultepec whose homes had been destroyed. When the neighborhood residents saw the patients, they immediately set out to help them. Within three hours they had evacuated all of them from the hospital. Many adolescents and young men found or made stretchers and began carrying the patients who could not support themselves.

One victim whose house had been destroyed realized that a list of supplies had to be made. Having no paper, she began writing on facial tissue. Patients began asking the victims in the neighborhood to find their families or to give them clothes. No telephones were working, so the victims waved down cars. Soon a system developed. Some neighborhood victims would write the names and addresses of the patients while other victims waved down cars asking them to take the patients home. Before the day was out, most patients were safely deposited with their families, even though many of them were very ill (Poniatowska, 1988). These anecdotes show that the victims of Armenia and Mexico City were not unorganized; in fact, they took the steps necessary to take care of each other, illustrating that the fears of irrational breakdowns in the emergency period immediately after a disaster are more myth than reality.

Immediately after the Event

No matter how much destruction a community has suffered, the first observers will likely find a temporary sense of well-being emerging among the victims. This phenomenon was first described by Fritz (1957), who said that disaster victims feel a sense of goodwill toward family, kin, and friends. People share with each other as they never have before. They react altruistically to each other and to their common problems (Drabek & Key, 1984). This form of altruism has been referred to as the *therapeutic community* (Barton, 1969) and has been corroborated in Italy (Cattarinussi & Tellia, 1978) and in France (Chandessais, 1980).

Menninger (1952) was the first to point out that during this altruistic period immediately after a disaster, people experience a world out of the ordinary, without social distinctions; many individuals experience such a heightened sense of energy that they feel more alive than they ever have before. People reason that such pain as was caused by the disaster cannot be without significance. The temporary well-being they experience following a disaster offers them a glimpse of a better world and gives significance to their being victimized.

In a comparative study of Hurricane Hugo and the Loma Prieta earthquake, Aptekar (1990) discovered that people began forming groups to help in the immediate work that was needed. Volunteering made people feel better about themselves. One female victim, who had grown up near the tidewater marshes on the South Carolina coast, remembered a previous storm, Hurricane Hazel, that destroyed her neighbor's house but did not damage her own home. At that time she felt "saved from God's will." This time, when Hurricane Hugo hit, she was not so lucky. The house she and her husband had built with their meager retirement money was almost entirely demolished. They lived in a neighborhood with many of their lifelong friends whose houses were also severely damaged. Rather than cleaning the mud from their own house, Ida and her husband went to help their neighbors. By keeping busy with the problems of other victims Ida was able to avoid her own. By working to save the community in which she lived, she helped reduce the possibility that this vital structure in her life would be obliterated.

During the Loma Prieta earthquake Susie Redface's five-year-old daughter, Rita, was taking a dance class in a building that collapsed.

Because she was on the wrong side of a damaged bridge closed to traffic, Susie was not able to pick up her daughter from dance class. In the hours of anxiety until she could learn what had happened to her, Susie helped her neighbors. "What kept me sane during the several hours it took for me to be reunited with my daughter was my being able to comfort my neighbors. At least I could help somebody. I just didn't want to be alone and not help. I knew someone would help me. I prayed they were helping Rita." As long as she could help, she could imagine that her plight was not as bad as that of the people she was helping.

The breadth and magnitude of the altruism displayed—almost everyone studied in both disasters demonstrated some of it—made the phenomenon appear almost religious in nature. By doing something for someone else, people could feel relatively at peace; at least they were not so victimized that they could not be helpful. In showing kindness in spite of so much difficulty, they felt redeemed from whatever anger they had experienced. Perhaps dealing with such basic and raw emotions was the reason volunteers commonly used the language of religion. Two women commented on their volunteer efforts, "This is God's plan," "God would want it this way," "It is my moral duty," "The ten commandments tell me to help my neighbor" (Aptekar, 1991, p. 12).

Barton (1969) demonstrated that people with definitive roles to play after a disaster cope much better than those who have no specific duties. By helping each other after the Mexico City earthquake, citizens took on the role of volunteers. What motivated their volunteerism is difficult to determine—that is, whether they helped out of a genuine sense of ethical commitment or because they found that by helping they felt better about their own plight. No one, perhaps not even the helpers themselves, can say for sure. In any event, giving assistance helped them cope with their trauma.

Consuelo Romo waited for days in front of the Nuevo Leon Hotel in Mexico City after the 1985 earthquake imprisoned her daughter and three grandchildren in that structure. She was waiting to see if they would be brought out of the ruins alive. She reported that while she was waiting, a girl came up to her and asked her if she wanted to distribute water while she was waiting. For the next several days Consuelo gave out water and food; finally she was forced to acknowledge that she must give up hope of seeing her relatives alive. "I lost the only thing I had. . . . I had no one else, only them. I was left completely alone" (Poniatowska, 1988, p. 9). She recalled crying for the next several days while she was distributing food, but she would not give up her volunteer work. "Then I put more and more and more love into being a volunteer" (Poniatowska, 1988, p. 10). One of the relief personnel draped a makeshift volunteer sign around Consuelo's shoulders. Through helping others she helped herself.

Fritz (1961) was the first to note that disasters provide an opportunity to mark the boundaries between old and new. Disasters serve as time markers, and for some people they offer a chance to begin again. Several writers have noted that some disaster victims become more religious and less materialistic after surviving a disaster, as if they realized that material things are not nearly so important as life and human connections. From the disaster they found important meaning in life (Drabek & Key, 1984; Leik et al., 1982; Ollendick & Hoffman, 1982).

As strange as it sounds, being victimized by a disaster might produce a change for the better. After Cyclone Tracy in Australia damaged a prison, the inmates were able to escape. Instead of leaving the scene, however, they stayed to help other storm victims. In the end, they had made the right choice because they were granted pardons; but the important point is that they acted against their apparent interests by giving up an opportunity to flee in order to help others (Haas, Cochrane, & Eddy, 1976).

Wallace (1956) noted that disasters not only place people in stress but also provide the opportunity for leadership. Weber (1968) also believed that disasters produced charismatic leaders. Two studies from the United States (Bolin, 1982; Taylor, 1977) and one from Sri Lanka (Patrick & Patrick, 1981) have shown that survivors' mental health improved after a disaster. The notion that all people respond to disasters by becoming panicked, irrational, and hysterical has long been invalidated (Drabek & Quarantelli, 1967). Likewise, the idea that it is common for disaster victims to develop a particular kind of severe mental problem, post-traumatic stress disorder (PTSD), should be questioned.

Freud (Freud & Breuer, 1957) outlined many symptoms of PTSD in his studies of hysteria: physical manifestations of mental tensions, inability to concentrate, fixation on childhood trauma, and so on. Horowitz (1986b) has traced the history of PTSD from the description of shell shock in World War I to the symptoms outlined in the *Diagnostic and Statistical Manual*, third edition revised (American Psychiatric Association, 1987). PTSD comprises several symptoms caused by a stressor beyond the range of common human experience. Common human experiences would be the normal loss of a loved one, the loss of a business or a job, or the loss of marital partner. Uncommon human experiences that would produce PTSD symptoms might be having one's life threatened by an attacker, being in a war, or being in an airplane or car crash. PTSD may also come about from a sudden loss of one's home or community, which often occurs after environmental disasters (Horowitz, 1986b; Horowitz et al., 1980).

A person might have experienced an event of such unusual proportions as to account for PTSD, and indeed develop some its symptoms, but if the symptoms are not long lasting and debilitating, the person cannot be diagnosed as having PTSD.

The symptoms of PTSD can range from extreme and enduring to mild and transitory. One symptom is intrusive thoughts—those the person feels she or he cannot control, get rid of, or prevent from occurring. Intrusive thoughts include the appearance of unwanted images either in sleep or during the day, repetitive nightmares, and sleep-disturbing dreams.

Another symptom of PTSD is denial, a process of mentally reorganizing the event to reduce or eliminate its pain. An example of denial was the response of Jessica Bright who lives near McClellanville, South Carolina. During Hurricane Hugo the roof of her house was blown off and the interior was destroyed by the rain. In addition, her ten-month-old baby had died a month before the storm. Three weeks after the storm the insurance adjuster had still not visited her house. When asked how she was handling the slow pace of the insurance claim process, she said, "I don't really mind. A lot of people are worse off than me" (Aptekar, 1991, p. 16).

After the Buffalo Creek flood, many victims were afraid of water and were hypervigilant around it; they were uncomfortable hearing sounds that reminded them of running water. In addition, for many years some had dreams about water. As a result, they tended to orient their lives in such a way as to reduce the possibility of experiencing that fear. They were fearful of bathing; they would not swim, even if they had enjoyed it before. Some people even refused to drive over bridges (Titchener & Kapp, 1976).

As a rule some denial is apparent immediately after the event, but complete denial is not. The person must experience some anxiety and fear before being able to cope effectively with the extreme stressor. If denial is complete, the unwanted thoughts and images associated with PTSD are more likely to intrude later (Horowitz, 1986b). Denial is often coupled with social withdrawal and frequently leads to depression, especially if denial is severe (Wilkenson & Vera, 1985).

Commonly, for a short period of time there is an intense emotional reaction when a person experiences stimuli similar to those that pro-voked the disorder. A victim may go to extremes to avoid anything that might resemble or bring back memories of the original event. Some victims may even develop a psychogenic amnesia of the event. Immediately after the event most people usually experience what has been described as a "psychic numbing": a reduced responsiveness to the outside world. The person feels detached and loses the ability to enjoy what had previously brought pleasure. Some victims cannot feel any emotions, particularly those of tenderness or intimacy.

Wilkenson and Vera (1985) described a six-year-old girl who, stand-ing only six feet away, saw her mother killed in a disaster. Rather than admit that her mother was dead, the girl maintained that she was on a trip. When her pet cat was killed several days later, the child described the event in a matter-of-fact, emotionless way.

Terr (1990) described a Japanese boy of Hiroshima who had been in the eighth grade in 1945. As he was looking for his family after the atom bomb had been dropped on that city, he saw many bodies so badly burned that the people's skin was hanging off. A woman came by drag-ging a child so destroyed that he couldn't tell if it was a girl or a boy. A young man without his legs was crawling in the dirt. As he described this scene he said, "I cannot imagine what state of mind I was in—to see all of those horrors without feeling shocked or frightened, to feel nothing at all" (Terr, 1990, p. 81). Immediately after a traumatic event sleep disturbances are common. Victims may have difficulty going to sleep or staying asleep. Some people have recurrent nightmares of the event or even daytime flashbacks. During the day many victims often report problems in concentrating. They become hypervigilant, a behav-ior that can even turn into phobic responses. No one is sure how many disaster victims suffer symptoms severe enough to be considered PTSD. The figure is elusive, as the contradictory results at the begin-ning of the chapter indicate. Another problem is that the existing data are essentially from developed countries. Of the 297 references from a National Institute of Mental Health bibliography on natural disasters and mental health, only thirteen deal with less developed countries

(Ahearn & Cohen, 1984). A review of the 120 studies summarized in a National Institute of Mental Health bibliography of technological disasters and mental health shows no references to studies in less developed countries (Raigrodski, 1987).

It is also difficult to know the extent of PTSD because not all the symptoms occur immediately after the disaster; sometimes they do not manifest themselves until weeks or even months later. Some believe that humans have a "stimulus barrier" (Horowitz, 1986b) that shields the psyche from an overload of distress by using all symptoms as a way of denying or blocking out reality. The barrier, however, is not effective forever. When it loses its capacity to ward off the fright, symptoms begin to appear. A similar notion is the theory of "trauma membrane," a concept described by Lindy (1985) in his study of bereaved families following a fire in a Kentucky nightclub. He too maintained that the psyche, like a human cell, has a surrounding barrier. This barrier serves as a protective device by denying what is too painful to accept.

Another difficulty in assessing the impact of PTSD is that many of the symptoms are associated with the normal sequence of reactions to disasters (Wilkenson & Vera, 1985). Numbing and denial, followed by intrusive thinking, often end in resolution. The work of Wortman (1983) provides more information about the normal responses of people to disaster. Wortman's interest in people's response to traumatic circumstances, such as being told they have terminal cancer, gave a frame of reference for how people would respond to being victimized. She noted that normal emotional reactions last considerably longer than imagined; many incest victims, for example, were still responding 20 years after the event occurred. She was able to illustrate that it was in the victims' best interest not to keep "a stiff upper lip, but to get angry and to focus not only on the positive but also on the negative. Victims rarely heal all at once, and coping should not be examined in its entirety but broken down into pieces.

There is a cyclical rhythm or seasonal variation to disaster reactions (Green, Lindy, & Grace, 1985). Victims often experience anniversary reactions to disasters, times that make the person reexperience the event. Phifer and Norris (1989) noted this for floods and Bolin and Bolton (1983) for tornado victims. Anniversary or seasonal reactions were much more likely to occur if the disaster impact went beyond the individual to include a level of destruction for the whole community.

The Second Wave of Responses

From a comparative study of the Loma Prieta earthquake and Hurricane Hugo it is possible to determine how the various symptoms of PTSD might influence victims and those who come to help them (Aptekar, 1991). Much of the cognitive confusion of the victims subsided within the first week after the hurricane, and, because of the aftershocks, within two to three weeks after the earthquake. Likewise, altruistic behavior faded. As people began to think beyond the disaster, they looked for an explanation of why they were victimized. They gave the event the status of a divine act: God punished us or saved us; it was part of God's plan. As Jim Colt of Watsonville said, "Thirty minutes and it destroys your whole life. Who knows why, but it was God's will."

People also reorganized their thinking. They distorted the memory of the disaster, they forgot parts of what happened, and most important, they denied the magnitude of the disaster's impact and their reactions to it. One way to explain the psychological function of denial and other memory changes is to see them as a way for the psyche to master the experience (Freud & Breuer, 1957; Schur, 1966). Similarly, it is possible to see these coping devices as functioning to provide emotional distance from the event (Goffman, 1971).

Research has shown that denial is effective in helping people cope with overwhelming events (Caplan, 1981; Horowitz, 1986b), but it sets up other difficult problems. Denial has an impact on victims and volunteers and it has important implications for researchers and practitioners. One problem after Hurricane Hugo was that denial by the survivors made it hard for volunteers to help them. When volunteers offered their aid, it was often rejected by the victims. If victims had accepted help, it would have been an admission that they were in need of it. Rejecting the volunteer's help can be interpreted as being in the psychological interest of the victims, but it was a source of frustration for the volunteers.

Denial was in evidence among high school students in the area after the earthquake. Administrators, teachers, and counselors at a high school near Watsonville began serving the mental health needs of the students immediately after the earthquake. They organized their efforts and met regularly to discuss the emotional status of the students. They initiated a daily mental health briefing, but the briefings did not accomplish as much as they could have because school personnel were not aware of the power of denial. Although a good deal of information exists that informs people about the immediate state of mental confusion that follows a disaster (Blom, 1986; Cohen & Ahearn, 1980; Crabbs, 1981; Farberow & Gordon, 1981; Howard, 1980; Klingman, 1987; Raphael, 1975; Seroka, Knapp, Knight, Siemon, & Starbuck, 1982; Tuckman, 1973), there is little information about the second wave reactions, and thus school officials were not prepared for the stage of denial. Denial, if not carried on for too long, is considered functional (Horowitz, 1990), and thus the school staff's lack of knowledge about its value was unfortunate.

The mental health briefing group from the high school sent out requests to the local universities for help soon after the earthquake. When the university volunteers arrived they were told by one of the counselors that "everything is back to normal. There are more counselors than we can use." Likewise, when the volunteers asked what problems the students were facing, they were told that the students had had problems, but that things were now back to normal. Then the school team talked about attendance. Noting that more than a quarter of the students were absent, the university volunteers asked if this might be related to the earthquake. The members of the emergency team thought it was not, and found it very difficult to entertain the possibility that it might be.

A similar phenomenon was observed by the state mental health workers who were summoned to California's Santa Cruz County immediately after the Loma Prieta earthquake. In the second week after the earthquake the state of California sent nearly ninety volunteers from San Bernadino County to Santa Cruz County. A week later other counties sent sixty more volunteers to Santa Cruz County. By this time the process of denial had taken hold. One Orange County mental health worker said that he was "kicked out" of a Red Cross shelter because the person in charge said there was no reason to talk to people. Their emotional problems were over. Another mental health volunteer was told, "People have talked as much as they need to. We don't want to continue talking with them about the quake." In fact, three weeks after the earthquake most mental health workers were apparently unable to find people who needed their services. In the shelters in the first days following the disaster people were demonstrating the clear and commonly accepted signs of the mental problems that come immediately after a disaster. These symptoms included mental confusion, lack of concentration, uncontrolled crying, and nightmares. For the vast majority of people these symptoms disappeared quite quickly, and officials in the schools and in the mental health agencies were unaware of what was to follow—the extensive use of denial.

Factors That Influence the Onset of Symptoms

In determining the impact of a disaster on mental health, the actual experience of the victim is much more important than is a general description of the disaster (severe earthquake, extensive flooding, and so on). Compare the stories of two California neighbors. Evelyn Escarpe, an elderly woman living in Watsonville at the time of the Loma Prieta earthquake, broke her hip when the major earthquake struck. Unable to move and not having relatives who would seek her out, she sat in her home for almost twenty-four hours fearing the aftershocks would bring what was left of the roof down upon her. When she was finally found, she lost her freedom, not only by having to enter a nursing home but also by being forced to accept public assistance because she had no insurance. In contrast, her next-door neighbor was not at home at the time of the earthquake. She escaped physical injury and her house was not damaged. She also had no hours of fear. To report this earthquake only in terms of the overall Richter scale indicates nothing about what it did to individual people, and thus of how likely they are to develop some form of psychopathology. It is the exposure to fear that ultimately determines the psychological sequel (Gleser, Green, & Winget, 1981). For people in situations like Evelyn's, the longer they experience the impact of the disaster, the greater is the likelihood that their resources will be drained.

Also affecting the mental state of victims is the magnitude of the disaster: the more severe it is, the more damage it will have inflicted to property. In a severe disaster there is also greater likelihood that social support networks will be interrupted (Perry & Lindell, 1978). There is a relationship between victims' psychopathology and the degree of damage to both social support (Drabek, Key, Erickson, & Crowe, 1975) and property damage (Wallace, 1956).

If property is considered a record of a person's cultural heritage and personal identity, the connection between loss of property and stress is quite apparent. Given only one object that people might take from a burning home they almost always chose photographs or a treasured heirloom rather than the most expensive item. Material objects take on symbolic value. In a disaster the loss of an object that has little value but is treasured greatly can produce severe stress.

The victims who show the greatest psychopathology are those who lose close friends and relatives (Gleser, Green, & Winget, 1981). The threat to one's own life is not nearly so terrorizing as actually observing the death of others, particularly of loved ones. The more gruesome the observations, the worse the mental outcome for the victim (Sowder, 1985). People's grief increases greatly if they feel they could have done something to prevent the death of a loved one. In this case the grief reaction is profound and enduring. In some cases not only do people lose loved ones but they also lose the community in which they lived. One reason so many cases of mental disorders were reported following the Buffalo Creek flood was that it literally meant the destruction of "place" for its survivors (Erikson, 1976b; Lifton & Olson, 1976). A finding from a comparative study of two floods in Kentucky demonstrated that survivors of a community disaster were victimized to a far larger degree than were victims of disasters in which the community survived to offer help to its victims. "Although personal loss was required for psychological distress, it was the concurrent level of community destruction that determined the longevity of these symptoms" (Phifer & Norris, 1989, p. 215)."

A study of different community responses to environmental disasters would be helpful in understanding the role of the community in the recovery process (Soloman, 1989). Just as the lack of community erodes people's ability to cope, so can the power of the community provide mental health support to victims (Cohen & Ahearn, 1980). This finding is supported by studies done after the Peruvian avalanche in Yungay (Oliver-Smith, 1977), by reports from Australian tornado victims (Henderson & Bostock, 1977), and by studies after the Teton Dam collapse in the United States (Golec, 1983).

Another factor that influences the onset of symptoms is the victim's predisaster mental health. Fenichel (1945), representing the psychoanalytical point of view, stated that the degree to which there is trauma following a tragedy depended on the individual's preexisting personality, as well as situational factors surrounding the trauma. This opinion reflects the views of Freud, who believed that trauma was related to the meaning that stress had for the individual (Freud & Breuer, 1957).

In short, reactions to trauma depended upon the victim's idiosyncratic response to the traumatic event.

In the latest psychoanalytic position and the most detailed account, Horowitz (1986b, 1990) outlined six predisaster personality characteristics that could account for difficulty in responding to disasters. People who excessively connect illogical thinking to behavior or people who have a psychological conflict that could be exacerbated by the disaster have more trouble responding to disasters. Other personality factors that might make people susceptible to disasters include a primitive system of psychological defense mechanisms, such as an excessive degree of denial or an overuse of fantasy to ward off psychological danger, a particularly low self-concept, emotional fatigue, or physical symptoms caused by emotional difficulties.

Psychology, like history, tends to repeat itself. Those people susceptible to stress before disasters are likely to remain so when disaster strikes. In fact, the way people coped with stress before the disaster is the best predictor of how they function after it—a finding that is supported by studies of disaster victims in the United States (Quarantelli & Dynes, 1977) and in Italy (Pelanda, 1981) following the Friuli earthquakes.

Not all studies agree with this view, however. Hocking (1965, 1970a, 1970b) wrote that the existence of PTSD was not related to preexisting personality factors. He argued that the stress involved with reacting to environmental disasters is so large and leaves such significant emotional impacts that it overrides any pre-event personality characteristics that may have existed.

These findings are important because they address a long-standing and fundamental question: whether a person can change, either from deliberate slow intervention such as therapy or from drastic one-time learning events like disasters. Clearly the importance of knowing the degree to which prior mental health determines postdisaster psychology has significance beyond the domain of disaster study.

The degree to which a victim can help others also influences that person's mental health. In many cases across cultures it appears that victims who are able to help other victims and who participate in the rebuilding of their community become less emotionally disturbed than those without this experience (Gleser, Green, & Winget, 1981). One cross-cultural study of the United States and Japan found that there was a difference in the degree to which people helped each other immediately after a disaster by volunteering. In Japan there was much less volunteering (Drabek, 1987). If the Japanese offer less help it might mean they are more vulnerable to emotional problems. Further cross-cultural research is needed to verify this hypothesis.

People expect to be helped if they were to find themselves in any terrible situation through no fault of their own. One study examined this phenomenon by comparing the same Kentucky victims who were unfortunate enough to experience two severe floods within a three-year time span (Kanlasty, Norris, & Murrell, 1990). As a rule, the perceptions of what help they would get was fairly accurate. Those who expected a lot of assistance received it, while those who did not have high expectations received less. However, nearly half the victims felt the help was not adequate. This study suggested that the people who received less help than they thought they would get were particularly prone to stress.

Psychological Reactions in Special Groups

The very young and the very old are more susceptible to mental disorders and to dying from environmental disasters. In a devastating series of events—a cyclone, flooding, and consequent famine in the Bay of Bengal in 1970 and 1971—nearly 30 percent of those who died were children younger than five years of age. Another 20 percent were people over seventy years of age (Lechat, 1976). Similar statistics were found after an earthquake in the former U.S.S.R. (Beinin, 1981). Because of the high degree of risk disasters pose to these groups, an explanation of their psychological reactions is particularly useful.

The Elderly

The elderly are especially vulnerable to becoming emotionally disturbed in a disaster. They are often very attached to the place where they live, they are slower to make changes, and less likely to recover from being physically or emotionally damaged (Raphael, 1986). After living in the same city for eighty-six years, it came as a complete surprise to Rose Baldwin when Hurricane Hugo destroyed her aging house. Before the storm, Rose was able to live alone. In spite of some waning of her physical abilities, her mental capacity allowed her to keep things well organized. After the storm, although she had no physical injuries, her children found that she was no longer able to care for herself (Aptekar, 1990).

In spite of anecdotal evidence, such as this, and research findings about the elderly, the same split opinion exists about the long-term effects of disasters on this group as for other victims of disasters (Phifer & Norris, 1989). Many researchers (Kilijanek & Drabek, 1979) feel the elderly are particularly at risk and therefore more likely to develop psychopathology than other age groups. Different research suggests that no age per se is more vulnerable than another to psychological problems following a disaster (Cohen & Poulsock, 1977). Still other researchers have found the elderly to be more resilient than other age groups (Bell, Kara, & Batterson, 1978; Bolin & Klenow, 1983;).

Phifer and Norris (1989) had begun to study the reactions of the elderly to a single episode of severe flooding in Kentucky when another flood came. The two floods provided the researchers with longitudinal data that helped to eliminate the bias associated with retrospective telling of prior events. While the elderly victims in the study often coped by excessive worrying, anxiety, and depression, the magnitude of their problems did not reach the level that would fulfill the symptoms of mental disorders. Phifer and Norris found that about 40 percent of the symptoms of the elderly victims could be accounted for by their predisaster mental health. Far fewer symptoms could be accounted for by age.

Children

Many studies have described children as a particularly vulnerable group after a disaster. They have been found to have sleeping difficulties, anxieties, and phobias (Frederick, 1977; Howard, 1980; Ollendick & Hoffman, 1982; Terr, 1981a; 1981b; Titchener & Kapp, 1976). Some authors have suggested that adverse effects could be so severe that disaster victims would pass fear and insecurity onto their children—even those yet to be born—by replacing in their child-rearing a sense of a secure world with a fearful worldview (Lifton & Olson, 1976).

A well-known study of the mental health of English children who had survived the German bombings of World War II showed that the children's responses were directly related to how their parents reacted (Freud & Burlingham, 1944). The children "copied" their parents. If their parents were calm, the children remained calm; if their parents were highly anxious, so were the children (Carey-Trefzer, 1949). Similarly, a longitudinal study of Australian primary school children who had been in grass fires showed that debilitating emotional reactions among the children had more to do with their family's adverse reactions than with the children's actual experience of the fire (McFarlane, 1984, 1986).

Three American studies noted that if children's parents were nearby to support them, the children did not have emotional problems (Benedek, 1985; Kinster & Rosser, 1974; Perry, Silber, & Black, 1956). The children of Belfast who lived through violent civil disturbances without their parents close by suffered far more severely than the children who endured similar trauma but were shielded by their parents' protection (Frazer, 1973). Yugoslavian elementary children who were separated from their parents after an earthquake developed hoarding behaviors and feared being abandoned (Singer, 1982).

The point of view that children's behavior could be understood only in the context of their parents existed in child psychiatry for generations (Terr, 1990). There was little information about children's subjective experience of trauma without reference to their parents. After reviewing the literature on methodological problems associated with disaster research, Garmezy (1986) noted that as a result of this bias there was also almost no information about the resilient ways in which children do cope with trauma.

Only in 1956 was an early experimental study done of children's emotional reaction to an environmental disaster. In that year children watching a movie in a Mississippi theater were hit by a tornado that devastated the building, injuring many. Because of the damage, parents could not reach their children immediately. Two studies (Bloch, Perry, & Silber, 1956; Silber, Perry, & Bloch, 1957) using unstructured interviews with the parents produced information about the children's emotional reactions. The authors concluded that the well-being of the children was largely a result of the way their families responded to them. The children's symptoms included regressive dependency needs, enuresis, night terrors, and phobic and avoidance responses. Although the children were not interviewed, the study did look directly at their behavior following the event.

The 1972 Buffalo Creek flood also yielded considerable data on children's responses (Newman, 1977). Two hundred twenty-four children were asked to draw a picture of the disaster, to draw human figures, and to tell the researcher their three wishes. The data were taken from children who were away from their parents at the time the test was given. Several factors influenced the children's drawings and reactions: the children's developmental level, their perceptions of their parents' reactions, and the degree of impact or the amount of horror that the children experienced. The author concluded that the children were very troubled with phobias concerning the natural world and weather, with sleep disturbances that included insomnia and nightmares, with separation anxieties, and with regression in their behavior.

Galante and Foa (1986) documented the aftermath of an extremely destructive earthquake that struck the mountainous region of Lombardy, Italy on November 23, 1980. One hundred sixteen villages were damaged, more than 4,000 people were killed, and tens of thousands lost their homes. As the homes collapsed, the charming narrow streets in the villages were inundated with tons of rubble. They soon became death traps without escape. It was several days before Italy's relief teams could get to many of the villages. While children watched, survivors tried to rescue victims whose voices could be heard crying from under the rubble. Right after the earthquake the children demonstrated extreme signs of apathy and aggression (Galante & Foa, 1986).

A study of Israeli children held hostage outlined several similar important factors for lives, predicting a child's reaction to disasters (Ayalon, 1982). These include the intensity of the stressor, the child's history of stress, the developmental period of the child, and the degree to which the child was able to gain a sense of mastery during the experience. Gleser, Green, and Winget (1981) also noted variables that were important for understanding children's responses after the Buffalo Creek flood. First, there was a gender difference. At every age girls were more affected than boys. Perhaps the girls were more aware of their feelings than boys. Being better able to express their feelings, they might have appeared more troubled when in fact they were not. Second, there was a race factor. Whites at every age had more problems than African Americans, a result that has not been found in every study (Aptekar, 1990). In another American study, boys were found to become more aggressive after being victimized by an environmental disaster (Burke et al., 1982). Similar results were found in Australia by McFarlane (1984, 1986).

Other studies draw attention to age differences as well as a child's predisaster state of mental health (Chamberlin, 1980; Malmquist, 1986). One pointed out that the oldest child in a family is the most vulnerable to mental health problems as a result of a disaster (Bloch, Perry, & Silber, 1956; Frazer, 1973; Raphael, 1983). Other studies show that the youngest children are the most vulnerable (McFarlane, 1984; Milne, 1977). Some children seem to be more resilient than others, regardless of age (Anthony, 1986a, 1986b; Garmezy 1986), a finding postulated to be the result of environmental and biological factors (Anthony, 1986a, 1986b; Werner & Smith, 1982).

Terr has done considerable work with children who have been traumatized (1981a, 1981b, 1990). She has noted that children react to trauma very similarly in spite of differences in their sociocultural backgrounds, family psychopathology, and previous psychological problems. This conclusion, however, was not corroborated by another study of bereaved children. Although these subjects were not traumatized by violence, each before the age of thirteen had lost a parent (Furman, 1983). These children's symptoms varied, and there was "no syndrome that [told] the clinicians, 'this is a bereaved child'" (p. 242). Perhaps the different types of traumas faced by the subjects in the two studies accounts for the different findings.

Several studies found a high level of emotional problems among children-victims, independent of the demographic variables and the other factors that have been associated with elevated mental disturbance. Eighty percent of children in one study (Titchener & Kapp, 1976) were identified as having a "traumatic neurosis," which was identified as obsessive thinking, phobic and other anxiety responses, sleep disturbances, and grief reactions. One twenty-six-month-old child victim of Buffalo Creek, was unable to take a bath without screaming. He wet his bed frequently and screamed in his sleep. He had seen his father barely escape death, had witnessed his house swept downstream by the flood, and watched his father unable to rescue his friend who was screaming (Newman, 1976).

In October of 1966 a landslide in the mining town of Aberfan, Wales, destroyed an elementary school, killing more than 100 children (Lacey, 1972). The local psychiatrist saw more than fifty surviving children over the next five years. He described the children's play as being relentlessly monotonous, as if its purpose was not pleasure but the working through of internal conflicts, which he ascribed to the disaster experience.

It appears that immediately after a disaster children and adults react similarly. Both groups are anxious but thankful for surviving. Both look for their loved ones and try to unite with them. The anxiety responses that adults feel, which include hypervigilance and phobic reactions, are also evident in children. These reactions have been described for children following the Darwin, Australia, cyclone (Milne, 1977), an Omaha, Nebraska, tornado (McIntire & Sadeghi, 1977), a Mississippi tornado (Silber, Perry, & Bloch, 1957), severe winter storms in the United States (Burke et al., 1982), and fires in Australia (McFarlane, 1984). Raphael (1986) has suggested that children show greater separation anxiety than do adults, but many adults also become very dependent on their families and friends and become anxious when they are separated from them.

A comparison of psychological reactions between child and adult victims of Buffalo Creek (Gleser, Green, & Winget, 1981) showed that children exhibited fewer symptoms than adults. About a third of the children showed minor symptoms, another 20 percent were severely affected, while the remaining 50 percent exhibited no symptoms. Milne (1977) noted that a quarter of the children who were victimized by Cyclone Tracy developed psychiatric problems.

One study of the children of the Three Mile Island disaster correlated symptoms with developmental level (Handford et al., 1986). Coping became more cognitively focused with age, although all children showed some regression. Children younger than eight years of age showed almost no recognition of the danger. Children from eight to twelve years of age intertwined fantasy with reality. Another study showed that children's reactions take different forms depending upon their age (Lystad, 1984).

Reactions of adolescents are more similar to those of adults than to those of small children (Carey-Trefzer, 1949; Lifton, 1967; Silber, Perry, & Bloch, 1957). Drabek (1986) reported that Italian studies of older children show far fewer problems than do the studies of younger children.

Researchers' failure to distinguish between children and adolescents could partly explain why studies of children produce inconsistent results; but it cannot explain why some studies show that younger children have more problems than older children while other studies show the reverse. It may be that younger children do not understand the seriousness of the situation they are in, and if their parents are supportive, they may experience the events as exciting rather than as terrifying (Raphael, 1986). Also, young children who are not separated from their parents react differently from those who are. Studies that do not make these circumstances clear confound the findings. For a recent review of the literature on children's reactions to disasters, see Aptekar and Boore (1990).

As in the study of adults, another problem with research into children's reactions is the psychological reality of denial. A study of parents' responses to children exposed to several natural disasters in Australia showed that many parents were also victimized. Being in the disaster with their children brought up many childhood memories in the parents, and in many cases parents had unresolved memories of being frightened by events beyond their control, like the sudden death of their parents, that made it difficult for them to help their children deal with what they were experiencing (Valent, 1983, 1984). As a result, they tended to avoid reporting the children's problems.

Parents in the aftermath of Hurricane Hugo and the Loma Prieta earthquake who denied their own problems had a great deal of difficulty seeing their children's dysfunction (Aptekar, 1991). Several other disaster studies note that parents tend to minimize or deny their children's problems, whether these are related to disaster or to other trauma (Burke, et al. 1982; Kinzie, Sack, Angell, Manson, & Rath, 1986; Sack, Angell, Kinzie, & Rath, 1986; Terr, 1981a). Teachers also denied the children's problems; in addition to dealing with children at school, they had their own children and damaged houses to contend with. In each case, children and adults played upon the denial of each other. For example, children, sensing that their parents were bereft, were afraid to show their own fears and therefore denied having them. These children felt that because their parents were greatly upset, they must be on good behavior. This attitude did not develop out of a sense of altruism. The children reasoned that if they caused any further problems at home (or at school), then the shattered threads of normalcy that were left in their homes might be totally torn apart and this was too frightening to consider. They tried to carry on as if nothing had happened, or as if what had happened was over and under control. Therefore there was no need to worry about it.

Family dynamics also changed. Because they did not know how to respond to the circumstances, some parents were unsure of how to discipline their children. One forty-year-old Mexican-American man in Watsonville asked his eleven-year-old son to pick up some of the fallen tree branches in their yard. When his boy said, "I don't want to pick up any more limbs," his father did not know how to respond. The father was not sure whether he should demand that his boy do his share or make special allowances for him during that stressful time. This scene was repeated countless times and it was not easily resolved, in great part because many parents were unaware of their own disaster fears. One study (Titchener & Kapp, 1976) noted that adult victims reexperienced many of their childhood anxieties rather than responding more directly to the current stressor. Because of their own powerful emotions, parents had an investment in helping their children deny the event since it reduced their own tensions.

Given these types of emotional issues, it is very difficult to determine whether the parents' or the teachers' point of view is most valid. The issue comes down to deciding whether the children indeed did not have problems, or that they had more problems than the teachers and parents were reporting. The literature (Benedek, 1985) demonstrates that when parents and clinicians are overwhelmed they tend to minimize the victims' problems and thus inadvertently help them avoid talking. In the Loma Prieta and Hurricane Hugo study, Aptekar (1990) concluded that parents and teachers were denying the dimensions of the problem for their own mental health. Clearly, the interaction between denial and mental health needs further exploration.

Another problem created by denial is that it causes symptoms to be manifested in strange ways, making it difficult for health care workers to ascertain who was having problems and how severe they were. Symptoms often come months, if not years, after the disaster and often appear in somatic (as physical complaints) forms (McFarlane, 1986, 1990). Indeed, the Loma Prieta and Hurricane Hugo study (Aptekar, 1990) found a strange set of symptoms that made the pathway between the disaster and the symptoms of distress very diverse and rarely straightforward. This was particularly true for pre-puberty (pre-operational) children who manifested their emotions either through tears about lost toys or in grief about toy planes being broken but rarely through any symptom easily seen to be related to the disaster. Thus, although victims might have appeared to be functioning adequately, the extent of their emotional distress became apparent if one was aware of how unusual the manifestation of symptoms could be.

An example is a fourth-grade boy in McClellanville. He was known to the counselor before the hurricane because he was timid and had few friends. He had been to the dentist and was given an antibiotic shortly before the storm. Three weeks after the hurricane he was sent to the counselor's office complaining about a toothache. As he spoke with the counselor he said his tooth ached. When he was asked again about the hurricane he said he was doing fine. He had not lost his house, and he and his family had not been separated from each other. If the counselor had not understood the denial of postdisaster psychology she could easily have ignored the psychological implications of the child's toothache. But she suspected that he was masking symptoms, so she asked him to describe what happened to him during and immediately after the hurricane. At this the child burst into tears. During the storm he had been able to tolerate seeing his environment literally fall apart, but when this was coupled with seeing his mother for the first time break down and cry, he could no longer manage his fear.

Other studies have shown that children tend to display their symptoms in ways that might not be expected by adults (Bloch, Perry, & Silber, 1956; Burke et al., 1982; McFarlane, 1984). When the symptoms do appear, they may be triggered by a symbolic and seemingly neutral occurrence that has activated recollection of the traumatic event (Blauford & Levine, 1972; Lindy, 1985; Terr, 1981a).

In addition, the manifestations of symptoms do not appear in every part of the child's life. Several studies have been done of Cambodian children who were forced to leave their homes because of persecution from the Pol Pot regime (Kinzie et al., 1986; Sack et al., 1986). These children suffered torture, loss of family members, and forced labor before coming to the United States. The children were found to have symptoms of PTSD and depression, but they were characterized as diligent learners in school. Their good school performance was attributed by the authors to cultural factors that prize school success. Such selective manifestation might be another reason beyond denial or avoidance that several studies have described parents who seem unaware of their children's problems (Kinzie et al., 1986; Sack et al., 1986; Terr, 1981a, 1981b). The parents of children who experienced the Three Mile Island incident (Handford et al., 1986) reported far fewer symptoms in their children than the children themselves reported.

Some research has shown that use of intrusive thoughts in children takes a different form from what it does in adults. The children in Chowchilla who were kidnapped in their school bus interpreted unrelated events preceding the trauma as "omens" foretelling of the kidnapping. This helped them explain the trauma to themselves and to find some meaning in the events. Although, the use of omens is not unknown among adults, it was used far more frequently than is common by the children of Chowchilla (Terr, 1981a, 1981b, 1990).

Whereas the psychological purpose of healthy children's play is to have the ego gain mastery through fantasy (Erickson, 1950), in posttraumatic play children compulsively repeated the event that caused the trauma. Because they reenacted a pattern that did not produce mastery but increased their anxiety, Terr (1990) interpreted this play as being different from healthy play, even though the children were using fantasy to master their fears, as do all children.

The children of Chowchilla did have many of the adult signs of PTSD. They had repeated traumatic dreams and they had continued daytime visions of the event. Their play featured many reenactments of the event, a phenomenon described by Anna Freud from her work with children in England during the bombing of London in World War II (Freud & Burlingham, 1944).

The essential symptom of adult PTSD, intrusively reexperiencing the traumatic event, has been observed in children who show anxiety, sadness, and aggression (Rescorla, 1986). Horowitz (1990) noted that children with anxiety and affective disorders also have intrusive thoughts and repetitive emotional patterns. It is difficult, therefore, to separate children with traumatic reactions from children with preexisting disorders.

Families

Family deaths from disasters have long-lasting effects. In the abrupt absence of the deceased family member, other family members interact with each other differently. Family dynamics change. Responsibilities among family members are shifted, the planning of everyday events is altered, and routines become different. Children's lives are altered, their mentorship is suspended or eliminated, and conflicts are interrupted so as to make their resolutions difficult. The children's view of authority regresses and they become dependent (Bolin, 1982; Milne, 1977).

Conflict often arises among the survivors in the family over the deceased person's role: who will fill that role and how it will be done? When the space in the family left by the deceased is taken by another family member, that shift produces also produces a gap that must be filled, and this too has the potential to produce stress. All of these changes are likely to be highly emotional for all the family members.

Several studies of a variety of disasters have examined families' reactions to these (Drabek, 1983; Drabek & Key, 1976; Drabek, Key, Erickson, & Crowe, 1975; Erickson, Drabek, Key, & Crowe, 1976; Trost & Hultaker, 1983). Immediately after a disaster, victims first turned to their nuclear family for help, then to family members who were close to the nuclear family and eventually to distant cousins, whom they may not have seen for years. No matter how neglected distant family ties had been, in the time following the disaster, extended families including cousins far removed in kinship were expected to help. Such expectations are less common in the United States, where extended families are not so functional as they are in developing countries.

In all cultures, however, it is the family who first supports victims (Smith et al., 1986; Solomon, 1985), particularly in places where the predisaster kin relationships are strong. Where kin relationships are less solid, the greatest help tends to come from people who are not related (Perry, Hawkins, & Neal, 1983). In these societies, when the expected help from official sources does not come, the resentment is directed toward kin, rather than non-kin (Bar-Tal, Bar-Zohar, Greenberg, & Hermon, 1977).

In the aftermath of a disaster, differences between traditional and modern families became important, according to an earthquake recovery study in Italy. Traditional families were less likely to use the new social support opportunities and consequently were slower to recover (Pelanda, 1981). A comparison of family responses following a Managua, Nicaragua, earthquake and a flash flood in South Dakota (Bolin & Bolton, 1983) showed that relatives were seen as more central to helping in Nicaragua than they were in South Dakota, where victims relied more on the government for help. The difference between the two studies might be from cultural differences or from the social class differences in the samples.

In the United States, among poorer families there is greater potential for family disruption following disasters than among those who are more affluent (Bolin & Bolton, 1983). U.S. families who have no insurance have more problems than families with insurance, and minority group families or those with elderly and disabled members are also more prone to disintegration after disasters (Drabek & Key, 1984).

In communities where disasters recur and where both parents are routinely away from their children, disaster-related factors are part of the way children are raised. Fears of disasters are incorporated into family life, as are the procedures to follow should a disaster occur. This constant awareness of an impending disaster alters the personality of children as they grow up; it also affects their parents. This attitude can be seen in Israeli children raised in kibbutzim that were constantly under siege from hostile neighbors (Bettleheim, 1969).

Hultaker and Trost (1976) compared the reactions of American and Swedish women forced after a disaster to go into a shelter without their children; the researchers found that Swedish women were much more distressed than the Americans by this necessity. The authors explained that because more American women than Swedish women worked outside the home, they were more likely to be separated from their families in times of normal stress, and American children were more accustomed to being without their parents. The families were thus by necessity prepared to deal with separation from each other during emergencies.

If the family is forced to go into a shelter together, family dynamics are also altered. The whole family is forced to be dependent on others—in this case, those responsible for maintaining the shelter. This reliance goes against societal norms in this country, where families are ordinarily expected to look after themselves, and also affects the roles of members within the family (Bates et al., 1963; Taylor, Zurcher, & Key, 1970). In shelters a woman's accustomed role is taken over by a formal bureaucrat who happens to be working on a particular day as a server of meals and a distributor of clothes. Because of the dependency shelters require, many families find them degrading.

That same distaste for being dependent may explain why disaster victims in the United States have resisted using mental health services. Other reasons might be that families truly do not need this help or that they find sufficient support from nonprofessionals. After the initial impact, families may be able to cope and return to normal functioning, or they may have extended family to help, or they may receive help from friends. As a consequence, many of the emotional needs of the victims might be taken care of before aid agencies arrive (Mileti & Nigg, 1984). Perceptions also can influence whether one seeks aid for emotional difficulties. Victims in the United States often do not seek help from mental health agencies because of the stigma that is sometimes attached to such a need (Yates, Anson, Bickman, & Howe, 1989).

A comparative study between the United States and Japan showed that Americans tended to avoid shelters more than the Japanese did (Perry & Hirose, 1983). The authors concluded that a major reason for this difference was that Japanese homes were smaller than American homes; therefore it was more difficult for neighbors to take in evacuees. In support of this point of view are other findings from the United States, which show that the poor, the elderly, and people without family support are the groups most likely to use public shelters (Moore, Bates, Layman, & Parenton, 1963; Quarantelli, 1980, 1990). An examination of victim behavior after an earthquake in Nicaragua and a flood in Rapid City, South Dakota, both in 1972, showed that families in both cultures went to shelters only if no help from relatives or neighbors was possible. Both the Nicaraguan and American families realized that many of their customary family roles changed when they moved into shelters. Loss of the important nurturing function might have accounted for the large incidence of mental health problems found among the women in shelters (Bolin, 1976, 1982; Bolin & Trainer, 1978; Bolin & Bolton, 1983).

Among the important changes faced by both Nicaraguan and American women in the study was a severe curtailment of their social life: they no longer had the financial resources to be able to spend time with family and friends. They had to refuse social invitations for the family because of fear that they could not reciprocate with return engagements. Many poor people in both countries strictly limited their social lives and stayed at home more often (Bolin 1976; Bolin & Trainer, 1978). This response is by no means universal. In some cultures, particularly traditional societies, people are accustomed to recurring disasters and have altered their social ceremonies to use less food and to find ways of sharing the whole community's resources among all people (Firth, 1959; Kirby, 1974; Torry, 1979b).

Disasters in developed societies also result in daily family changes, largely attributable to economic problems. These include the disappointment and frustration of not being able to pay off the family's house mortgage or to reduce other debts. Families must spend more time on the basics. Getting to work often becomes complicated and time-consuming, and free time must be devoted to looking for housing to replace the family home if it was damaged or lost in the disaster. These tasks are even more difficult if the city's mass transit system has also been affected by the disaster.

Having to relocate outside of the old neighborhood brings additional problems to families hit by disasters in developed nations. Such problems include being in an unknown place, the added time burden of having to travel to see old friends who formerly might have been just across the street, the sense of social isolation, and unfamiliarity with the facilities in the new neighborhood. Having to live outside of the accustomed neighborhood was particularly stressful for victims in both the United States and Nicaragua in the Bolin and Trainer study (1978).

Almost all families in the region are changed by the disaster experience, even if they have not lost a family member or their home. They often use the disaster as a time marker. Nearly fifty years after a 1929 hurricane in the Bahamas, families were interviewed about their memories of the event. They all seemed to have the event in their family lore, and other family events were placed in the time context of the hurricane (Westgate, 1978).

In spite of all of these changes the results of the studies of families in disaster are as mixed as the data about children and the elderly. Two studies (Drabek, 1983; Drabek & Key, 1984) concluded that disasters can help families pull together; other authors, however, have shown that disasters increase family tension (Bolin, 1982; Penick, Powell, & Sieck, 1976; Titchener & Kapp, 1976). Whether the studies are about children, the elderly, or the general population, the results are not clear. Some studies demonstrate severe pathology; others describe transitory problems. The Buffalo Creek studies support the idea that disasters produce long-term pathology in adults and children, as do studies from other cultures. Many other studies, both in the United States and other countries, describe a period of crisis immediately after a disaster but suggest that people return to the level of functioning they had prior to the event. Sometimes, as in the case of the Three

Mile Island nuclear scare, different studies of the same disaster show different results. Several methodological reasons contribute to the conflicting results, such as how long after the disaster the data were collected and whether results were based on individual experiences or aggregated information.

Many disaster-related myths—for example, that people will panic or become looters—are rarely found by researchers. Concerning the effects of a disaster on individuals, it appears that for people to suffer PTSD several factors must come into play. Some of these include the person's psychological resilience, the degree of personal impact the disaster has had on the individual, the type of disaster that occurred, and the degree of support the person has received. What happens to victims in the long run and how people deal with the help that is forthcoming after a disaster is the topic of the next chapter.

6

Postdisaster Recovery

Studies of the psychology of disaster victims, in spite of variation in their conclusions, all generally find one uniform result: the victims cope rather well with the initial disastrous event. They tend to act altruistically toward each other and they form a therapeutic community. The initial reaction to the disaster is to help each other. Victims reach out to families, friends, neighbors, and others within the community. This behavior has been recorded not only in the United States (Drabek, 1986) but also in Italy (Boileau et al., 1978), in Cyprus (Loizos, 1977) and in Nicaragua, where the extended family accounted for 95 percent of the total help given (Davis, 1975). Cross-cultural evidence suggests that the first people to help victims are other victims. Help comes either from individuals or from groups who emerge to offer assistance (Wenger, James, & Faupel, 1985). Only later does help from established relief agencies arrive (Aptekar, 1990; Wenger, James, & Faupel, 1985).

Alonso Mixteca came to Mexico City from his native state Guerrro just in time to be victimized by the 1985 earthquake there. As he watched, the building where he worked as a parking lot watchman collapsed, killing his wife and seven children who were inside. In the time it takes to walk across the street, his status changed from husband and father to widower without children. As he was walking through the rubble someone placed a water bottle in his hand and told him to give water to those who needed it. "Then I started handing out the water to those who waited for their relatives just like me, to the volunteers, to the people who were working, to the soldiers. Then they had me distribute food" (Poniatowska, 1988, p. 9). He relates how the simple routine tasks, first of giving water, later of carrying food trays, helped him withstand the tremendous trauma he had experienced.

When assistance arrives in disaster communities, victims are often treated as if they were irrational, helpless, and capable of destructive acts such as looting. In fact, as Mileti and Nigg (1984) pointed out, "It would be more prudent to view a victimized public as a resource to assist with disaster response than as a problem" (p. 100).

Once victims and relief agencies begin to interact, a new set of psychological phenomena emerge. Slowly but inevitably the mood shifts. As people become official "disaster victims," they begin a difficult adjustment, marked by a series of responses to the people and organizations that come to help. To understand how these phenomena come about, it is necessary to examine the way relief organizations operate.

Initiating the Relief Effort

In many ways the media are the first channel for redefining a harrowing event as an official disaster. They inform the public about it. The resulting public awareness often determines the level of attention the relief agencies pay to the disaster. An example of this interaction occurred with the Ethiopian famine in the 1970s and 1980s (Green, 1977; Morentz, 1976). For years Ethiopians had died of starvation but received little outside aid until a group of English television journalists placed the faces of suffering children on the international television networks. People all over the developed world, the would-be donors, were aghast at what they saw.

At the same time the world was seeing the images of starving African children there were approximately fifty other major world disasters (Kent, 1987). Although two million Ethiopians were dying from famine, there were five million Argentinians suffering from floods, another five million Indians nearly ruined by a cyclone, and more than ten million Brazilian victims of drought (Kent, 1987). However, the powerful television images of starving children in Ethiopia mobilized the public to contribute donations to their aid agencies for relief in that country.

When one compares the amount of media attention given to the Three Mile Island incident, which killed no one, or the Chernobyl accident, which killed fewer than a hundred people in its first months, to the 1976 Tangshan earthquake in China where more than 250,000 people were reported dead, the relationship between media attention and relief efforts becomes clear. Both the TMI and Chernobyl incidents generated extensive media coverage, but the Tangshan earthquake did not. The first two areas received considerable aid, the latter very little.

Why certain tragic circumstances gain the media's attention and others do not is not always easy to ascertain. The local press failed to report the 1977 cyclone in Andhra Pradesh, India. The political parties were using the government's relief policy as part of their political campaign so the media, in an effort not take sides, chose to refrain from publishing anything about the cyclone (Caldwell, Clark, Clayton, Malhotra, & Reiner, 1979). This restraint had the effect of slowing aid from the international relief community.

It is interesting that the severity of the disaster is not what establishes it as newsworthy (Adams, 1986). In a cross-cultural study of thirty-five severe disasters that occurred outside the United States between 1972 and 1985, the number of people who died accounted for only 5 percent of the variance in the amount of news coverage given to the disaster by the U.S. media. The largest amount of variance was explained by the country's popularity with the U.S. tourist trade (Adams, 1986).

Once an event gains the attention of the media, they generally give it a high degree of exposure. The Bhopal chemical accident and the Ethiopian drought received the second and third largest amounts of news coverage in 1984, a year of U.S. presidential elections, several international crises and armed conflicts, and a worldwide recession (Wilkins, 1987). Almost twice as many American readers are interested in disaster stories as they are in political information (Sood, Stockdale, & Rogers, 1987).

In a comparison of how four different disasters were covered by the media in Japan and in the United States, Quarantelli and Wenger (1990) found that despite some minor differences in the reporting of the events there were many similarities. In all cases there was a lack of accurate information. Equally as striking, each story was covered in a nearly identical manner, so much so that the study's authors hypothesized a universal culture for media coverage of disasters. They claimed that although a Nigerian and a Chilean reporter might have different audiences, their techniques for covering disaster stories and the way the stories would be presented would be identical. Not only does this uniformity lead to the spread of myths about how people will react to disasters but it also ignores whatever cultural differences exist in reactions to disasters.

A study of five quick-onset disasters, both within and outside the United States, showed that after each event most media reported on the number dead, the amount of property lost, and then, after time, human interest stories of victims or volunteers (Sood, Stockdale, & Rogers, 1987). After a few days the statistics no longer catch the public's attention and the reporting begins to emphasize certain parts of the whole disaster story. This emphasis has the effect of creating themes. In the case of the humanly induced disaster the theme is the fear of the unknown, of what might happen. An example of this theme came from the Three Mile Island accident. The media focused on the unbridled power of nuclear energy and the incompetence if not corruption of designers, operators, and federal regulators. The readers and viewers were left with a nonspecific but all-pervasive fear. In the Bhopal chemical accident the theme was the irresponsibility and greed of the multinational corporations working in poor countries. In the case of the Ethiopian famine the theme was the wealthy world's indifference to the less fortunate and its responsibility to suffering children. The deadly Bengal cyclone of 1970 turned into a story of West Pakistan's indifference to East Pakistan, which was tied to the larger human interest story of people's inhumanity to others. The theme of a disaster gives the public justification for their beliefs and helps them identify with what is happening. Themes greatly influence public opinion. They also sell copy.

The way the disaster is reported not only influences public opinion but also focuses on where and how relief is given. In Bhopal, where the theme was the greed of the multinational corporations, disaster relief was focused on getting money from the company to pay off the relief efforts. Unfortunately, the media cannot always be correct in their facts or complete in the portrayal of events. After the Andhra Pradesh Indian cyclone of 1977, ABC news reported that there was an outbreak of cholera when in fact there were few cholera deaths. However, the reports in the media started an immense outpouring of cholera vaccine, which had two effects: the vaccine was provided at great but unnecessary expense, and the amount of this medicine being sent to India prevented it from going where it was truly needed (Drabek, 1986). A similar phenomenon occurred after the 1970 cyclone in the Bay of Bengal (Kent, 1987).

One reason for inaccuracy in reporting events from the less developed nations is that often the journalists who are reporting come from developed countries. They often view events from an ethnocentric viewpoint that does not match the culture they are observing; they may have limited contact with the disaster area or may not understand the language spoken in that country. Journalists also have varied abilities to deal with the death and destruction they see in disasters. Many simply avoid the tragedy of so many dying, often using secondhand sources so they do not have to enter the camps themselves. There were reports that some journalists who dropped their notebooks were afraid to touch them because they feared getting infected with cholera. They were also afraid of eating or drinking whenever they were near victims (Kent, 1987).

For many reasons, journalists often rely mostly on officials for their information. In a study of five disasters, more than three-fourths of the information reported came from official sources (Quarantelli & Wenger, 1990; Sood, Stockdale, & Rogers, 1987). Since officials often are not able or do not want to give the kinds of information that might grab the public's attention, journalists frequently turn to people on the fringes of the story such as religious or political opportunists, business people looking for profits, or victims with high interest stories to tell. The validity of information from these sources is questionable since the sources are motivated by personal interests or have a limited view of the effects of the disaster. The reality is that evaluating information is very difficult. People have their own points of view or their own constituencies to defend, or their own personal reasons to emphasize certain information.

People from different cultures want different kinds of information. This was found in a comparative study of the English and Italian public and what they wanted from the media in reporting the flooding of the art treasures in Florence. Italians wanted human interest stories; the English desired information about the lost art (Alexander, 1980).

Cross-cultural reviews suggest that the media's focus on the dramatic conveys the impression of more damage and destruction than there is. This exaggeration has been confirmed in the United States (President's Commission on the Accident at Three Mile Island, 1979), Canada (Scanlon, 1980), Yugoslavia (Anicic, 1980), Nicaragua (Kates et al., 1973), and several other developing nations (Mader, Spangle, & Blair, 1980). The tendency for the media to portray events dramatically means that the public sees the worst damage on television, hears about the most awful destruction on radio, and reads about the most catastrophic events in the press. The public assumes a worst-case scenario.

Not only do the media control the public's knowledge of disasters; they can also determine when the public is informed—that is, how long after the event occurs information is released. Even in countries with a free press, like the United States, it can be difficult to get the facts from government officials. This is particularly true when the government may be implicated in chemical spills, nuclear leaks, or other human-induced disasters. Although governments with free presses are much more likely to yield timely and accurate information than media in more oppressive regimes, even these can be less than forthcoming. A comparative study of media coverage of the Chernobyl accident and its reporting of the Three Mile Island incident in the United States demonstrated a considerable difference in the public's knowledge of the events in their own country (Rubin, 1987). Within hours after the radioactive leak occurred, the press began reporting the events of TMI. In the United States the public's right to know took precedence over the problems associated with the unknown consequences of TMI. This was not the case in what was then the Soviet Union. It was sixty-seven hours before anyone outside of an inner circle knew of the Chernobyl accident. Public awareness and access to information were severely restricted.

Rubin (1987) did find some cross-cultural similarities. Officials in both countries tried to ignore the bad news, particularly about the amount of radiation in the atmosphere. In both cases the media tried to find someone at fault. This was the common theme of the news coverage of the two disasters. Assigning blame for humanly induced disasters changes how victims cope with them. It contributes to victims' ability to displace their problems onto an outside source. Although at first this might have some therapeutic value, after a while it delays the process of having to cope with the events at the personal level. It also contributes to difficult exchanges between relief agencies and victims.

First Stages of Relief

Relocating victims after disasters is one of the first things that official relief agencies must do. How this is carried out has important social and psychological ramifications for victims. Several studies around the world have shown how difficult it is for people to find shelter once they arc forced to leave or stay away from their communities. Victims resist moving into houses or into communities that are different from their own. This reluctance was observed in Nicaragua after an earthquake (Cuny, 1977; Davis, 1975), in Yugoslavia after an earthquake (Davis, 1977), and in India after flooding (Cuny, 1977). In all cases relocation prolonged the stress associated with being victimized.

After two earthquakes in one year, residents of a stricken town in Italy said the largest stressor they had was not the unpredictable continual stress of another earthquake but the inability to rebuild their destroyed homes in the same place (Geipel, 1982). Victims want to return to normal—to the past as it was—rather than to begin anew, even if they can do so with a more modern life-style. This preference for the old life has been demonstrated in Italy, in Yungay, Peru, after the 1970 earthquake and avalanche, in Mexico after the 1985 earthquake, and in Nicaragua after the 1972 earthquake (Kates, 1977).

Two studies of the 1974 cyclone that destroyed Darwin, Australia (Milne, 1977; Parker, 1977), showed that victims who could not return to their homes were the ones who showed the greatest and most enduring stress. Trainer and Bolin (1976) reported in a cross-cultural study of relocation after the Nicaraguan earthquake and a flood in South Dakota that temporary housing tends to impede the emotional recovery of victims. Similar results were found in Sweden (Bjorklund, 1981). The problem is particularly acute when the temporary housing is outside the victims' accustomed social milieu because this dislocation slows the reestablishment of social interactions with past friends and neighbors.

By the time relocation has started, it is clear to the members of the community that they are being "helped" and that further social and psychological changes are inevitable. Groups within the community are changed by the relief effort in three ways (Dynes, 1970b; Stallings, 1978; Tierney, 1989). First, groups that are already established in the community must do more than their regular jobs. Police and fire departments are much busier, working long hours without relief. Some established groups in the community must offer their services in new ways. A social service agency that ordinarily provides welfare benefits only in their office may begin going into the community to offer services.

Second, groups begin offering new types of services. This would be the case, for example, with a public housing agency that begins to offer mental health counseling. Other examples would include parent or social groups composed of business people that provide food to shelters, such as the Lions or Kiwanis clubs.

Finally, new community groups emerge. Almost invariably people begin to work together to deal with new issues they face because of the disaster (Mileti, Drabek, & Haas, 1975). Among other activities they seek to fill the gaps in needed services (Saunders & Kreps, 1987). This could result in a collection of people looking for lost relatives or people coming together to provide long-term aid to certain types of victims such as the elderly. Groups also emerge to work on previously existing problems (Parr, 1970). If a disaster worsens an existing housing shortage, for example, a group might emerge to lobby for long-term housing policies (Forrest, 1977).

It seems likely that groups forming in response to disasters would have life histories similar to those of groups forming in response to other social crises (Drabek, 1987). They either grow out of previously existing groups, which was the case after the bi-coastal American disasters of 1989 (Aptekar, 1990), or they come from existing organizations that have expanded their roles following a disaster. This was the situation in Sweden after a large mudslide (Syren, 1981). Emergent group leadership is often from people who had some type of prestige in the community prior to the disaster or who have certain skills that are needed, such as military or political experience.

Each of the three types of groups has its own problems after a disaster. Often tensions arise among those who want to volunteer help, the victims, and those in a group whose responsibilities are being expanded and stretched. Shortly after the Loma Prieta earthquake, victims were sheltered at various places in the city. One Mexican-American man who lived near one shelter arrived with several boxes of food he had taken from his home. He approached three of the National Guard who were patrolling the boundaries of the shelter, saying he had food to give. They told him that food could not be given to people in the shelter directly but must be taken to a central food bank where the person in charge would inspect it. The man decided that instead of driving across town he would give the food to the victims as they entered the shelter. Because the people in the shelter already had ample food provided for them, these victims stored the man's food donation in their tents, an

act that was in violation of the camp's public health rules. This disobe-
dience contributed to the tensions between the victims and the National
Guard who now felt obliged to enforce the rules. As a consequence the
victims staying in the camp, who already had complained that they felt
like they were living in a military base, felt further forced to accept additional orders (Aptekar, 1990).

Another frequently observed problem in established groups is the
stress caused from overwork. This results when groups are asked to
take on more functions, generally without additional manpower.
Members of police and fire departments often find it hard to meet the
additional demands they face. Working long hours under stressful conditions, they understandably become tired and less accommodating.
After Hurricane Hugo one African-American man simply wanted to take
some food out of his kitchen, walk it over to a shelter a few short blocks
from his house, and give it to the very people he often shared food with
at his dining room table. When the police at the door told him he could
not give food unless he drove across town and dropped it off at a centralized bureaucratic center he became angry. He explained to the officer that he wanted to give food to his friends, and he did not want to
see his donation mixed with thousands of pounds of other donated food,
which would, after being inspected and sorted, be sent to the various
official shelters. The policeman, having worked without rest for nearly
sixty hours, stared blankly at the man, who finally left frustrated and
angry. The well-meaning volunteer had given little thought to the
health requirements involved with having large numbers of people living together in close space for long periods of time. Yet the clumsy way
he was handled contributed to his feeling of being victimized and to the
changed feeling within the community (Aptekar, 1991).

Personnel in the second type of group, those that have extended
their focus of work—such as people accustomed to working in a housing agency office who have shifted to providing services door-to-door—
often find it hard to adjust to their new roles. What was normal and
expected has already been disrupted because of the disaster, and the
further shift in scope of services is often very difficult to cope with. To
groups that are expanding their roles by providing new services, like
the Lion's Club or the PTA, there is the problem of how to accept all
the volunteers who show up to help. These expanding groups also have
problems supervising volunteers and difficulty fitting the volunteers
into their organizational framework.

After learning through radio and television about the great need for Spanish-speaking volunteers in Watsonville, California, following the Loma Prieta earthquake, three bilingual young adults from San Jose filled their cars with clothes and drove the hour and a half to the town (Aptekar, 1991). When they arrived in Watsonville they went to one relief group where they were told that rather than clothes, the victims needed money so they could buy their own clothes. The relief worker said this allowed victims to make their own choices and to get a sense of regaining some control of their lives.

Feeling frustrated, the volunteers went to a mental health agency that was giving clothes to victims. When they arrived they were told that there were already plenty of clothes. A large warehouse was over-flowing with them and workers were having difficulty just sorting the garments. In spite of their growing frustration at having their offerings rejected, particularly after the public service announcements had asked volunteers to bring donations with them, the three went to another relief agency, a local nonprofit clothing and food distribution center which prior to the earthquake had operated as a church group. Here, they were also informed that clothes were no longer needed but were told that their bilingual skills might be used at a Red Cross shelter across town. That shelter, they soon discovered, was being patrolled by the National Guard. The guardsman did not allow them to give clothes because the person in charge of taking donations was not on duty when they arrived.

The experiences that the bilingual volunteers had were in great part the result of the difficulties expanding groups had with organizing so many volunteers and changing from one type of work to another. However, rejecting volunteers, or making them feel as if their help was not needed, led to a number of further problems. Those in turn changed the sense of community from one of goodwill to one of ill temper (Aptekar, 1991).

The *San Jose Mercury News* of November 6, 1989, had the following headline: "Quake relief work big and clumsy." The article told of a man who went into the Red Cross office offering his services. They were unable to give him a task at the moment. He explained to them that wherever he went he kept receiving similar rejections, which in his words meant that he was "passed from Red Cross to Red Cross" (Aptekar, 1991, p. 23). Not being able to volunteer through the estab-lished channels the man took the problems associated with coordinating many volunteers as a personal rejection. He then organized his own relief effort, which put him in competition with the established relief agencies. Although he gained a good deal of laudatory attention from friends and from the local press, a more careful analysis of his work illustrated that uncoordinated help actually hinders the relief effort.

One established agency is the Second Harvest Food Bank. After the earthquake it received many donations from volunteers. It phoned donators and organized a group of volunteers to pick up food, load it onto several trucks, and drive the trucks to a shelter. When the trucks arrived to drop the food off the drivers discovered that the shelter already had received a food delivery from the man who had started up his own independent relief effort. He had organized the food delivery without notifying other relief agencies. Without any room to store additional food, the shelter had to reject the donation from Second Harvest Food Bank (Aptekar, 1991).

Many volunteers have had bad experiences with established relief agencies similar to those reported above. As a result, they purposely avoid the agencies, giving help directly to victims without notifying the relief agencies. This is more problematic than it might seem as it forces relief agencies into making mistakes about how much and what services are needed. To avoid these mistakes, relief agencies, already pressed for time and money, have been forced to hire more personnel to carry the additional burden of replanning their efforts. Further efforts have entailed having to undo the poor work of an untrained volunteer or to reclaim the goodwill of victims who were led to believe bad things about the relief agency. With volunteers giving help of all kinds in all directions with no central control, the burden of trying to coordinate aid is greatly increased for the relief agencies. It is impossible for them to know which victims need what aid; consequently their task of organizing a directed aid effort becomes much more difficult. Similar phenomena were described after the 1985 Mexico City earthquake (Comfort, 1988), the 1987 Ecuador earthquake (Comfort, 1990), and the 1988 Armenian earthquake (Mileti, 1989). The same situation applied to the 1989 oil spill in Valdez, Alaska, to Hurricane Hugo (Aptekar, 1990; Comfort, 1988, 1990), and to the Loma Prieta earthquake (Aptekar, 1991). In all cases relief personnel experienced problems in communicating with one another and with victims. Not being able to coordinate their efforts caused a delay in relief. Their added burdens resulted in increasing the psychological problems of victims.

The third change communities face in the postdisaster recovery period comes from the formation of new groups. As a rule, new groups emerge because they see an unfilled need; either they try to fill the need by direct action or they become advocates for satisfying the need through legislative action. (For a review of the role, problems. and typology associated with emergent groups see Stallings and Quarantelli, 1985).

Studying communities affected by the California earthquake and Hurricane Hugo of 1989, Aptekar (1990) noted that in both places new groups formed to fill some community needs. He observed that the behavior of each group in acting to fulfill these needs was consonant with the predisaster political tradition of each community. Watsonville, California, in the previous decade, had a substantial history of political activism that affected how the community responded to the earthquake recovery. Three events in the previous two years were particularly important to the development of its political consciousness. First, two years before the earthquake there was an eighteen-month cannery strike. Almost all the cannery workers were Mexican and Mexican-American women. The strike was successful not so much for the wage concessions it won but because it created a sense of solidarity and community. The second event was in 1988 when Mexican-Americans protested against the citywide system of city council elections, which they claimed was biased against Mexican Americans. When they did not receive an adequate reply to their protest from the city council, they filed a suit that was eventually decided in their favor by the California Supreme Court. The third event came after the earthquake. It was the formation of a new group made up of people who were headquartered in a tent city in the center of town at Calahan Park. The group was established to protest the long-term affordable housing needs exacerbated by the earthquake.

On the other side of the country was McClellanville, South Carolina, hard hit by Hurricane Hugo. The nonwhite majority of McClellanville had no political movement. The formation two years earlier of a private school, Rutledge Academy, was seen by them as an effort by some white families to keep their children from attending integrated schools. This incident never received a clear counter-statement from the African-American community.

There was also no sustained and organized effort to press the government for more than emergency, disaster-relief services after the hurricane. Instead, a group of white men from upstate South Carolina came into the African-American section of McClellanville that was hit hardest by the storm "in order to help them help themselves." These men started a new group called Dupree Association for Repair, or DARE, named for Dupree Street where it began. The focus of the group was giving aid to hurricane victims.

The comparisons between the political traditions of the two communities reflect the different ways in which groups emerged after the disaster. Watsonville had a strong recent past of political activism by and for its minority population; this tradition was lacking in McClellanville. In Watsonville the political process for the poor and working class was effective and confrontational. These people were aware of their civil rights, knew how to form political movements to demand what was their due, and, based on their past experience, felt successful in getting satisfaction. In McClellanville politics were subdued and unorganized. The political process was neither public nor confrontational.

The political process reflected the different underlying attitudes of the populace in the two towns, and these attitudes were important in determining how people reacted to the governmental agencies in charge of repairing destruction. The differences can be seen by comparing two new groups in each city: the ad hoc shelter tent city in Watsonville's Calahan Park, and DARE, the housing and community group in McClellanville.

At the first DARE meeting in McClellanville, Gordon, a fifty-five-year-old, African-American, long-term resident of the community was selected as leader. One reason the outsiders chose Gordon to be the political power broker was that he had traditionally been the Democratic Party's liaison to the African-American community. During the meeting other African-American community members began complaining about the services they felt were going to the white community. Gordon took the microphone. In the mid-day sun of what once had been a family's front yard, now filled with sea mud from the storm, he told the crowd, "Now is the time to be humble. In this time of crisis, don't rock the boat" (Aptekar, 1990, p. 86).

In contrast, at Calahan Park twenty-one-year-old Arturo used the timing of the disaster to pressure the Watsonville city authorities on the long-term problem of housing. He crafted a power base by organizing a group of people from the tent city, using media coverage to keep the tent city park highly visible and making sure that the fifty or so families in the park maintained their sense of value. He constantly reassured them of their importance and told them that as long as they stayed together their basic needs would be satisfied.

Gordon, on the other hand, tried to keep the media out of DARE, preferring to negotiate privately behind the scenes. He also asked that people return to their homes to wait for the aid to come to them rather than to draw attention to themselves as a group. Rather than taking a confrontational stance as a political group by uniting the victims toward a common goal and seeing that they stayed united, Gordon worked toward having each person represent his or her own case to the authorities, not on their home turf but in governmental offices.

These two different groups, one based on accommodation, the other on confrontation, had different effects on the community and relief organizations. The Red Cross did not want to get involved with local political issues. This was in line with Gordon's point of view but in exact opposition to Arturo's. At first the Red Cross refused to give services to Calahan Park residents because the park was not an official shelter. However, Arturo's group used media coverage and the high visibility of the park to embarrass the city for refusing to give assistance. This strategy eventually forced the city to lobby the Red Cross, which agreed to bring hot food to Calahan Park three times a day. This victory raised the spirits of the Mexican-American Calahan Park victims.

A similar phenomenon did not exist in McClellanville. There the African-American people were unwilling to use confrontation to influence the authorities; consequently, help was slow to come and small in amount, a situation that added to their sense of helplessness. In Watsonville, Mexican Americans had recently profited from their successful cannery strike and from the favorable Supreme Court decision on municipal elections. The Mexican-American community was already in the midst of successfully establishing its power when the disaster struck.

Emergent groups serve their membership in several ways. In Watsonville, for example, the predisaster issue of the lack of affordable housing received a boost from the Calahan Park group. The group not only worked toward solving the immediate housing needs of its victims resulting from the disaster, but also worked to establish a political coalition that would seek long-term housing solutions. It also served to increase the self-esteem and political efficiency of the people involved in it. Mexicans working in the United States but without American citizenship learned more about their civil rights and how to secure them.

Emergent groups are a cross-cultural side effect of disasters; they influence the ways victims cope with their disaster experience. Cattarinussi and Tellia (1978) reported on an emergency tent city that formed after an earthquake in Italy. The new group revived many old customs that had almost disappeared since World War II. It helped women become viable members of the political process for the first time. It helped victims begin to take charge of their circumstances. In short, the Italian group was able to help victims shed the sense of fatalism that had characterized their attitude toward government prior to the earthquake. Working together in an emergent group they were able to force their mayors and city council members to leave office, paving the way for a more representative government.

After the 1976 Guatemalan earthquake, emergent groups formed around the issues of rebuilding community structures and homes. These groups were helpful in teaching peasants how to gain control over the political process (Bates, 1982). They became so successful that the central government perceived them as a threat and after a few years abolished them.

Disasters come to places with a particular history and they are met by people with particular experiences, both personal and political. Comparing the ways new groups form and operate in their respective communities illustrates how politics and history come to be significant in times of crisis. Understanding the process by which existing groups expand or offer new services also focuses attention on how communities change following the introduction of disaster relief.

The Difficulty of Providing Aid

Although every emergency cannot be planned for in advance, there is a great need for predisaster planning, as can be seen from the problems associated with volunteering, the problems of new groups emerging with their own political agendas, and the problems that existing community groups have in coordinating relief efforts. Aid agencies need to prepare for their role in disaster relief and to understand the community they are planning to help.

International relief began in 1863 when Henry Dunant created the Red Cross. A few years earlier, Dunant had been in the Battle of Soferino. He saw the tremendous suffering the wounded endured while lying on the battlefield waiting to be helped. The Red Cross was formed to aid those hurt in battle, regardless of the side they fought on. A year later, in 1864, the first Geneva convention adopted Dunant's international rules for the care of war victims.

The Red Cross continued its work with war victims and slowly began assuming the role of providing relief for disaster victims. Because it was primarily a volunteer agency, it simply did not have the funds to meet all needs for all kinds of emergencies. It encountered tremendous problems with logistics. To assist in the global effort, several other international relief agencies emerged—as well as a number of national groups. With many of these working on disasters outside their own countries, problems of coordination developed, many of which still exist.

Imagine the coordination problems of a typical desk officer in the United Nations Children's Fund (UNICEF). Green (1977) notes that such an officer might receive more than 50 emergency telexes a day. He reports an incident in which a desk officer reading such a telex was asked to send a particular type of serum, but the official failed to read the part of the message requesting syringes. He found and sent the serum but not the needles. When he heard about his mistake, he had to find the syringes and send them. This took time. As a result of his mistake, which in large part was a result of the excessive coordination demands of the job, there was a serious cost in human suffering.

There are also logistical difficulties in international aid. How could those in charge of relief find the equipment to cut through reinforced concrete to rescue victims after the 1985 Mexico City earthquake? Once the equipment was located how might it be delivered to the area where it was needed? How would the equipment be serviced? Logistical problems are immense.

After the volcanic eruption in Armero, Colombia (Podesta & Olson, 1988), the logistical difficulty was to find rapidly sufficient numbers of people to dig victims out of the mud. Tools had to be located. Food and shelter for the victims were needed. Visas for foreign workers had to arranged. A system of getting materials through customs had to be devised.

It is extremely difficult for relief workers to be efficient when they have little predisaster information about the disaster site. The lack of a good population census or a serviceable communication system are common obstacles. If relief agency workers are unaware of the ethnic differences within a country and merely respond to "victims" in the abstract, they might prove to be extremely ineffective. Ethiopia is good case in point. In the highlands of Ethiopia there are Amharic-speaking farmers, in the midlands there are the Oromo herders, and in bush dry-lands there are the Afar nomads. Not only does each group have its own language, its own culture, and its unique relationship to the political system, but each group is affected by the drought in different ways, so that each group needs a different kind of relief. Because the Afar nomads have lost their animals in the last several years of the drought, it will take considerable time and special relief efforts for them to regain their way of life or to adapt to a different life-style. The farmers from the highlands need only to wait for rain. Temporary relief until it comes might be sufficient for them because when the rain arrives they may well be able to continue their traditional way of life. In short, each group needs its own unique assistance strategy (Anderson & Woodrow, 1989).

Not only is cultural understanding essential in providing relief that is appropriate; warnings of a disaster can also be contingent on cultural differences. A comparative study of thirty-one sites in different cultures demonstrated that over 50 percent of the public did not receive warnings (Leik, Carter, & Clark, 1981). The most common reasons for this were "ideology, politics, and values" (p. 19) and not the hardware of the warning system (Schware & Lippoldt, 1982). A number of West Bengali villages received no warning before the 1970 cyclone. There was no failure of the highly acclaimed technological warning system that had recently been installed; the unwillingness rested with the political party in power who would not give the warning to people who were of different and conflicting parties (Burton, Kates, & White, 1978); even if the system had been used, the migrant workers in the Bay would not have understood the language used to warn them of the coming storm (Schware, 1982).

One central problem with disaster management is organizing the tremendous influx of goods and people that always follows a tragic event (Mileti, Drabek, & Haas, 1975). In a comparison of several relief efforts in large-scale disasters, Dynes (1970b) showed that supplies usually arrive in excess of what is called for, and often the supplies do not include the items that are most needed. This situation arises because individuals who want to give assistance and the helping agencies themselves, across cultures, almost always underestimate the extent of help the community is able to provide for itself (Mileti, Drabek, & Haas, 1975; Quarantelli & Dynes, 1972). As a result, there are too many volunteers. They take up valuable time receiving orientation, work assignments, and on-the-job supervision; often they have to be helped to deal with their own emotional reactions to the disaster.

Given the problems associated with disaster relief, mistakes are not surprising. After the earthquake in Guatemala, canned food was sent in; but the indigenous people would not eat food from cans because they associate food in cans with dog food (Olson & Olson, 1977). Guatemalans also received unmatched shoes, which were useless, and heavy clothing, which could not be worn in their tropical climate (de Ville de Goyet, del Cid, Romero, Jeannee, & Lechat, 1976). Culturally inappropriate housing schemes occurred in Peru, Yugoslavia, and Turkey (Davis, 1977).

Any donation, useful or not, must be inventoried and stored, all of which takes local time and money. Inventorying places an additional burden on the personnel who are already busy giving direct aid. Often extra people must be enlisted to help and as a consequence they may be taken from other places where they are really needed. The problems associated with having a large amount of donations in a disaster area go beyond the logistical difficulties of the relief agencies. There is also the adverse economic factor that a large influx of free goods has on the local economy. For example, if highly subsidized grain is sent into a drought area, local farmers and merchants cannot sell the local grain and are consequently inhibited from making a living. Such situations have been reported in Guatemala (Bates, 1982) and Ethiopia (Green, 1977).

If there is an excess of donations coming into an area in a less developed nation, people from outside the disaster area will flock in to claim a share of the free goods. They may need these commodities to survive, but more commonly, they come because the imported goods are better than what is available locally—and often they are free (Dudasik, 1980). The victims of the 1970 Peruvian earthquake were so inundated with aid that not only did the national government lose control of what was being sent, but "victims" appeared from many states outside the disaster area to claim a portion (Green, 1977). In Colombia after the

Armero volcanic eruption, excess aid caused a significant number of nonvictims to appear seeking to share in the donations (Parker, 1989).

International relief agencies have problems of coordination, primarily because in most international relief efforts there are many donors. Any large-scale disaster will probably draw relief workers from the international community, from within the government, and from several regional countries. Each group expects similar recognition from the media and from the host government. Each group might also have its own political agenda. Every group in disaster relief eventually seeks to justify its work to the people who provide its operating expenses. "It has been argued—with justification—that most information produced by international relief organizations about their work is designed to enhance the agencies' reputations, to satisfy past funding sources, and to elicit future support" (Green, 1977, p. 31).

The United Nations has established the United Nations Disaster Relief Organization (UNDRO) whose task is to coordinate relief efforts. UNDRO has done a great deal to prevent the kinds of coordination problems that Biafra and Peru faced, but it has seen other problems emerge. Most people without experience assume that relief is motivated only by goodwill; those who are knowledgeable, however, understand that there are serious political considerations associated with giving disaster relief. When Kurt Waldheim was the Secretary-General of the United Nations, he is reported to have said he first had thought that humanitarian aid was above politics, but after some experience on the job he knew that humanitarian aid *was* politics (Kent, 1987).

Politics exists within and between disaster relief organizations, and political factors contribute to how many relief decisions are made. If a community were to list the problems it might face, disasters would be near the bottom. This is not a denial of their existence; rather, the placement reflects the intermittent nature of disasters and the reality that other welfare problems the community might have to deal with are more predictable and regular (Wright & Rossi, 1981). Thus, there is little political pressure to deal with disasters before they occur.

Within most national governments the people who are responsible for disaster relief are not in positions of great power (Kent, 1987). They do not have easy access to the ultimate decision maker and they lack authority in the final decision process. People in charge of national disaster relief must seek their support from agencies within the government that are already funded. As a result they are constantly forced to make the case that it is in the best interests of the agency to give its resources for disaster aid. In the United States, for example, foreign disaster relief is in the hands of the State Department principally through the Office of Foreign Disaster Assistance and the Agency for International Development. But the State Department has many concerns and many people competing for its resources. The decision about whether and how much aid should be given often depends upon whether the aid will promote the causes of the State Department. The decision for the United States to give money to Pakistani victims of the 1970 cyclone had more to do with President Nixon's desire to win the good-will of China, which was backing Pakistan, than it did with easing the pain of the victims (Kent, 1987).

Political connections are always important in determining how much aid a country will get. This was the case in Micronesia where a small but strategically important place received a great deal of funds, while less important but more needy places suffered (Marshall, 1979). In the mid-1980s the United States argued in the United Nations that Ethiopia should ask for aid from the Soviet Union and not from the United States since Ethiopia was a supporter of the Soviets. Similar arguments were made when Angola and Mozambique asked for aid. Western Europe was reluctant to give assistance after the Nicaraguan earthquake of 1976 because they were afraid of getting into a conflict with the United States (Green, 1977; Kent, 1987). Giving aid to a country might be interpreted as formal recognition of a political group within that country, and the donor government might not want to do this. Such a situation affected aid during the famine in Ethiopia when the Eritreans and the central government in Addis Ababa were engaged in civil war. The United States argued that the Soviet Union and not the United States should aid the Soviet client, Ethiopia. Neither the Soviet Union nor the United States wanted to recognize Eritrea, so that country suffered from lack of aid.

International trade and fluctuations in the world economy can also affect relief efforts. An example of this occurred in the early 1970s when large droughts struck the Indian continent. At the same time there were also droughts in the Sahel and weather-related low harvests in China and the Soviet Union. In all these places people were attempting to buy grain on the world market. Because of shortages and high demand, grain prices rose. As the world's major seller of grain, the United States had its own economic interests. Because of very high oil prices and the recession at home the United States decided to sell its grain only through competitive bidding.

India, also highly dependent on oil, was short of cash. it was at that time in a war with Muslim Pakistanis. Bangladesh was suffering severe famine but received no help from its two neighbors, Pakistan and India. The two countries were unwilling to help Bangladesh because they were at that time paying very high prices for oil and for wheat. At least in part because of this complex series of events, over a million people died of starvation (Hewitt, 1983a).

Still other political situations affect the way aid is administered once it reaches the field. In almost all disasters many groups of people are involved in helping victims. However, because they are separate groups they have their own interests to maintain and their own objectives to pursue. These conflicting goals often make aid-givers competitors and at times adversaries. In a longitudinal study of the effects of aid following the Guatemalan earthquake, Bates (1982) recognized six separate interest groups whose differences led to conflict in Guatemala. These included the national government, the private sector, church and other volunteer agencies, the local community sector, household and kinship networks, and the foreign governmental aid agencies. Ad hoc or emergent volunteer groups should be added as a seventh interest group.

The national government in the country where the disaster occurs also has to face the demands of several ad hoc groups. In Guatemala there was an alliance of business people who wanted the contracts for rebuilding. The national government was under pressure from international organizations who wanted it to award building contracts only after competitive bidding. If the power shifted to either the local business interests or to the demands of the international relief agencies, certain elements within the national government lost power. The ruling party in the government felt that its power was in jeopardy, a perception that strongly motivated its reactions. This fear within the government influenced the way aid was obtained and to whom it was distributed.

Similar phenomena have been observed in other localities. The way local governmental officials handed out aid depended on how they reacted to several competing groups. On one hand, they needed to satisfy their superiors at the state and national level who wanted to be sure that the recipients of aid were aware of government's part in the aid distribution. On the other hand, the officials could not alienate other powerful groups, such as the church and the business sector. The church wanted its fair share for rebuilding and wanted its constituency to know that the church was taking care of them. Likewise the local business groups wanted to ensure that they were given the contracts for rebuilding. They resented any outside influences, especially the demand by international agencies that competitive bidding take place.

As it turned out, in Guatemala the international relief agencies initially won out. They devised a housing plan that gave power to local emerging groups. As these groups gained power they developed leaders who learned how to build a political base, to make political demands, to rally supporters, and to build consensus with other ad hoc groups. These emerging skills made it difficult for local and national officials to maintain the paternalistic system of government. They saw their hold on power eroding. As a result, they were not going to give any further aid to their potential rivals who they thought would use these local emerging groups to oppose the waning power of the government. The phenomenon of politics affecting aid is, of course, not peculiar to Guatemala. It was observed after the 1972 Nicaraguan earthquake (Bates, 1982) as well as many other disasters (Anderson & Woodrow, 1989; Green, 1977; Kent, 1987; Parker, 1989).

An account of the relief efforts in Armero, Colombia, after the 1985 volcanic eruption is instructive in showing how internal political processes influence relief as well as what happens when there is an excess of donated goods (Parker, 1989). The Colombian government's response to the volcanic eruption was primarily based on its internal political situation. From the beginning of Colombia's independence from Spain in 1820, that country has been split into two political camps: the liberal and the conservative. In 1959 the military took over the government and a new political faction formed: the leftist guerrillas who began functioning clandestinely. The government and guerrillas fought until 1984 when they began a tenuous cease-fire. At the time of the volcanic eruption in 1985 President Bentancourt was desperately trying to shore up his party to take firm control of the government while avoiding the appearance of being too lenient with the guerrillas.

While the president struggled with the government, in another part of the country, a disaster was about to occur. Nevado de Ruiz, the mountain overlooking the Armero Valley, had erupted twice before, the last time over a hundred years earlier. However, because it had been quiet for so long, people inhabited the valley, drawn there because of

been distributed it had gone to groups who were not victimized or to wealthy people who did not really need it. The materials that were distributed to peasants were described as being the least valuable and least needed of all the goods received from the aid agencies. Some peasants said they had to pay for the aid that was supposed to be given to them. The international agencies sponsoring the relief were unaware of the problems the recipients reported. They said they made their decision to give material to local groups because those groups knew more about local customs than did the international agencies.

Whether or not corruption actually occurred in the distribution of the materials, the farmers felt they had received unfair treatment. Half the recipients of aid said they were worse off than before the storm. The results of Snarr and Brown's study found no economic difference between those victims who got aid and those who did not. The study concluded, "The Honduran peasant, like subsistence peasants throughout the world, are at the mercy of forces beyond their control; the weather, multinational corporations, the various levels of their own government, and persons of means in their own communities, such as those responsible for distributing the aid materials" (Snarr & Brown, 1984, p. 486).

Giving aid for reconstruction can be difficult because of the choices that must be made in the ways it is distributed. These can take three different forms. The money can be based on the value of what was lost. Those who have lost more receive more. The problem with this way is that it often maintains the status quo; everyone remains where he or she was before the disaster, leaving the poor who were more vulnerable to disaster as much at risk as ever.

A second type of aid is also based on need, but in this case the money is calculated by a formula that combines loss and financial ability to rebuild. This system favors the poor over the upper and middle classes.

A third type of aid gives the same amount and type of assistance to all victims, independent of their income levels. If, for example, a thousand houses of the same type are donated, then every victim gets equal access to them. This method benefits the poor because they find themselves living in much closer contact with the wealthy than before.

Obviously each situation has certain side effects, both real and imagined. When groups are upset about who does and does not get aid, it is commonplace to hear accusations of corruption. While some of those charges are well founded, many other claims of corruption are in fact something quite different. In many places in the world it is common for disaster victims to take relief items they are given and trade them for things they have a greater need for, or to sell them for money (Kent, 1987). After a flood in the Bay of Bengal, Bengalis without homes were given woolen blankets. When the rains came, the blankets became wet and heavy. A local market sprang up to trade them for other items the victims needed. Traders from Calcutta came to buy the blankets from the local marketers. They moved them to Calcutta where wool blankets were in short supply. This type of trading can be seen as corruption.

The problem is really with the original donors. Their help would be much more effective if they gave either money or materials that are truly needed. Often, rather than learning what victims need and then supplying those items, donors take the cheaper and less time-consuming route and give what is available. As long as this practice continues, it will fuel the systems of postdisaster bartering that often are labeled corrupt.

Another practice often leads people in charge of distributing donated goods to feel that fraud is taking place. In many places in the world, victims register several times so they can get more aid. Officials see this as corruption; victims consider themselves as merely fulfilling obligations to their extended families. While some fraud does occur, most of what is called corruption can be explained in cultural contexts. The principal damage caused by this charge is that it seriously reduces the amount donors are willing to give (Kent, 1987).

The Difficulty of Accepting Aid

Even when it is offered, not everyone wants aid. Some traditional societies prefer dealing with disaster on their own because the mere fact of the disaster has special meaning, and accepting aid from outsiders would disturb the recovery of the culture. After Cyclone Isaac, in order to show community solidarity, victims in Tonga preferred to change their living arrangements and move in with nonfamily rather than accept outside relief (Oliver & Reardon, 1982).

Religion also plays an important part in how disaster relief is received. In countries where the Catholic church is strong, it provides a permanent apparatus for distributing aid soon after it is delivered. The church was the major aid-giver after the 1976 Friuli earthquakes in

Italy, and all aid had to be filtered through church auspices (Cattarinussi & Tellia, 1978).

Cultural factors also account for whether a country accepts or refuses aid. Clifford found in his study (1956) of two flood communities along the Mexican and American border that the Mexicans refused aid because they did not trust the authorities who were offering it. The Mexicans relied more on family and kin, whom they trusted. The Americans relied less on kin and more on authorities, whom they trusted to give them accurate information and unbiased help.

When aid does come, the long-term results do not always benefit its recipients, at least according to a cross-cultural comparison of several anthropological case reports of traditional societies (Torry, 1979a). These studies concluded that disaster assistance promoted dependence, and the more outside help a society received, the more its local coping skills were reduced (Cuny, 1983).

As examples, after unseasonal frosts in New Guinea, foreign aid agencies brought in food to help the people survive the loss of their crops. The people developed such a dependence on the "exotic goods" that they preferred them to their own, ruining the local economy (Waddell, 1975). A similar situation happened in Guatemala where so much grain came into the country that it ruined the local market for grain. This placed a severe hardship on local farmers (Riding, 1977). In yet another example, so much food aid came into Bangladesh after the civil war in 1971 that the local market for rice plummeted. Farmers planted less, thereby reducing production. This prompted more food aid to come from the international relief community. Ships filled with food lined up in the Bay of Bengal. In order to get a fair price for their rice, local farmers began illegally selling what they had to Indians. It was months before the director of the World Food Program realized what was happening. When he did, he asked the international relief agencies to stop bringing in food (Wijkman & Timberlake, 1988).

As early as the 1906 San Francisco, earthquake marshals were called in to prevent pillage. Citizens found that the police prevented them from going into their own homes to rescue what they could (Morren, 1983). Left unattended, the homes were looted and ironically, the homeowners lost much more than they would have if they had not had police protection. After an earthquake in the French Antilles in 1989, troops, thinking that it would be unsafe to let people leave the shelters and return to their homes, prevented farmers from feeding their animals (Morren, 1983). As a result, peasants lost much of their livestock, resulting in additional hardships.

Most studies of disaster victims in developed countries who get aid have shown that they end up with increased debt (Rossi et al., 1983; Vinso, 1977). Contrary evidence exists in Sweden, where a superb national insurance program helps people recover completely (Bjorklund, 1981). Not all developed countries have adequate insurance protection, however, and payment by insurance companies is often less than expected. After Hurricane Hugo many African-American victims, such as Sylvia, whose story is told below, complained bitterly about how insurance failed to help them recover their losses (Aptekar, 1990).

Sylvia, a fifty-four-year-old African American and a single mother of three boys, was born and raised in McClellanville. At eighteen she had her first child. A year later she married the father whom she stayed with through the birth of her two other sons. Sylvia felt unhappy and trapped in her marriage and finally left her husband. She raised her three children alone.

She worked out of the ground floor of her house as a seamstress. The house was filled with a thirty-year accumulation of sewing patterns. Hurricane Hugo did not knock down her house, but a six foot tidal surge swept through it and left a foot of red sea mud and silt. Sylvia was not allowed to clean her house until it had been inspected by insurance agents and representatives from FEMA. She talked to researchers while she carried her drenched and muddied sewing patterns in a wheelbarrow to the front lawn where they were to be carried away by a bulldozer. Sylvia spoke rapidly, her words pouring out like coins from a slot machine. When she got to the painful points she began to stutter. She had wisely purchased $100,000 of home insurance and $50,000 of insurance for its contents. When the insurance agent visited her home he measured the water line at six feet and told her that she was covered for winds, but not for floods. He offered to pay for the damages above the water line, but not below, and wrote out a check for $4,600. Unhappy with the offer, Sylvia did not sign the check. She called her agent several times to talk about the settlement but he would not answer her calls. When disaster relief comes in the form of insurance, it is often inadequate.

In addition to the economic and political reasons assistance can inhibit people's recovery, there is also a psychological factor that retards victims' recovery. People do not like being in the role of victim

(Taylor, 1983). Victims do much to resist being dependent, in large part because they feel better if they take their own action to reduce their losses. Ironically, the helpers who come to give them relief make it difficult for victims to shed their dependence. Relief workers like being helpers; it is often their one chance to be heroic and virtuous. Many have reported how much they enjoy being able to leave their prior roles behind and become involved with people of various social classes and walks of life, an opportunity that was not open to them before they worked in disaster relief (Aptekar, 1991). When personnel from the official relief agencies arrive, many volunteer helpers become angry because they must give up their posts to them. They often feel their own work, based on personal commitment, is more valuable than the impersonal bureaucratic work of the aid agencies (Taylor, 1983).

Because there can be no helpers without victims, there is a natural desire among the helpers to keep victims dependent. The media contribute by dramatizing the extent of the disaster, encouraging even more volunteers. These helpers, true volunteers as well as those from organized agencies, routinely underestimate the degree to which the disaster community can help itself. The result is far more relief personnel than victims needing help. The volunteers end up fighting for the few victims available, increasing the propensity to keep victims dependent (Aptekar, 1991). The more dependent victims are, the slower they will be in taking control of their circumstances and beginning the recovery process.

Psychology of Disaster Workers

Working in a disaster is not simple; many people are not able to cope with what they see and what they must do. Even those with experience often need outside emotional assistance to help them cope with their work. The study of the mental health of disaster workers began with Rayner (1958) who noted that nurses often responded to stressful cases by over-intellectualization. Further work related to disasters was carried out by Burkle (1983), who found that at first disaster workers feel ebullient, but eventually their work becomes stressful, particularly if they are exposed to gruesome sights. This is a particularly difficult situation in many cultures such as the United States (Krell, 1978), Australia (Raphael, 1979), and New Zealand (Taylor & Frazier, 1980).

The normal and common process of denial on the part of the victims can affect the psychology of the disaster workers. After the Loma Prieta earthquake (Aptekar, 1991), denial by the victims reduced the pool of victims to be helped by volunteers. However, the call for volunteers came before denial set in so there was an overabundance of mental health volunteers. A problem emerged with what to do with the volunteers. Some volunteer counselors went immediately to counsel, while others had to wait or were placed in less direct service jobs where they were performing paper work. Volunteers in the more favored positions defined and defended their territory. When they perceived that someone might cross over into their domain they became defensive or even argumentative. Because volunteerism was so often based on self-esteem and the need to help others, volunteers who were not in direct counseling service found themselves substantially less happy with volunteering than they had imagined.

Different types of disasters have a different effect on disaster workers (Lindy, Grace, & Green, 1981). A plane crash affects only a small part of the local community, a flood affects the people living in low-lying areas, hurricanes demand the attention of nearly everyone. In the first case disaster workers do not receive much support that lasts beyond the dramatic events; in the other cases they might be heroes in their local community. There are also differences with humanly induced disasters. Workers are sometimes seen as part of the establishment that is being blamed for the occurrence of the disaster. In this case they might be the objects of tremendous amount of displaced anger from victim

The help that many disaster workers require is similar to crisis counseling. Such connections were first noted from studying the victims of the Coconut Grove fire (Cobb & Lindemann, 1943; Lindemann, 1944). Cobb and Lindemann suggested that victims (like disaster workers) are overwhelmed. If they can get rapid help that is consistent with their usual means of dealing with difficulty, they will be helped. They also suggested that clients be limited to talking only about the areas where they feel distress rather than about their more chronic problems.

7

Conclusion

As the victims of Hurricane Hugo, trapped in Lincoln High School, watched the water rise all around them, they prayed for relief. They were willing to make amends for past wrongdoings, to promise to go forth and live a better life should they be saved. But when, miraculously, they walked out into the daylight, had they truly changed? What did the experience mean to them?

The research suggests that they probably changed very little. Those who were functioning well before they endured the storm would emerge to help their neighbors and to rebuild what was left of their homes. Other would continue to lead somewhat dysfunctional lives, returning to the same means of coping that had helped them in the past.

Had this costly disaster of property also been costly in human lives, and only some of the victims in the high school been able to escape, the survivors would have found that the tragedy had left longer-lasting psychological scars. If the survivors had had to save themselves by climbing over human bodies to find an escape, or if they had lost relatives in the hurricane, their recuperation would have been even more difficult. Only the more resilient would have been able to shake loose totally from the horrendous memories.

Psychologically, in spite of the ordeal they had been through, the Lincoln High School victims probably returned to the same level of functioning they had operated on throughout their lives. It is difficult to imagine, however, that their experience will not become an important life event. One can also imagine that having been in the high school late at night without light and with the roar of the tidal surge filling the black void, these people will draw on that experience to generate many stories. Their recollections will be repeated many times—to spouses, to children, to grandchildren. There is power in stories. Clearly, one reason researchers are drawn to studying disaster victims is to tap the powerful experiences that are captured in these stories.

Research about disaster victims almost always comes from the developed world; therefore, it is difficult to know whether victims in the developing world would react like the victims of these studies. We do know that people of traditional societies have changed considerably as a result of environmental disasters. In some societies, these changes have affected almost every aspect of life. After the 1970 avalanche in Yungay, Peru, the Inca and mestizo peoples endured weeks of burying dead family members, but as a result of their ordeal they achieved a sense of power that forced the government in Lima to give them appropriate postdisaster relief. Following floods and droughts in Andhra Pradesh, poor Indians also became knowledgeable for the first time about the political process and were successful in getting equitable relief. After droughts and flooding, the Zapotec of southern Mexico developed a plan for sharing wealth. The Fulanai learned to diversify their herds, change their farming techniques, and expand their trading as a result of drought.

Among the !Kung bushmen of the Kalahari desert, drought now determines where and how they live. Among the Navajo, alliances between kin and family groups changed as a result of drought. Because of drought the Tikopia of the South Pacific rescheduled their adult initiation ceremonies to occur much later, thus introducing what for them was a new developmental phase of life: adolescence. After an earthquake the Inca of Huarez, Peru, moved from a local bartering economy to an urban service economy. Typhoons on the island of Yap caused Yapians to abandon their traditional values and adopt a European lifestyle. Because of Typhoon Ophelia the people of the Micronesian island of Ulithi changed the food they ate, the style of homes they lived in, their habits of work, the way men and women related to each other, their form of government, and even their religion.

The numbers of disaster deaths and injuries are tremendously higher in the developing world than they are in the developed world. Sixty-five people died in the Loma Prieta earthquake in California; a quarter of a million deaths occurred because of the 1976 Tangshen earthquake, which was of similar intensity. There was one death, from a heart attack, during the hurricane in McClellanville; nearly a thousand died from the same storm in the Caribbean and many thousands were left homeless.

Fewer than a hundred died from the 1972 Buffalo Creek flood in West Virginia, but because it was considered so horrendous a disaster it received considerable attention from disaster researchers, many of whom focused on the destruction of the Buffalo Creek community of about 5,000. In the same year Managua, Nicaragua, was destroyed by an earthquake. It killed thousands of people, left tens of thousands homeless, and ultimately caused the collapse of the government—but generated few studies.

For months the attention of the press and much of the nation was focused on the human interest stories that sprang from Hurricane Hugo and the Loma Prieta earthquake. At the same time it was rather difficult to find much information about the numbers of disaster-related tragedies going on in the developing world, even though in the Bay of Bengal between 200,000 and 400,000 people died in a single storm and millions were dying from drought in Africa. Ironically, the immensity of disasters in the developing world obscures the degree of suffering they involve. The numbers of victims are so huge that it becomes difficult to humanize the personal suffering of one individual.

In the developed world almost no one starves as a result of becoming a disaster victim. In the developing world mass starvation is routinely associated with disasters, as the Sahelian and Indian droughts have illustrated. Loss of a home is certainly tragic, but in the developed world this tragedy is relatively mild; homes are almost always replaced through private or government insurance. The developing world has no comparable programs. The events that follow disasters in the developing world often bring on serious political upheavals. In the developed world disasters are rarely, if ever, associated with political changes.

Disasters in the developed world can be explained largely by referring to the physical phenomenon that triggered the catastrophe. This is not true in the developing world where disasters must be understood in the context of how people become vulnerable to environmental hazards. A combination of economic factors drives people to live in vulnerable places in developing countries. They build shacks on the steep hillsides surrounding many Third World cities because it is the only affordable place they can find. A single flood on the Yellow River in China killed almost four million people who lived next to the river, not because they were ignorant of its dangers but because it provided them sustenance.

Economic factors also account for people's choice of what type of house to build. If flimsy wood and cardboard are the only affordable materials with which to build houses in storm areas, the poor will remain particularly vulnerable. If building a house of adobe is the only way a poor person can have a home, those in earthquake zones will continue to be victims.

There has been little change in the number and regularity of extreme environmental events over the centuries, but for economic reasons the numbers of people dying from disasters has increased dramatically in the developing world. At the same time the numbers of victims have decreased in the developed world. The difference between the haves and have nots is found not only in vital health statistics but also in disaster statistics. For each disaster-related death somewhere in the developed world, however poor it might be in comparison to other places in the developed world, there are more than fifteen disaster deaths in developing countries. In the next decade the planet will experience a million thunderstorms; it is unlikely that the most severe of them will cause as much suffering in the developed world as the least severe will cause in the less developed world. In spite of such information, relatively little is known about how the people of the developing world cope with being victimized by disasters.

For the few hours that the victims of Lincoln High School were held hostage to the elements they were able to understand how victims of disasters in other places in the globe must feel when they face similar terror. Reduced to the basics of human emotions, the Lincoln High School victims passed through a cultural barrier that opened the door to understanding some basic human needs and values. This is why they used so many references to God in explaining what had happened to them, and it is why they felt such altruism toward others after they emerged unscathed. The expanded sense of humanity that came to the Lincoln High School victims can be transferred to the victims in the developing world. Such a transfer occurred in the case of the Ethiopian famine. When the media portrayed the human suffering in that country and viewers experienced that pain, although vicariously, there was an outpouring of human response. Seeing the faces of particular children helped viewers feel the human misery in a faraway place.

Such mass altruism certainly helps postdisaster victims, but it fails to get at the root causes of why there are such high numbers of victims in developing countries. People help others for a variety of reasons. It is far more common to help victims of acts of fate (earthquakes, floods, storms) than it is to give help to the poor. Since people are less likely to help the poor until after a disaster strikes, such human suffering is not likely to be reduced.

Large-scale efforts by the international relief agencies are also unlikely to reduce people's vulnerability to disasters. Since there are more disasters than resources can cover, international relief agencies often make decisions about where to send aid based on political factors. In any event, there is little money for the preventive assistance that would help reduce vulnerability.

What constitutes a disaster has also changed over time. Historically, as the world became more industrialized the fear of traditional disasters receded while the fear of humanly induced disasters increased. Sometime in the fifteenth century an earthquake destroyed the major ceremonial buildings of the Mayan culture. Because the social hierarchy of Mayans rested on the assumption that Mayan leaders were in contact with the divine, the destruction caused by the earthquake indicated that the leaders were not in divine grace. All over the empire people lost faith in their leaders and destroyed temples. Some historians have postulated that the sudden and definitive demise of Mayan culture came about because of the fear that the earthquake brought, a fear based on the unknown and unlimited power of the Mayan gods (MacKie, 1961).

By the time of the Lisbon fire in the mid-eighteenth century, many people in the developed world no longer feared extreme natural events as the Mayans did. People of the Enlightenment had adopted a scientific frame of reference for environmental disasters. In spite of our scientific sophistication a degree of fear like that of the Mayans still exists. The fear has been transferred from natural events to those caused by humans— nuclear accidents, poisonous chemical leaks, destructive oil spills, and holes in the ozone layer.

In "traditional" disasters, victims knew relatively quickly how badly they had been hurt. It is difficult to know how badly victimized a person has been in a humanly induced disaster. Only the descendants of Chernobyl victims will know the real level of destruction caused by that incident. Unlike the Lincoln High School victims who can say the hurricane was God's will, the victims of a Chernobyl or a Bhopal know that it was the work of humans who caused their misfortune. Because these victims cannot know how badly they are hurt, they must rely on experts. The victims' fears are changed into anger by the frustration of not knowing the facts, of fearing the worst, and of not trusting the government to tell them how badly they are likely to suffer.

People's anger from humanly induced disasters can be powerful. Many argue that the Chernobyl nuclear disaster of April 26, 1986, contributed to the unraveling of the Soviet Union (Cullen, 1992). On that fateful day radioactive clouds covered much of Byelorussia and Ukraine, yet the Communist government of Ukraine insisted on having its May Day parade as if the radioactive skies posed no problems to the participants. The national government lost its credibility by denying the disaster and misleading people about its consequence. According to Yuri Shcherbak, the current president of Ukraine, "Chernobyl blew the empire to hell. It gave the lie to all the propaganda because it showed that Soviet technology was worthless. The ideological work was false. They had tried to fool their own people. All the flaws of the system came out in Chernobyl" (Cullen, 1992, p. 40).

The countries of the developed world are no longer in danger of being destroyed by traditional disasters; their danger comes from those created by humans—as does the danger to the entire planet. What will future students of disasters say about how we dealt with the threat of humanly produced disasters? One possibility is that there will be no world or students. Another possibility is that the fear associated with the unknown, like the fear the Mayans had of the earthquake and the current fear of humanly induced disasters, will expand to one based on disasters not of this planet but of the solar system. Following the trends of history the magnitude of the potential destruction of environmental disasters will increase. Larger and larger consequences will come from environmental hazards as the forces of nature are incrementally released by human efforts and the boundaries between natural environment and human technology are further blurred.

In 1991 Biosphere II, a controlled environment mimicking a miniature earth, was built outside Tucson, Arizona. (Biosphere I is the real earth.) Eight "biospherians" have committed themselves to live for two years inside the artificially created world. Biosphere II, like the earth, is a closed system that filters air, cleans water, and is capable of producing food. The biospherians will not be able to bring in clean water, fresh air, or new seeds—as indeed we biospherians cannot do.

There are many ways in which these biospherians are unlike earthlings. Rather than living in a world that continually produces more people, they have agreed to refrain from having children. They have planned their resources and have anticipated what their environment can support. They do not face the extremes of weather nor the misfortunes of poverty nor the plagues of war. They are unlikely to have to deal with humanly induced disasters.

In spite of all these differences their experiment still serves as a reminder that the earth is a closed system, frail and endangered. Like those eight, we must be keenly aware of each other, how we treat the environment, and how we get along with one another. Our survival depends upon it. If we can learn to be aware of the individual people who suffer from storms in the Bay of Bengal, from drought in the Sahel, or from radioactivity in Ukraine, we can begin to see how the survival of our world hinges on our ability to depend on others.

Afterword

Recently on a trip to Brazil I had the opportunity to spend a few hours on a beach south of the mouth of the Amazon. After a bus ride, my friends and I were left on the red sand streets of a small town next to the ocean. In the mid-day tropical sun we walked through the town. People were sleeping in hammocks, a few burros were grazing. Our anticipation mounted as we got closer to the sea, waiting for our first sight of a pristine beach. Indeed, the first sight of the white sands and the palm trees held the promise, but as we began to walk along the beach we noticed that something didn't feel right. At first, we were not sure what the black ooze was, and then we knew. It was oil. Our hands smudged as we tried to wipe it off. When we tried wiping our hands on our bathing suits they too were smeared. We tried scraping the oil off with stones, but it only spread more.

As we walked back into town to catch the bus we stopped for something to eat and began to tell the shopowner about our misfortune. Immediately he sent us to the pharmacist who, it turned out, had been making and packaging a special oil cleaner for some time. Our experience was no surprise to him or to the local people. Was the real tragedy the fact that they had already grown accustomed to this human-caused disaster?

Bibliography

Adams, W. C. (1986). Whose lives count?: TV coverage of natural disasters. *Journal of Communications, 36*(2), 113–122.

Adams, David. (1970, January–February). The Red Cross: Organizational sources of operational problems. *American Behavioral Scientist, 13*, 392–403.

Ahearn, Frederick, Jr. (1981, Summer). Disaster mental health—A pre-earthquake and post-earthquake comparison of psychiatric admission rates. *Urban and Social Change Review, 14*, 22–28.

Ahearn, Frederick, & Cohen, Rachel. (1984). *Disasters and mental health: An annotated bibliography*. Rockville, MD: National Institute of Mental Health, Center for Mental Health Studies of Emergencies, U.S. Department of Health.

Alexander, David. (1980, January). The Florence floods—What the papers said. *Environmental Management, 4*, 27–34.

American Psychiatric Association. (1987). *Diagnostic and statistical manual of mental disorders* (3rd ed. rev.). Washington, DC: Author.

Anderson, Mary, & Woodrow, Peter. (1989). *Rising from the ashes: Developing strategies in times of disaster*. Boulder, CO: Westview Press.

Anderson, William. (1969). *Disaster and organizational change: A study of long-term consequences in Anchorage of the 1964 Alaska earthquake*. Columbus: Disaster Research Center, Ohio State University.

Anderson, William. (1970, January–February). Military organizations in natural disasters: Established and emergent norms. *American Behavioral Scientist, 13*, 415–422.

Anderson, William, & Dynes, Russell. (1976). Civil disturbances and social change—A comparative analysis of the United States and Curacao. *Urban Affairs Quarterly, 12*(1), 37–56.

Andrade, Eva Salgado. (1988). Epilogue: One year later. *Oral History Review, 16*(1), 21–31.

Angotti, Thomas. (1977). Playing politics with disaster: The earthquake of Fruili and Belice (Italy). *International Journal of Urban and Regional Research*, *1*, 327–331.

Anicic, D. (1980). *Montenegro, Yugoslavia earthquake, April 15, 1979.* Berkeley, CA: Emergency Earthquake Research Institute.

Anthony, E. James. (1986a). The response to overwhelming stress: Some introductory comments. *Journal of the American Academy of Child Psychiatry*, *25*, 299–305.

Anthony, E. James. (1986b). Terrorizing attacks on children by psychotic parents. *Journal of the American Academy of Child Psychiatry*, *25*, 326–335.

Aptekar, Lewis. (1990). A comparison of the bicoastal disasters of 1989.*Behavior Science Review*, *24*(1–4), 73–104.

Aptekar, Lewis. (1991). *The psychosocial process of adjusting to natural disasters.* Natural Hazards Research and Applications Information Center, Working Paper No. 70. Boulder: Institute of Behavioral Science, University of Colorado.

Aptekar, Lewis, & Boore, J. (1990). The emotional effects of disaster on children: A review of the literature. *International Journal of Mental Health*, *19*(2), 77–90.

Aronoff, Marilyn, & Gunter, Valerie. (1992). Defining disaster: Local construction for recovery in the aftermath of chemical contamination. *Social Problems*, *39*(4), 345–365.

Ayalon, O. (1982). Children as hostages. *The Practitioner*, *224*, 1773–1781.

Baisden, Barbara. (1979). Crisis intervention in smaller communities. In E. J. Miller & R. P. Wolensky (Eds.), *The small city and regional community*, Proceedings of the Second Conference (pp. 325–332). Stevens Points: University of Wisconsin Foundation Press.

Baker, Earl. (1979). Predicting response to hurricane warnings: A reanalysis of data from four studies. *Mass Emergencies*, *4*, 9–24.

Baker, George, & Chapman, Dwight (Eds.). (1962). *Man and society in disaster.* New York: Basic Books.

Ball, N. (1979). Some notes on defining disaster: Suggestions for a disaster continuum. *Disasters*, *3*, 3–7.

Barkun, Michael. (1974). *Disaster and the millennium.* New Haven, CN: Yale University Press.

Barkun, Michael. (1977). Disaster in history. *Mass Emergency*, *2*, 219–231.

Bar-Tal, D., Bar-Zohar, Y., Greenberg, M. S., & Hermon, M. (1977). Reciprocity in the relationship between donor and recipient and between harmdoer and victim. *Sociometry*, *40*, 293–298.

Barton, Allen. (1969). *Communities in disaster: A sociological analysis of collective stress situations.* New York: Doubleday.

Bates, Frederick. (1982). *Recovery, change, and development: A longitudinal study of the 1972 Guatemalan earthquake* (Vol. 1–3). Athens: University of Georgia Press.

Bates, Frederick, Fogleman, Charles, Parenton, Vernon, Pittman, Robert, & Tracy, George. (1963). *The social and psychological consequences of a natural disaster*. National Research Council Disaster Study 18. Washington, DC: National Academy of Sciences.

Bates, Frederick, & Killian, Charles. (1982). An assessment of impact and recovery at the household level. In Federick Bates (Ed.), *Recovery, change, and development: A longitudinal study of the 1976 Guatemalan earthquake* (Vol. 3, pp. 731–791). Athens: University of Georgia Press.

Bates, Frederick, & Peacock, Walter. (1987). Disaster and social change. In Russell Dynes, Bruna de Marchi, & Carlo Pelanda (Eds.), *Sociology of disasters: Contributions of sociology to disaster research* (pp. 291–330). Milano, Italy: Franco Angeli.

Baum, Anthony. (1985). *Toxins, technology, and natural disasters* (Cassette Recording No. 154-297-86A). Washington, DC: American Psychological Association.

Baum, Anthony, & Davidson, Laura. (1985). A suggested framework for studying factors that contribute to trauma in disaster. In B. Sowder (Ed.), *Disasters and mental health: Selected contemporary perspectives* (pp. 29–40). Washington, DC: U. S. Government Printing Office.

Baum, Anthony, Fleming, R., & Davidson, K. (1983). Natural disaster and technological catastrophe. *Environment and Behavior, 15*, 333–354.

Baumann, Duane, & Sims, John. (1974). Human response to the hurricane. In *Natural hazards: Local, national, and global* (pp. 25–30). New York: Oxford University Press.

Beinin, L. (1981). An examination of health data following two major earthquakes in Russia. *Disasters, 5*(2), 142–146.

Belardo, Salvatore, Pazer, Harold, Wallace, William, & Danko, William. (1983, Fall). Simulation of a crisis management information network: A serendipitous evaluation. *Decision Sciences, 14*, 588–606.

Bell, Bill, Kara, Gail, & Batterson, Constance. (1978). Service utilization and adjustment patterns of elderly victims in American disasters. *Mass Emergencies, 3*, 71–81.

Belshaw, C. (1951). Social consequences on the Mount Lamington eruption. *Oceana, 21*, 241–248.

Benedek, Elissa. (1985). Children and disaster: Emergency issues. *Psychiatric Annals, 15*(3), 168–172.

Bennet, G. (1970). Briston floods 1968. Controlled survey of effects on health of local community disaster. *British Medical Journal, 3*, 454–458.

Berren, Michael, Santiago, Jose, Beigel, Allan, & Timmons, Sue. (1989). A classification scheme for disasters. In Richard Gist & Bernard Lubin (Eds.), *Psychosocial aspects of disaster* (pp. 40–58). New York: John Wiley.

Berren, Michael, Beigel, Allan, & Ghertner, Stuart. (1980, Summer). A typology for the classification of disasters. *Community Mental Health Journal, 16*, 103–120.

Bettleheim, Bruno. (1969). *Children of the dream.* New York: MacMillan.

Bjorklund, Birgitta. (1981). *Skredet I TuvelFmailjenoch Dess Bostadssituation* (English Summary). Disaster Studies, 13. Uppsala, Sweden: Department of Sociology, Uppsala University.

Black, G. (1981). *Triumph of the people—the Sandinista revolution in Nicaragua.* London: Zed Press.

Blauford, H., & Levine, J. (1972). Crisis intervention in an earthquake. *Journal of Social Work, 19*, 16–17.

Bloch, David, Perry, Stewart, & Silber, Earle. (1956). Some factors in the emotional reaction of children to disaster. *American Journal of Psychiatry, 113*, 416–422.

Blom, Gaston. (1986). A school disaster—Intervention and research aspects. *Journal of the American Academy of Child Psychiatry, 25*(3), 336–345.

Bode, B. (1974). *Explanation in the 1970 earthquake in the Peruvian Andes* (Ph.D. dissertation, Tulane University). Ann Arbor, MI: University Microfilms.

Boileau, A. M., Cattarinussi, B., Delli Zotti, G., Pelanda, C., Strassoldo, R., & Tellia, B. (1978). *Friuli: La Prova del Terremoto* (in Italian). Milano, Italy: Franco Angeli.

Bolduc, Jean-Pierre. (1987). Natural disasters in developing countries. *Emergency Preparedness Canada, 14*, 12–15.

Bolin, Robert. (1976). Family recovery from natural disaster. *Mass Emergency, 1*, 267–277.

Bolin, Robert. (1982). *Long-term family recovery from disaster.* Boulder: Institute of Behavioral Science, University of Colorado.

Bolin, Robert. (1985). Disaster characteristics and psychosocial impacts. In B. Sowder (Ed.), *Disasters and mental health: Selected contemporary perspectives* (pp. 3–28). Washington, DC: U.S. Government Printing Office.

Bolin, Robert, & Bolton, Patricia. (1983). Recovery in Nicaragua and the U.S.A. *International Journal of Mass Emergencies and Disasters, 1*(1), 125–145.

Bolin, Robert, & Burton, Patricia. (1986). *Race, religion, and ethnicity in disaster recovery.* Boulder: University of Colorado, Institute of Behavioral Science.

Bolin, Robert, & Klenow, Daniel. (1983). Response of the elderly to disaster: An age-stratified analysis. *International Journal of Aging and Human Development, 16*, 283–296.

Bolin, Robert, & Trainer, Patricia. (1978). Modes of family recovery following disaster: A cross-national study. In E. L. Quarantelli (Ed.), *Some basic themes in sociological studies of disasters* (pp. 233–247). Beverly Hills, CA: Sage.

Bommer, Julian. (1985). The politics of disaster—Nicaragua. *Disasters, 9*(4), 270–279.

Breslau, N., & Davis, G. (1987). Post-traumatic stress disorder: The stressor criterion. *Journal of Nervous and Mental Disease, 175*(5), 255–264.

Britton, Neil. (1978, March). The social implications of earthquake predictions and warnings on and for organizations. *Bulletin of the New Zealand National Society for Earthquake Engineering, 11*, 15–18.

Britton, Neil. (1981). What have New Zealanders learned from earthquake disaster in their country? *Disasters, 5*(4), 384–390.

Bromet, Evelyn. (1989). The nature and effects of technological failures. In Richard Gist & Bernard Lubin (Eds.), *Psychosocial aspects of disaster* (pp. 120–139). New York: John Wiley.

Bromet, Evelyn, & Dunn, L. (1981). Mental health of mothers nine months after the Three Mile Island accident. *Urban and Social Change Review, 14*, 12–15.

Bromet, Evelyn, Parkinson, D., & Schulberg, H. (1982). Mental health of residents near the Three Mile Island reactor: A comparative study of selected groups. *Journal of Preventive Psychiatry, 1*, 225–276.

Burke, Jack, Borus, Johnathon, Burns, Barbara, Millstein, Kathleen Hannigan, & Beasley, Mary. (1982, August). Change in children's behavior after a natural disaster. *American Journal of Psychiatry, 139*, 1010–1014.

Burkle, F. M. (1983). Coping with stress under conditions of disaster and refugee care. *Military Medicine, 148*, 800–803.

Burton, Ian, Kates, Robert, & White, Gordon. (1978). *The environment as hazard*. New York: Oxford University Press.

Butcher, J. N. (1980). The role of crisis intervention in an airport disaster plan. *Aviation, Space and Environment Medicine, 512*, 1260–1262.

Butler, John. (1976). *Natural disasters*. Richmond, Victoria, Australia: Heinemann Educational Australia.

Caldwell, Nick, Clark, Andrew, Clayton, Des, Malhotra, Kuldip, & Reiner, Dag. (1979). An analysis of Indian press coverage of the Andhra Pradesh cyclone disaster of 19 November 1977. *Disasters, 3*(2), 154–168.

Cantril, H. (1940). *The invasion from Mars: A study in the psychology of panic*. Princeton, NJ: Princeton University Press.

Caplan, G. (1981). Mastery of stress: Psychological aspects. *American Journal of Psychiatry, 138*, 413–420.

Carey-Trefzer, C. G. (1949). The results of a clinical study of war-damaged children who attended the child guidance clinic. *Journal of Mental Science, 95*, 535–559.

Carter, Michael, Kendall, Stephanie, Clark, John. (1983). Household response to warnings. *International Journal of Mass Emergencies, 1*(1), 95–104.

Cattarinussi, B., & Tellia, D. (1978, April–June). Social response to disaster: The Fruili earthquake (in Italian). *Studi di Sociologia,* 236–254.

Chamberlin, R. J. (1980). Mayo seminars in psychiatry: The psychological aftermath of disaster. *Journal of Clinical Psychiatry, 41*(7), 238–244.

Chandessais, Charles. (1980). The work of Le Centre d'Etudes Psycho-Sociologiques des Sinistres et de leur Prevention (CEPSP) in France. *Disasters, 4*(2), 223–229.

Ciborowski, Adolf. (1967). Some aspects of town reconstuction (Warsaw and Skopje). *Impact, 17,* 31–48.

Clifford, Roy. (1956). *The Rio Grande flood: A comparative study of border communities.* National Research Disaster Study No. 7. Washington, DC: National Academy of Sciences.

Cobb, S., & Lindemann, E. (1943). Neuropsychiatric observations after the Coconut Grove fire. *Annals of Surgery, 117,* 814–824.

Cockburn, A. (1989, November 27). Beat the devil. *The Nation,* 628–629.

Cohen, Elias, & Poulsock, Walter. (1977). Societal response to mass relocation of the elderly. *The Gerontologist, 17,* 262–268.

Cohen, Raquel, & Ahearn, Frederick Jr. (1980). *Handbook for mental health care of disaster victims.* Baltimore, MD: Johns Hopkins University Press.

Colson, Elizabeth. (1979, Spring). In good years and in bad: Food shortages of self-reliant societies. *Journal of Anthropological Research, 35,* 18–29.

Colton, Harold. (1932). Sunset crater: The effects of a volcanic eruption on an ancient Pueblo people. *Geographical Review, 32,* 582–591.

Comfort, Louise (Ed.). (1988). *Managing disaster: Strategies and policy perspectives.* Durham, NC: Duke University Press.

Comfort, Louise. (1990). Turning conflict into cooperation: Organizational designs for community response in disasters. *International Journal of Mental Health, 19*(1), 89–108.

Copans, Jean. (1979). Droughts, famines, and the evolution of Senegal (1966–1978). *Mass Emergencies, 4,* 87–93.

Covello, Vincent. (1983). The perception of technological risks: A literature review. *Technological Forecasting and Social Change, 23,* 285–297.

Crabbs, M. A. (1981). School mental health services following an environmental disaster. *Journal of School Health, 51*(3), 165–167.

Cullen, Robert. (1992, January 27). Report for Ukraine. *The New Yorker,* 37–57.

Cuny, Frederick. (1977). Refugee camps and camp planning: The state of the art. *Disasters, 1*(2), 125–143.

Cuny, Frederick. (1983). *Disasters and development.* Oxford: Oxford University Press.

Cuthbertson, B., & Nigg, Joanne. (1987). Technological disaster and nontherapeutic community: A question of true victimization. *Environment and Behavior, 19*, 462–483.

D'Souza, Frances. (1984, November–December). Disaster research—Ten years on. *Ekistics, 309*, 496–506.

Dacy, Douglas, & Kunreuther, Howard. (1969). *The economics of natural disasters*. New York: Free Press.

Dames and Moore, Inc. (1989). *A social report on the October 17, 1989, Loma Prieta earthquake*. Los Angeles: Author.

Davis, Ian. (1975, January). Disaster housing: A case study of Managua. *Architectural Design*, 42–47.

Davis, Ian. (1977). Emergency shelter. *Disasters, 1*(1), 23–40.

Davis, Morris, & Seitz, Steven. (1982). Disasters and governments. *Journal of Conflict Resolution, 26*(3), 547–568.

de Ville de Goyet, C., del Cid, E., Romero, A., Jeannee, E., & Lechat, M. (1976). Earthquake in Guatemala: Epidemiologic evaluation of the relief effort. *Bulletin of the Pan American Health Organization, 19*(2), 95–109.

Dohrenwend, B. P., Dohrenwend, B. S., Kasl, S., & Warheit, G. (1979). *Report of the Public Health and Safety Task Force on Behavioral Effects to the President's Commission on the Accident at Three Mile Island* (Stock No. 052-003-00732). Washington, DC: U.S. Government Printing Office.

Dombrowsky, Wolf. (1987). Critical theory in sociological disaster research. In Russell Dynes, Bruna de Marchi, & Carlo Pelanda (Eds.), *Sociology of disasters: Contribution of sociology to disaster research* (pp. 331–356). Milano, Italy: Franco Angeli.

Downs, J. R. (1965). The social consequences of a dry well. *American Anthropologist, 67*, 1388–1416.

Drabek, Thomas. (1983, Fall). Shall we leave? A study on family reactions when disaster strikes. *Emergency Management Review, 1*, 25–29.

Drabek, Thomas. (1986). *Human system response to disaster: An inventory of sociological findings*. New York: Springer-Verlag.

Drabek, Thomas. (1987). Emergent structures. In Russell Dynes, Bruna de Marchi, & Carlo Pelanda (Eds.), *Sociology of disasters: Contributions of sociology to disaster research* (pp. 259–290). Milano, Italy: Franco Angeli.

Drabek, Thomas, & Key, W. H. (1976). The impact of disaster on primary group linkages. *Mass Emergencies, 1*, 89–105.

Drabek, Thomas, & Key, William. (1984). *Conquering disaster: Family recovery and long-term consequences*. New York: Irvington Publishers.

Drabek, Thomas, Key, William, Erickson, Patricia, & Crowe, Juanita. (1975, August). The impact of disaster on kin relationships. *Journal of Marriage and the Family, 37*, 481–494.

Drabek, Thomas, & Quarantelli, E. L. (1967, March). Scapegoats, villains, and disasters. *Transactions, 4,* 12–17.

Dudasik, Stephen. (1978). *The socio-cultural effects of natural disaster in a Peruvian highland community* (Ph.D. dissertation, University of Florida). Ann Arbor, MI: University Microfilms.

Dudasik, Stephen. (1980). Victimization in natural disaster. *Disasters, 4*(3), 329–338.

Dudasik, Stephen. (1982). Unanticipated repercussions of international disaster relief. *Disasters, 6*(1), 31–37.

Dupree, Herb, & Roder, Wolf. (1974). Coping with drought in a preindustrial preliterate farming society. In Gilbert White (Ed.), *Natural hazards: Local, national, global* (pp. 115–119). New York: Oxford University Press.

Dworkin, J. (1974). *Global trends in natural disasters 1847–1973.* Natural Hazards Working Paper, No. 26. Boulder: Institute of Behavioral Science, University of Colorado.

Dynes, Russell. (1970a, January–February). Organizational involvement and changes in community structure in disaster. *American Behavioral Scientist, 13,* 430–439.

Dynes, Russell. (1970b). *Organized behavior in disaster.* Lexington, MA: D. C. Heath.

Dynes, Russell. (1972). Cross-cultural studies in disasters. In *Proceedings of the Japan-United States Disaster Research Seminar Organizational and Community Responses to Disasters.* Columbus: Disaster Research Center, Ohio State University.

Dynes, Russell. (1974). *Organization behavior in disasters.* Columbus: Disaster Research Center, Ohio State University.

Dynes, Russell. (1975). The comparative study of disaster: A social organizational approach. *Mass Emergencies, 1,* 21–31.

Dynes, Russell. (1988). Cross-cultural international research: Sociology and disaster. *International Journal of Mass Emergencies and Disasters, 6,* 101–129.

Dynes, Russell, de Marchi, Bruna, & Pelanda, Carlo (Eds.). (1987). *Sociology of disasters: Contributions of sociology to disaster research.* Milano, Italy; Franco Angeli.

Dynes, Russell, & Quarantelli, E. L. (1971). The absence of community conflict in the early phases of natural disaster. In Clagett Smith (Ed.), *Conflict resolution: Contributions to the behavioral sciences* (pp. 200–204). South Bend, IN: University of Notre Dame Press.

Dynes, Russell, & Quarantelli, E. L. (1976a). The family and community context of individual reactions to disaster. In Howard Parad, H. L. Resnick, & Libbie Parad (Eds.), *Emergency and disaster management: A mental health sourcebook* (pp. 231–245). Bowie, MD: Charles Press.

Dynes, Russell, & Quarantelli, E. L. (1976b). Community conflict: Its absence and its presence in natural disasters. *Mass Emergencies, 1*, 139–152.

Ebert, Charles. (1986). Consequences of disasters in developing nations. In Robert Maybury (Ed.), *Violent forces of nature* (pp. 283–292). Mt. Airy, MD: Lamond Publishing.

Edberg, Anna-Karin, & Lustig, Britt-Inger. (1983). *Solidarity and conflict* (in Swedish with English summary). Disaster Studies No. 14. Uppsala, Sweden: University of Uppsala.

Eiser, J. Richard, Hannover, Bettina, Mann, Leon, Morin, Michel, Van Der Plight, Jood, & Webley, Paul. (1990). Nuclear attitudes after Chernobyl: A cross-national study. *Journal of Environmental Psychology, 10*, 101–110.

Ember, Carol, & Ember, Melvin. (1992). Resource unpredictability, mistrust, and war. *Journal of Conflict Resolution, 36*(2), 242–262.

Ember, Carol, Ember, Melvin, & Russett, Bruce. (1992). Peace between participatory politics: A cross-cultural test of the 'democracies rarely fight each other' hypothesis. *World Politics, 44*(4), 573–599.

Ericksen, Neil. (1974). Flood information, expectation, and protection on the Opotiki Floodplain, New Zealand. In Gilbert White (Ed.), *Natural hazards: Local, national, global* (pp. 60–70). New York: Oxford University Press.

Erickson, Eric. (1950). *Childhood and society.* New York: Norton.

Erickson, Patricia, Drabek, Thomas, Key, William, & Crowe, Juanita. (1976). Families in disaster: Patterns of recovery. *Mass Emergencies, 1*, 203–216.

Erikson, Kai. (1976a). *Everything in its path.* New York: Simon & Schuster.

Erikson, Kai. (1976b). Loss of community at Buffalo Creek. *American Journal of Psychiatry, 133*, 302–305.

Farberow, N. L., & Gordon, N. S. (1981). *Manual for child health workers in major disasters.* Rockville, MD: U.S. Department of Health and Human Services.

Federal Emergency Management Association. (1990). *Interagency hazard mitigation team report, Hurricane Hugo.* No. 843 DR/SC. Washington, DC: Federal Emergency Management Agency.

Feldman, Shelley, & McCarthy, Florence. (1983, March). Disaster response in Bangladesh. *International Journal of Mass Emergencies and Disasters, 1*, 105–124.

Fenichel, Otto. (1945). *The psychoanalytical theory of neurosis.* New York: Norton.

Fernandez, Aloysius. (1979). The relationship between disaster assistance and long-term development. *Disasters, 3*(1), 32–36.

Festinger, Leon. (1954). A theory of social comparison processes. *Human Relations, 7*, 117–140.

Festinger, Leon, Riecken, H., & Schachter, S. (1956). *When prophecy fails.* Minneapolis: University of Minnesota Press.

Firth, Raymond. (1959). *Social change in Tikopia.* New York: Macmillan.

Flynn, C. B., & Chalmers, J. A. (1980). *The social and economic effects of the accident at Three Mile Island.* Tempe, AZ: Mountain West Research.

Forrest, Robert. (1977). Group emergence in disasters. In E. L. Quarantelli (Ed.), *Disasters: Theory and research* (pp. 87–1050). Beverly Hills, CA: Sage.

Frazer, M. (1973). *Children in conflict.* Greenwood, Victoria, Australia: Penguin.

Frazier, Kendrick. (1979). *The violent face of nature.* New York: William Morrow.

Frederick, Calvin. (1977). Current thinking about crisis or psychological intervention in United States disasters. *Mass Emergencies, 2,* 43–50.

Frederick, Calvin. (1980). Effects of natural versus human induced violence upon victims. *Evaluation and Change* (Special issue), 71–75.

Freud, Anna, & Burlingham, D. (1944). *War and children.* New York: International University Press.

Freud, Sigmund, & Breuer, Joseph. (1957). Studies in hysteria. In J. Strachey (Ed.), *Standard edition of the complete psychological works of Sigmund Freud.* London: Hogarth Press.

Friesema, H. Paul, Caporaso, James, Goldstein, Gerald, Lineberry, Robert, & McCleary, Richard. (1979). *Aftermath: Communities after natural disaster.* Beverly Hills, CA: Sage Publications.

Fritz, Charles. (1957). Disasters compared in six American communities. *Human Organization, 16,* 6–9.

Fritz, Charles. (1961). Disasters. In Robert Merton & Robert Nisbet (Eds.), *Contemporary social problems* (pp. 651–694). New York: Harcourt.

Fritz, Charles. (1968). Disasters. In D. Sills (Ed.), *International encyclopedia of the social sciences* (pp. 202–207). New York: Macmillan.

Furman, Erna. (1983). Studies in childhood bereavement. *Canadian Journal of Psychiatry, 28*(4), 241–247.

Galante, Rosemarie, & Foa, Dario. (1986). An epidemiological study of psychic trauma and treatment effectiveness for children after a disaster. *Journal of American Academy of Child Psychiatry, 25,* 357–363.

Garmezy, Norman. (1986). Children under stress: Critique and commentary. *Journal of the American Academy of Child Psychiatry, 25,* 384–392.

Geipel, Robert. (1982). *Disasters and reconstruction: The Friuli (Italy) earthquakes of 1976.* London: George Allen & Unwin.

Glantz, Michael (Ed.). (1976). *The politics of natural disaster: The case of the Sahel drought.* New York: Praeger.

Gleser, Goldine, Green, Bonnie, & Winget, Carolyn. (1981). *Prolonged psychosocial effects of disaster: A study of Buffalo Creek.* New York: Academic Press.

Goffman, Erving. (1971). *Encounters: Two studies in the sociology of interaction.* New York: Bobbs-Merrill.

Goldstein, Raymond, Schorr, John, & Goldstein, Karen. (1984, November). What's the matter with those people: Rethinking TMI. *International Journal of Mass Emergencies, 2,* 369–387.

Golec, Judith. (1983, August). A contextual approach to the social psychological study of disaster recovery. *International Journal of Mass Emergency and Disasters, 1,* 255–276.

Graham, Frank. (1990, January). Matchsticks. *Audubon,* pp. 44–51.

Grecu, G., Csiky, K., & Munteanu, I. (1972, March). Study on a group of 87 patients with depressive states triggered by the floods of May 1970, in *Rumania. Neurologia, Psichiatria, Neurochirugia, 17,* 109–115.

Green, Bonnie. (1980). Prediction of long-term psychosocial functioning following the Beverly Hills fire (Ph.D. dissertation, University of Cincinnati). Ann Arbor, MI: University Microfilms.

Green, Bonnie. (1982). Assessing levels of psychological impairment following disaster. *Journal of Nervous and Mental Disease, 70,* 544–552.

Green, Bonnie, Lindy, J., & Grace, M. C. (1985). Post-traumatic stress disorder: Toward DSM-IV. *Journal of Nervous and Mental Disease, 173*(7), 406–411.

Green, Stephen. (1977). *International disaster relief: Toward a responsive system.* New York: McGraw-Hill.

Haas, Eugene, & Drabek, Thomas. (1973). *Complex organizations: A sociological perspective.* New York: Macmillan.

Haas, Eugene, Cochrane, Harold, & Eddy, Donald. (1976). *The consequences of large-scale evacuation following disaster: The Darwin Australia cyclone disaster of December 25, 1974.* Natural Hazards Research Working Paper No. 27. Boulder: Institute of Behavioral Science, University of Colorado.

Haas, Eugene, Kates, Robert, & Bowden, Martyn (Eds.). (1977). *Reconstruction following disaster.* Cambridge, MA: MIT Press.

Hagman, Gunnar. (1984). *Prevention better than cure.* Stockholm: Swedish Red Cross.

Hall, Jerry. (1983). The place of climatic hazards in food scarcity: A case study of Belize. In Kenneth Hewitt (Ed.), *Interpretations of calamity* (pp. 140–161). Boston: Allen & Unwin.

Hammarstrom-Tornstram, Gunhild. (1977). Warning process (in Swedish with English summary). *Disaster Studies, 5.* Uppsala, Sweden: University of Uppsala.

Handford, H. Allen, Dickerson, Susan, Mattison, Richard, Humphrey, Frederick, Bagnato, Stephen, Bixler, Edward, & Kales, Joyce. (1986). Child and parent reaction to the Three Mile Island nuclear accident. *Journal of the American Academy of Child Psychiatry, 25,* 346–356.

Hartsough, D. M., & Myers, D. G. (1985). *Disaster work and mental health: Prevention and control of stress among workers.* Rockville, MD: National Institute of Mental Health.

Hays, Walter. (1990). *The U.S. decade for natural disaster reduction.* Unpublished manuscript. Presented at the 15th Annual Hazards Research and Applications Workshop, July 17, Boulder, Colorado.

Helzer J. E., Robins, L. N., & McCuny, L. (1987). Post-traumatic stress disorder in the general population: Findings of the epidemiologic catchment area survey. *New England Journal of Medicine, 317,* 1630–1634.

Henderson, Scott, & Bostock, Tudor. (1977, July). Coping behavior after shipwreck. *British Journal of Psychiatry, 131,* 15–20.

Hersey, John. (1966). *Hiroshima.* Sydney: Penguin.

Hewitt, Kenneth. (1983a). Climatic hazards and agricultural development: Some aspects of the problem in the Indo-Pakistan subcontinent. In Kenneth Hewitt (Ed.), *Interpretations of calamity: From the viewpoint of human ecology* (pp. 181–201). Boston: Allen & Unwin.

Hewitt, Kenneth (Ed.). (1983b). *Interpretations of calamity: From the viewpoint of human ecology.* Boston: Allen & Unwin.

Hirose, Hirotada. (1979). Volcanic eruptions and local politics in Japan: A case study. *Mass Emergencies, 4,* 53–62.

Hocking, F. (1965). Human reaction to extreme environmental stress. *Medical Journal of Australia, 2,* 477–482.

Hocking, F. (1970a). Extreme environmental stress and its significance for psychopathology. *American Journal of Psychotherapy, 24,* 4–26.

Hocking, F. (1970b). Psychiatric aspects of extreme environmental stress. *Diseases of the Nervous System, 31,* 542–545.

Hodge, David, Sharp, Virginia, & Marts, Marion. (1979). Contemporary responses to volcanism: Case studies from the Cascades to Hawaii. In Payson Sheets & Donald Gray (Eds.), *Volcanic activity and human ecology* (pp. 221–248). New York: Academic Press.

Hogg, Sara Jane. (1980). Reconstruction following seismic disaster in Venzone, Friuli. *Disasters, 4*(2), 173–185.

Holy, Ladislav. (1980). Drought and change in a tribal economy: The Berti of Northern Darfur. *Disasters, 4*(1), 65–71.

Horowitz, Mardi. (1986a). Disaster stress studies: Conclusions. In James Shore (Ed.), *Disaster stress studies: New findings and methods* (pp. 141–149). Washington, DC: American Psychiatric Press.

Horowitz, Mardi. (1986b). *Stress response syndromes.* New York: Jason Aronson.

Horowitz, Mardi. (1990). Post-traumatic stress disorders: Psychosocial aspects of the diagnosis. *International Journal of Mental Health, 19*(1), 21–36.

Horowitz, Mardi, Wilner, N., Kaltreider, N., & Alvarez, W. (1980). Signs and symptoms of post-traumatic stress disorder. *Archives of General Psychiatry,* *37*, 85–92.

Houts, Peter, Miller, Robert, Ham, Sum Shik, & Tokuhata, George. (1980). Extent and duration of psychological distress of persons in the vicinity of Three Mile Island. *Proceedings of the Pennsylvania Academy of Science, 54,* 22–28.

Houts, P. S., & Goldhaber, M. K. (1981). Psychological and social effects on the population surrounding Three Mile Island after the nuclear accident on March 28, 1979. In J. Majumdar (Ed.), *Energy, environment and the economy* (pp. 152–164). Easton: Pennsylvania Academy of Sciences.

Howard, S. J. (1980). Children and the San Bernando earthquake. *Earthquake Information Bulletin, 12*(5), 190–192.

Hultaker, Orjan. (1976). Evacuate (in Swedish with English summary). *Disaster Studies, 2.* Uppsala, Sweden: University of Uppsala.

Hultaker, Orjan, & Trost, Jan. (1976). The Family and the shelters. *Disaster Studies, 1.* Uppsala, Sweden: Uppsala University.

Ikeda, Ken'ichi. (1982). Warning of disaster and evacuation behavior in a Japanese chemical fire. *Journal of Hazardous Materials, 7,* 51–62.

Irish, J. L., & Falconer, B. (1979). Reaction to flood warning. In R. L. Heathcote & B. G. Thom (Eds.), *Natural hazards in Australia* (pp. 313–329). Canberra: Australian Academy of Science.

Janis, I. L., & Mann, L. (1977). *Decision making: A psychological analysis of conflict, choice, and commitment.* New York: Free Press.

Jeffery, Susan. (1980). Universalistic statements about human social behavior. *Disasters, 4*(1), 111–112. p73

Kanlasty, Krzyztof, Norris, Fran, & Murrell, Stanley. (1990). Received and perceived social support following natural disaster. *Journal of Applied Social Psychology, 20*(2), 85–114.

Kates, Robert. (1977). Major insights: A summary and recommendations. In Eugene Haas, Robert Kates, & Martyn Bowden (Eds.), *Reconstruction following disaster* (pp. 261–293). Cambridge, MA: MIT Press.

Kates, Robert, Haas, Eugene, Amaral, Daniel, Olson, Robert, Ramos, Reyes, & Olson, Richard. (1973). Human impact of the Managua earthquake: Transitional societies are peculiarly vulnerable to natural disasters. *Science, 182,* 981–990.

Kasperson, R. E., & Pijawka, K. D. (1985). Societal response to hazards and major hazards events: Comparing natural and technological hazards. *Public Administration Review, 45,* 7–18.

Keesing, Felix. (1952). The Papuan Orokaive vs. Mount Lamington: Cultural shock and its aftermath. *Human Organization, 11*(1), 16–22.

Kelly, H. H. (1967). Attribution theory in social psychology. In D. Levine (Ed.), *Nebraska symposium on motivation* (Vol. 15, pp. 192–240). Lincoln: University of Nebraska.

Kent, Randolph. (1987). *Anatomy of disaster relief: The international network in action*. London: Printer Publishers.

Kilijanek, Thomas, & Drabek, Thomas. (1979). Assessing long-term impacts of a natural disaster: A focus on the elderly. *The Gerontologist, 19*, 555–566.

Killian, Lewis. (1952). The significance of multiple-group membership in disaster. *American Journal of Sociology, 57*, 309–314.

Kinster, Warren, & Rosser, Rachel. (1974, December). Disaster: Effects on mental and physical state. *Journal of Psychosomatic Research, 18*, 437–456.

Kinzie, J. David, Sack, William, Angell, Richard, Manson, S., & Rath, Ben. (1986). The psychiatric effects of massive trauma on Cambodian children: I, the children. *Journal of the American Academy of Child Psychiatry, 25*(3), 370–376.

Kirby, Anne. (1974). Individual and community response to rainfall variation in Oaxaca, Mexico. In Gilbert White (Ed.), *Natural disasters: Local, national, and global* (pp. 437–456). New York: Oxford University Press.

Klingman, A. (1987). A school-based emergency crisis intervention. *Professional Psychology: Research and Practice, 18*(6), 604–612.

Kreimer, Alcira. (1978). Post-disaster reconstruction planning: The cases of Nicaragua and Guatemala. *Mass Emergencies, 3*, 23–40.

Krell, George. (1978, August). Managing the psychosocial factor in disaster programs. *Health & Social Work, 3*, 139–154.

Kreps, Gary. (1985). Disaster and the social order. *Sociological Theory, 3*(1), 49–64.

Kreps, Gary. (1989). Future directions in disaster research: The role of taxonomy. *International Journal of Mass Emergencies and Disasters, 7*(3), 215–241.

Kunreuther, Howard. (1978). *Disaster insurance protection: Public policy lessons*. New York: Wiley.

Lacey, G. N. (1972). Observation on Aberfan. *Journal of Psychosomatic Research, 16*, 257–260.

Langer, William. (1958). The next assignment. *The American Historical Review, 63*, 283–304.

Lazarus, R., & Cohen, J. (1977). Environmental stress. In I. Altman & J. Wholwill (Eds.), *Human behavior and environment: Current theory and research* (pp. 89–127). New York: Plenum.

Lechat, Michel. (1976, June). The epidemiology of disasters. *Proceedings of the Royal Society of Medicine, 69*, 421–426.

Lee, R. B. (1972). !Kung spatial organization: An ecological and historical perspective. *Human Ecology, 1*, 125–148.

Bibliography   181

Leik, Robert, Carter, Michael, & Clark, John. (1981). *Community response to natural hazard warnings: Final report*. Minneapolis: University of Minnesota.
Leik, Robert, Leik, Sheila, Ekker, Knut, & Gifford, Gregory. (1982). *Under the threat of Mount St. Helens: A study of chronic family stress*. Minneapolis: Family Study Center, University of Minnesota.
Leivesley, Sally. (1977). Toowoomba: Victims and helpers in an Australian hailstorm disaster. *Disasters, 1*(3), 205–216.
Lessa, William. (1964). The social effects of the Typhoon Ophelia (1960) on Ulithi. *Micronesia, 1*, 1–47.
Levine, Adeline. (1982). *Love Canal: Science, politics, and people*. Toronto: Lexington.
Lifton, Robert Jay. (1967). *Survivors of Hiroshima: Death in life*. New York: Random House.
Lifton, Robert Jay, & Olson, Eric. (1976, February). The human meaning of total disaster: The Buffalo Creek experience. *Psychiatry, 39*, 1–18.
Lindemann, E. (1944). Symptomatology and management of acute grief. *American Journal of Psychiatry, 101*, 141–148.
Lindy, Jacob. (1985). The trauma membrane and other clinical concepts derived from psychotherapeutic work with survivors of natural disasters. *Psychiatric Annals, 15*(3), 153–160.
Lindy, Jacob, Grace, Mary, & Green, Bonnie. (1981, July). Survivors: Outreach to a reluctant population. *American Journal of Orthopsychiatry, 5*, 468–478.
Loizos, Peter. (1977). A struggle for meaning: Reactions to disaster amongst Cypriot refugees. *Disasters, 1*(3), 231–239.
Lystad, Mary. (1984). Children's responses to disaster: Family implications. *International Journal of Family Psychiatry, 5*(1), 41–48.
MacKie, Evan. (1961). New light on the end of classic Maya culture at Benque Viejo, British Honduras. *American Antiquities, 27*, 216–224.
Mader, George, Spangle, William, & Blair, Martha. (1980). *Land use planning after earthquakes*. Portola Valley, CA: William Spangle and Associates.
Malmquist, Carl. (1986). Children who witness parental murder: Posttraumatic aspects. *Journal of the American Academy of Child Psychiatry, 25*, 320–325.
Margolis, Maxine. (1979), Green gold and ice: The impact of frosts on the coffee growing regions of Northern Parana, Brazil. *Mass Emergencies, 4*, 135–144.
Mark, Hans, & Carver, Larry. (1987). Challenger and Chernobyl. *Interdisciplinary Science Reviews, 12*(3), 241–252.
Marshall, Mac. (1979, Fall). Natural and unnatural disaster in the Mortlock Islands of Micronesia. *Human Organization, 38*, 265–272.
Maybury, Robert (Ed.). (1986). *Violent forces of nature*. Mt. Airy, MD: Lamond.
Mayer, Jean. (1974, October). Coping with famine. *Foreign Affairs, 53*(1), 98–120. McFarlane, A. C. (1984). The Ash Wednesday bushfires in South

Australia: Implications for planning future post-disaster services. *Medical Journal of Australia, 141,* 286–291.

McFarlane, A. C. (1986). Long-term psychiatric morbidity after a natural disaster. *Medical Journal of Australia, 145,* 561–567.

McFarlane, A. C. (1990). An Australian disaster: The 1983 bushfires. *International Journal of Mental Health, 19*(2), 36–47.

McIntire, M. S., & Sadeghi, E. (1977). The pediatrician and mental health in a community-wide disaster. *Clinical Pediatrics, 16,* 702–705.

McLuckie, Benjamin. (1970). *A study of functional response to stress in three societies* (Ph.D. Dissertation, Columbus, Ohio State University).

McLuckie, Benjamin. (1977). *Italy, Japan, and the United States: Effects of centralization on disaster responses 1964–1969.* The Disaster Research Center Historical and Comparative Disaster Series, No. 1. Columbus: Disaster Research Center, Ohio State University.

Melick, M. E. (1985). The health of post-disaster populations: A review of the literature and case study. In J. Loube & S. Murphy (Eds.), *Perspectives on disaster recovery* (pp. 179–209). Norwalk, CT: Appleton-Century-Crofts.

Menninger, Carl. (1952, August). Psychological reactions in an emergency (flood). *American Journal of Psychiatry, 109,* 128–130.Merryman, James. (1982). Pastoral nomad settlement in response to drought: The case of the Kenya Somali. In Art Hansen & Anthony Oliver-Smith (Eds.), *Involuntary migration and resettlement: The problems and response of dislocated people* (pp. 105–120). Boulder, CO: Westview Press.

Merton, Robert. (1969). Foreword. In Allen Barton, *Communities in disaster: A sociological analysis of collective situations* (pp. vii–xxxvii). New York: Doubleday. Midlarsky, Elizabeth. (1968). Aiding responses: An analysis and review. *Merrill-Palmer Quarterly, 14,* 229–260.

Mileti, Dennis. (1983). Societal comparisons of organizational response to earthquake predictions: Japan versus the United States. *International Journal of Mass Emergencies and Disasters, 1*(3), 399–415.

Mileti, Dennis. (1987). Sociological methods and disaster research. In Russell Dynes, Bruna de Marchi, & Carlo Pelanda (Eds.), *Sociology of disasters: Contributions of sociology to disaster research* (pp. 57–69). Milano, Italy: Franco Angeli.

Mileti, Dennis. (1989). Social impact and emergency response. *Earthquake Spectra, 5* (supplement), 150–161.

Mileti, Dennis, Drabek, Thomas, & Haas, Eugene. (1975). *Human systems in extreme environments: A sociological perspective.* Monograph No. 21. Boulder: Institute of Behavioral Science, University of Colorado.

Mileti, Dennis, Hartsough, Donald, Madson, Patti, & Hufnagel, Rick. (1984, March). The Three Mile Island incident: A study of behavioral indicators of human stress. *International Journal of Mass Emergencies and Disasters, 2*, 89–113.

Mileti, Dennis, & Nigg, Joanne. (1984). Earthquakes and human behavior. *Earthquake Spectra, 1*(1), 89–106.

Milne, Gordon. (1977). Cyclone Tracy, 2: The effects on Darwin children. *Australian Psychologist, 12*, 55–62.

Milne, Gordon. (1979). Cyclone Tracy: Psychological and social consequences. In Joan Innes Reid (Ed.), *Planning for people in natural disasters* (pp. 116–123). Townsville, Queensland, Australia: James Cook University of North Queensland.

Mitchell, Jeffory. (1983). When disaster strikes . . . The critical incident stress debriefing process. *Journal of Emergency Medical Services, 8*, 36–39.

Mitchell, William. (1976a). Reconstruction after disaster—Gediz earthquake of 1970. *Geographical Review, 66*, 296–313.

Mitchell, William. (1976b). *The Lice earthquake of Southeastern Turkey: A geography of the disaster.* Final Report. Colorado Springs, CO: Department of Economics, Geography, and Management, United States Air Force Academy.

Moore, Harry. (1958). *Tornadoes over Texas.* Austin: University of Texas Press.

Moore, Harry, Bates, Frederick, Layman, Marvin, & Parenton, Verson. (1963). *Before the wind: A study of response to Hurricane Carla.* National Academy of Sciences/National Research Council Disaster Study No. 10. Washington, DC: National Academy of Sciences.

Moore, Herbert. (1958). Some emotional concomitants of disaster. *Mental Hygiene, 42*, 45–50.

Morentz, James. (1976). *The making of an international event: Communication and the drought in West Africa* (Ph.D. dissertation, Department of Political Science, University of Pennsylvania).

Morren, George. (1983). A general approach to the identification of hazards and responses. In Kenneth Hewitt (Ed.), *Interpretations of calamity: From the viewpoint of human ecology* (pp. 284–297). Boston: Allan & Unwin.

Nakano, Takamasa, & Matsuda, Iware. (1984, September–October). Earthquake damage, damage prediction and countermeasures in Tokyo, Japan. *Ekistics, 308*, 415–420.

Nakamura, Y. (1981). Helping behavior in a disaster. In Hirotada Hirose (Ed.), *Socio-scientific approach to disaster* (pp. 165–194). Tokyo, Japan: Shinyosha

Newman, Janet. (1976, March). Children of disaster: Clinical observations at Buffalo Creek. *American Journal of Psychiatry, 133*, 306–312.

Nolan, Mary Lee. (1979). Impact of Paricutin on five communities. In Payson Sheets & Donald Grayson (Eds.), *Volcanic activity and human ecology* (pp. 293–338). New York: Academic Press.

Ohta, Hideaki. (1972). Evacuating characteristics of Tokyo citizens. In *Proceedings of the Japan–United States disaster research seminar:*

Organizational and community responses to disasters (pp. 175–183). Columbus: Disaster Research Center, Ohio State University.

Ohta, Hideaki, & Abe, Kitao. (1977). Responses to earthquake prediction in Kawasaki City, Japan, in 1974. In C. Kisslinger & Z. Suzuki (Eds.), *Earthquake precursors: Proceedings of the U.S.–Japanese seminar on theoretical and experimental investigations of earthquake predictors* (pp. 273–282). Tokyo: Center for Academic Publications Japan, Japan Scientific Societies Press.

Okabe, Keizo. (1981). *A disaster warning and responses of residents: A study of evacuation behavior after a warehouse fire in Ohbu City*. Tokyo: Institute of Journalism and Communications, University of Tokyo.

O'Leary, Michael. (1980). Responses to drought in Kitui District, Kenya. *Disasters, 4*(3), 315–468.

Oliver, John. (1975). The significance of natural hazards in a developing area: A case study from North Queensland. *Geography, 60,* 99–110.

Oliver, John, & Reardon, G. F. (1982). *Tropical Cyclone Isaac: Cyclonic impact in the context of the society and economy of the Kingdom of Tonga*. Townsville, Queensland, Australia: Center for Disaster Studies, James Cook University.

Oliver-Smith, Anthony. (1977). Disaster rehabilitation and social change in Yungay, Peru. *Human Organization, 36*(1), 5–13.

Oliver-Smith, Anthony. (1979a). Post disaster consensus and conflict in a traditional society: The 1970 avalanche of Yungay, Peru. *Mass Emergencies, 4,* 39–52.

Oliver-Smith, Anthony. (1979b). The Yungay avalanche of 1970: Anthropological perspectives on disaster and social change. *Disasters, 3*(1), 95–101.

Oliver-Smith, Anthony, & Hansen, Art. (1982). Involuntary migration and resettlement: Causes and contexts. In Art Hansen & Anthony Oliver-Smith (Eds.), *Involuntary migration and resettlement: The problems and responses of dislocated people* (pp. 1–12). Boulder, CO: Westview Press.

Ollendick, Duane, & Hoffman, Sister Margeen. (1982, April). Assessment of psychological reactions in disaster victims. *Journal of Community Psychology, 10,* 157–167.

Olson, Robert, & Olson, Richard. (1977). The Guatemala earthquake of 4 February 1976: Social science observations and research suggestions. *Mass Emergencies, 2,* 69–81.

Pararas-Carayannis, George. (1986). The effects of tsunami on society. In Robert Maybury (Ed.), *Violent forces in nature* (pp. 157–168). Mt. Airy, MD: Lamond Publishing.

Parker, Gordon. (1977, June). Cyclone Tracy and Darwin evacuees: On the restoration of the species. *British Journal of Psychiatry, 130,* 548–555.

Parker, Ronald. (1989). Proyecto nueva vida Armero: Armero, Colombia. In Mary Anderson & Peter Woodrow (Eds.), *Rising from the ashes: Developing strategies in times of disaster* (pp. 157–183). Boulder, CO: Westview Press.

Parr, Arnold. (1970, January–February). Organizational response to community crisis and group emergence. *American Behavioral Scientist, 13,* 423–429.

Patrick, V., & Patrick, W. K. (1981, March). Cyclone 78 in Sri Lanka: The mental health trail. *British Journal of Psychiatry, 138,* 210–216.

Paulozzi, Leonard. (1980). Great myths in disaster relief—Epidemics. *Journal of Environmental Health, 43*(3), 140–143.

Peacock, Walter, & Bates, Frederick. (1982). Ethnic differences in earthquake impact and recovery. In Frederick Bates (Ed.), *Recovery, change, and development: A longitudinal study of the 1976 Guatemalan earthquake* (Vol. 3, pp. 792–892). Athens: University of Georgia Press.

Pelanda, Carlo. (1981). *Disaster and sociosystemic vulnerability.* Preliminary Paper 68. Columbus: Disaster Research Center, Ohio State University.

Penick, Elizabeth, Powell, B. J., & Sieck, W. A. (1976, January). Mental health problems and natural disaster: Tornado victims. *Journal of Community Psychology, 4,* 64–68.

Perry, Joseph, Hawkins, Randolph, & Neal, David. (1983, March). Giving and receiving aid. *International Journal of Mass Emergencies and Disasters, 1,* 171–188.

Perry, Ronald. (1983, January). Population evacuation in volcanic eruptions, floods, and nuclear power plant accidents: Some elementary comparisons. *Journal of Community Psychology, 11,* 36–47.

Perry, Ronald, & Greene, Marjorie. (1982, Fall). The role of ethnicity in the emergency decision-making process. *Sociological Inquiry, 52,* 306–334.

Perry, Ronald, Greene, Marjorie, & Mushkatel, Alvin. (1983). *American minority citizens in disaster.* Seattle: Battelle Human Affairs Research Center.

Perry, Ronald, & Hirose, Hirotada. (1983, August). Volcanic eruptions and functional change: Parallels in Japan and the United States. *International Journal of Mass Emergencies and Disasters, 1,* 231–253.

Perry, Ronald, & Lindell, Michael. (1978). The psychological consequences of natural disaster: A review of research on American communities. *Mass Emergencies, 3,* 105–115.

Perry, Ronald, Lindell, Michael, & Greene, Marjorie. (1981). *Evacuation planning in emergency management.* Lexington, MA: Lexington Books.

Perry, Ronald, Lindell, Michael, & Greene, Marjorie. (1982). Crisis communications: Ethnic differences in interpreting and acting on disaster warnings. *Social Behavior and Personality, 10*(1), 97–104.

Perry, Ronald, & Mushkatel, Alvin. (1984). *Disaster management: Warning response and community relocation.* Westport, CT: Quorum Books.

Perry, Stewart, Silber, Earle, & Black, Donald. (1956). *The child and his family in disaster: A study of the 1953 Vicksburg tornado.* National Academy of Sciences/National Research Council Disaster Study No. 5. Washington, DC: National Academy of Sciences. Petak, William, & Atkisson, Arthur. (1982). *Natural hazards risk assessment and public policy: Anticipating the unexpected.* New York: Springer-Verlag.

Phifer, James, & Norris, Fran. (1989). Psychological symptoms in older adults following natural disaster: Nature, timing, duration, and course. *Journal of Gerontology, 44*(6), 207–217.

Philips, Brenda. (1991). *Post-disaster sheltering and housing of Hispanics, the elderly and the homeless.* Dallas, TX: Department of Sociology, Southern Methodist University.

Plafker, George, & Galloway, John (Eds.). (1990). *Lessons learned from the Loma Prieta, California, earthquake of October 17, 1989.* United States Geological Circular 1045. Washington, DC: U.S. Government Printing Office.

Ploeger, A. A. (1970). A 1-year follow up of miners trapped for 2 weeks under threatening circumstances. In D. Spielberger & I. G. Sarason (Eds.), *Stress and anxiety* (Vol. 4). Washington, DC: Hemisphere.

Podesta, Bruno, & Olson, Richard. (1988). Science and the state in Latin America: Decisionmaking in uncertainty. In Louise Comfort (Ed.), *Managing disaster: Strategies and policy perspectives* (pp. 296–312). Durham, NC: Duke University Press.

Poniatowska, Elena. (1988, Spring). The earthquake: To Carlos Monsivais. *Oral History Review, 16*(1), 7–20.

Predescu, V., & St. Nica-Udangiu. (1979). Postseismic reactions. Observations on a group of patients displaying psychic disorders determined by March 4, 1977 earthquake in Rumania. *Revue Roumaine de Medecine-Neurologie et Psychiatrie, 17*(3), 179–188.

President's Commission on the Accident at Three Mile Island. (1979). *The need for change: The legacy of Three Mile Island.* Report of the Commission. Washington, DC: U.S. Government Printing Office.

Prince, Samuel. (1920). *Catastrophe and social change.* New York: Colombia University Press.

Py, Y. (1978). Comptements dans us cas de secours d'urgence (in French). *Le Travail Humain, 41*(1), 67–80.

Quarantelli, E. L. (1954). The nature and condition of panic. *American Journal of Sociology, 60,* 187–194.

Quarantelli, E. L. (1957). The behavior of panic participants. *Sociology and Social Research, 41,* 187–194.

Quarantelli, E. L. (1977). Panic behavior: Some empirical observations. In Donald J. Conway (Ed.), *Human response to tall buildings* (pp. 336–350). Stroudsbug, PA: Dowden, Huthchinson and Ross.

Quarantelli, E. L. (1979). Some needed cross-cultural studies of disaster behavior. *Disasters, 3*(3), 307–314.

Quarantelli, E. L. (1980). *Evacuation behavior and problems: Findings and implications from the research literature.* Columbus: Disaster Research Center, Ohio State University.

Quarantelli, E. L. (1984, November–December). Perceptions and reactions to emergency warnings of sudden hazards. *Ekistics, 309,* 511–515.

Quarantelli, E. L. (1988, Spring). Assessing disaster preparedness planning: A set of criteria and their applicability to developing countries. *Regional Development Dialogue, 9*(1), 48–69.

Quarantelli, E. L. (1990). *Some aspects of disaster planning in developing countries.* Disaster Research Center Preliminary Paper No. 144. Newark: University of Delaware.

Quarantelli, E. L., & Dynes, Russell. (1972, February). When disaster strikes (It isn't much like what you've heard and read about). *Psychology Today, 5,* 66–70.

Quarantelli, E. L., & Dynes, Russell. (1976). Community conflict: Its absence and its presence in natural disasters. *Mass Emergencies, 1,* 139–152.

Quarantelli, E. L., & Dynes, Russell. (1977). Response to social crisis and disaster. *Annual Review of Sociology, 3,* 23–49.

Quarantelli, E. L., & Wenger, Dennis. (1990). *A cross-societal comparison of disaster news reporting in Japan and the United States.* Preliminary Paper No. 146. Newark: Disaster Research Center, University of Delaware.

Raigrodski, E. (1987). *Technological disasters and mental health: An annotated bibliography.* Rockville, MD: National Institute of Mental Health.

Raphael, Beverly. (1975). Crisis and loss: Counseling following a disaster. *Mental Health in Australia, 1,* 118–122.

Raphael, Beverly. (1979). The preventive psychiatry of natural hazard. In R. L. Heathcote & B. G. Thom (Eds.), *Natural hazards in Australia* (pp. 330–339). Canberra: Australian Academy of Science.

Raphael, Beverly. (1983). *The anatomy of bereavement.* New York: Basic Books.

Raphael, Beverly. (1986). *When disaster strikes: How individuals and communities cope with catastrophe.* New York: Basic Books.

Rayner, J. F. (1958). How do nurses behave in disaster? *Nursing Outlook , 6,* 572–576.

Rescorla, L. A. (1986). Preschool psychiatric disorders: Diagnostic classification and symptom patterns. *Journal of the American Academy of Child Psychiatry, 25,* 162–182.

Riddington, Robin. (1982, Spring). When poison gas comes down like a fog—A native community's response to cultural disaster. *Human Organization, 41*(1), 36–42.

Riding, Alan. (1977, November 6). U.S. food aid seen hurting Guatemala. New *York Times*, p. 53.

Robins, Lee, Fischbach, Ruth, Smith, Elizabeth, Cottler, Linda, Soloman, Susan, & Goldring, Evelyn. (1986). Impact of disaster on previously assessed mental health. In James Shore (Ed.), *Disaster stress studies: New methods and findings* (pp. 21–48). Washington, DC: American Psychiatric Press.

Robins, Lee, & Smith, Elizabeth. (1983). *Diagnostic interview schedule/disaster supplement.* St. Louis: Washington University School of Medicine.

Rosengren, Karl, Arvisson, Peter, & Sturesson, Dahn. (1979). The Arsebak panic: A radio program as a negative summary event. *Acta Sociologica, 57*, 309–314.

Rossi, Peter, Wright, James, Weber-Burdin, Eleanor, & Pereira, Joseph. (1983). Victimization by natural hazards in the United States, 1970–1980. *International Journal of Mass Emergencies and Disasters, 1*(3), 467–482.

Rossi, Peter, Wright, James, Wright, Sonia, & Weber-Burdin, Eleanor. (1978). Are there long term effects of American natural disasters? *Mass Emergencies, 3*, 117–132.

Rossi, Peter, Wright, James, Wright, Sonia, & Weber-Burdin, Eleanor. (1978b). Are there long term effects of American natural disasters? Estimation of effects of floods, hurricanes, and tornadoes occurring 1960 to 1970 on U.S. counties and census tracts in 1970. *Mass Emergencies, 3,*117–132.

Rubin, Claire, & Popkin, Roy. (1991). *Disaster recovery after Hurricane Hugo in South Carolina.* Boulder: Institute of Behavioral Science, University of Colorado.

Rubin, David. (1987, June). How the news media reports serious nuclear power plant accidents. *Emergency Preparedness Digest, 14*, 10–14.

Rubonis, A., & Bickman. L. (1986). *A meta-analytic review of psychological impairment in the wake of disaster.* Unpublished manuscript. Nashville, TN: Program Evaluation Laboratory, Peabody College, Vanderbilt University.

Sack, William, Angell, Richard, Kinzie, J. David, & Rath, Ben. (1986). The psychiatric effects of massive trauma on Cambodian children: II, the family, the home, and the school. *Journal of the American Academy of Child Psychiatry, 25*(3), 377–383.

Saunders, Sarah Lee, & Kreps, Gary. (1987). The life history of the emergent organization in times of disaster. *Journal of Applied Behavioral Science, 23*(4), 443–462.

Scanlon, Joseph. (1980). The media and the 1978 terrace floods: An initial test of a hypothesis. In *Disasters and the mass media.* Proceedings of the Committee on Disasters and the Mass Media workshop, February, 1979, Committee on Disasters and the Mass Media. Washington, DC: National Academy of Sciences.

Schneider, David. (1957, Summer). Typhoons on Yap. *Human Organization, 16*, 10–15. Schur, M. (1966). *The id and the regulatory process of the ego.* New York: International University Press.

Schware, Robert. (1982, May). Official and folk flood warning systems: An assessment. *Environment Management, 6*, 209–216.

Schware, Robert, & Lippoldt, Douglas. (1982). An examination of community flood warning systems: Are we providing the right assistance? *Disasters, 6*(3), 195–202.

Scott, R. B. (1968). *The relevance of the prophets.* New York: Macmillan.

Seitz, Steven, & Davis, Morris. (1984, August). The political matrix of natural disasters: Africa and Latin America. *International Journal of Mass Emergencies and Disasters, 2*, 231–250.

Seroka, C. M., Knapp, C., Knight, S., Siemon, C. R., & Starbuck, S. (1982). A comprehensive program for postdisaster counseling. *Social Casework: The Journal of Contemporary Social Work, 67*(1), 37–44.

Shah, Bindi. (1983). Is the environment becoming more hazardous? A global survey 1947 to 1980. *Disasters, 7*(3), 202–209.

Shaw, Robert. (1979). Health services in a disaster—Lessons learned from the 1975 Vietnamese evacuation. *Military Medicine, 144*(5), 15–20.

Sheets, Payson. (1979). Environmental and cultural effects of the Hopango eruption in Central America. In Payson Sheets & Donald Grayson (Eds.), *Volcanic activity and human ecology* (pp . 525-564). New York: Academic Press.

Shore, James, Tatum, Ellie, & Vollmer, William. (1986a). The Mount St. Helens stress response syndrome. In James Shore (Ed.), *Disaster stress studies: New findings and methods* (pp. 77–98). Washington, DC: American Psychiatric Press.

Shore, James, Tatum, Ellie, & Vollmer, William. (1986b). Psychiatric reactions to disaster: The Mt. St. Helens experience. *American Journal of Psychiatry, 143*, 590–595.

Short, Patricia. (1979). Victims and helpers. In R. L. Heathcote & B. G. Thom (Eds.), *Natural hazards in Australia* (pp. 448–459). Canberra: Australian Academy of Science.

Silber, Earle, Perry, Stewart, & Bloch, David. (1957). Patterns of parent-child interaction in a disaster. *Journal of Psychiatry, 21*, 159–167.

Silver, R., & Wortman, C. B. (1980). Coping with undesirable life events. In J. Garber & E. P. Seligman (Eds.), *Human helplessness theory and applications* (pp. 279–375). New York: Academic Press.

Sims, John, & Baumann, Duane. (1972). The tornado threat: Coping styles of the north and south. *Science, 176*, 1386–1392.

Simpson-Housley, Paul, & Bradshaw, Peter. (1978, April). Personality and the perception of earthquake hazard. *Australian Geographical Studies, 16*, 65–72.

Singer, Timothy. (1982, March). An introduction to disaster: Some considerations of a psychological nature. *Aviation, Space, and Environmental Medicine, 53*, 245–250.

Sjoberg, Gideon. (1962). Disasters and social change. In George Baker & Dwight Chapman (Eds.), *Man and society in disaster* (pp. 356–384). New York: Basic Books.

Smith, Bob. (1989, October 19). It may not be over yet. *Watsonville Register-Pajaronian.*

Smith, D. I., Handmer, J., & Martin, W. (1980). *The effects of floods on health: Hospital admission for Lismore.* Canberra: Australian National University.

Smith, Elizabeth. (1984). *Chronology of disasters in Eastern Missouri.* Contract No. 83-MH-525181. Rockville, MD: National Institute of Mental Health.

Smith, Elizabeth, Robins, Lee, Przybeck, Thomas, Goldring, Evelyn, & Soloman, Susan. (1986). Psychosocial consequences of a disaster. In James Shore (Ed.), *Disaster stress studies: New methods and findings* (pp. 49–76). Washington, DC: American Psychiatric Press.

Smith, Keith, & Tobin, Graham. (1979). *Human adjustment to the flood hazard.* London: Longman.

Snarr, Neil, & Brown, Leonard. (1984, September–October). Disaster aid in rural Honduras: The villager's point of view. *Ekistics, 308*, 483–486.

Solomon, Susan. (1985). Enhancing social support for disaster victims. In Barbara Sowder (Ed.), *Disasters and mental health: Selected contemporary perspectives* (pp. 107–121. Washington, DC: U.S. Government Printing Office.

Soloman, Susan. (1989). Research issues in assessing disaster's effects. In Richard Gist & Bernard Lubin (Eds.), *Psychosocial aspects of disaster* (pp. 308–340). New York: John Wiley.

Sood, Rahul, Stockdale, Geoffrey, & Rogers, Everett. (1987, Summer). How the news media operate in natural disasters. *Journal of Communications, 37*(3), 27–41.

Sorokin, Pitirim. (1942). *Man and society in calamity.* New York: Dutton.

Sorenson, John, & Gersmehl, Philip. (1980, March). Volcanic hazard warning system: Persistence and transferability. *Environmental Management, 4*, 125–136.

Sowder, B. (1985). Some mental health impacts of loss and injury: A look outside the disaster field. In B. Sowder (Ed.), Disasters and mental health: Selected contemporary perspectives (pp. 74–106). DDHS Publication No. ADM 14-8521. Washington, DC: U.S. Government Printing Office.

Spencer, Harrison, Romero, Arturo, Feldman, Roger, Campbell, Carlos, Zeissig, Otto, Boostrom, Eugene, & Long, E. Croft. (1977, July 23). Disease surveillance and decision making after the 1976 Guatemalan earthquake. *The Lancet,* 181–184.

Spillius, James. (1957). Natural disaster and political crisis in a Polynesian society. *Human Relations, 10,* 3–27, 113–124.

Spitz, P. (1977). *Silent violence: Famine and inequality.* Geneva: United Nations.

Stallings, Robert. (1978). The structural patterns of four types of organizations in disaster. In E. L. Quarantelli (Ed.), *Disasters: Theory and research* (pp. 87–103). Beverly Hills, CA: Sage.

Stallings, Robert, & Quarantelli, E. L. (1985, January). Emergent citizen groups and emergency management. *Public Administration Review, 45,* 93–100.

Stein, Sherry. (1974). An earthquake shakes up a mental health system. In A. Tulipan, C. L. Attneave, & E. Kingstone (Eds.), *Beyond clinic walls* (pp. 34–45). University: University of Alabama Press.

Susman, Paul, O'Keefe, Phil, & Wisner, Ben. (1983). Global disasters, a radical interpretation. In Kenneth Hewitt (Ed.), *Interpretations of calamity* (pp. 263–283). Boston: Allen & Unwin.

Syren, Sverker. (1981). The Tuve landslide-organized activities (in Swedish with English summary). *Disaster Studies, 10.* Uppsala, Sweden: Uppsala University.

Takuma, Taketoshi. (1972). Immediate responses at disaster sites. In E. L. Quarantelli (Ed.), *Proceedings of the Japan–United States disaster research seminar: Organizational and community responses to disasters* (pp. 184–195). Columbus: Disaster Research Center, Ohio State University.

Taylor, Alan J. (1979). Directions for social research in disaster prevention, mitigation, and relief. *Disasters, 3,* 275–281.

Taylor, Alan J. (1983, March–April). Hidden victims and the human side of disasters. *UNDRO News, 12,* 6–9.

Taylor, Alan, & Frazier, A. (1980, April 23). Interim report of the stress effects on the recovery teams after the Mt. Erebus disaster, November, 1979. *New Zealand Medical Journal, 91,* 311–312.

Taylor, James, Zurcher, Louis, & Key, William. (1970). *Tornado: A community responds to disaster.* Seattle: University of Washington Press.

Taylor, S. E., Wood, J. V., & Lichtman, R. R. (1983). It could be worse: Selective evaluation as a response to victimization. *Journal of Social Issues, 39,* 19–40.

Taylor, Verta. (1977). Good news about disaster. *Psychology Today, 11*(5), 124, 126.

Taylor, Verta, Alexander, G., & Quarantelli, E. L. (1976). *Delivery of mental health services in disasters: The Xenia tornado and some implications.* Disaster Research Center Book and Monograph Series No. 11. Columbus: Disaster Research Center, Ohio State University.

Terr, Lenore. (1981a). Psychic trauma in children: Observations following the Chowchilla school-bus kidnaping. *American Journal of Psychiatry, 138,* 14–19.

Terr, Lenore. (1981b). Forbidden games. *Journal of the Academy of Child Psychiatry, 20*, 741–760.

Terr, Lenore. (1990). *Too scared to cry*. New York: Harper & Row.

Thompson, E. P. (1971). The moral economy of the English crowd during the eighteenth century. *Past and Present, 50*, 76–115.

Tierney, Kathleen. (1989). The social and community contexts of disaster. In Richard Gist & Bernard Lubin (Eds.), *Psychosocial aspects of disaster* (pp. 11–39). New York: John Wiley.

Tierney, Kathleen, & Baisden, Barbara. (1979). *Crisis intervention programs for disaster victims: A sourcebook and manual for smaller communities*. Rockville, MD: National Institute of Mental Health.

Tiranti, Dexter. (1977). The un-natural disasters. *New Internationalist, 53*, 5–6.

Titchener, James, & Kapp, Frederick. (1976). Family and character change at Buffalo Creek. *American Journal of Psychiatry, 133*, 295299.

Torry, William. (1978a, Fall). Bureaucracy, community, and natural disasters. *Human Organization, 37*, 302–308.

Torry, William. (1978b, July–October). Natural disasters, social structure and change in traditional societies. *Journal of Asian and African Studies, 13*, 167–183.

Torry, William. (1979a). Anthropology and disaster research. *Disasters, 3*(1), 43–52.

Torry, William. (1979b). Intelligence, resilience and change in complex social systems: Famine administration in India. *Mass Emergencies, 2*, 71–85.

Trabing, Wally. (1989, November 2). Fifteen minutes was all they got. *Santa Cruz Sentinel*.

Trainer, Patricia, & Bolin, Robert. (1976, October). Persistent effects of disasters on family activities: A cross-cultural perspective. *Mass Emergencies, 1*, 279–290.

Trost, Jan, & Hultaker, O. (1983). Family in disaster. *International Journal of Mass Emergencies and Disasters, 1* (Special Edition).

Tuckman, A. (1973). Disaster and mental health intervention. *Community Mental Health Journal, 9*, 151–157.

Turner, Ralph. (1976). Earthquake prediction and public policy: Distillations from a national academy of sciences report. *Mass Emergencies, 1*, 179–202.

Turner, Ralph. (1983, August). Waiting for disasters: Changing reactions to earthquake forecasts in Southern California. *International Journal of Mass Emergencies and Disasters, 1*, 307–334.

Turner, Ralph, Nigg, Joanne, Paz, Denise Heller, & Young, Barbara Shaw. (1981). *Community response to earthquake threat in Southern California. Part ten: Summary and recommendations*. Los Angeles: Institute for Social Science Research, University of California.

Tyhurst, J. S. (1951). Individual reactions to community disaster: Natural history of psychiatric phenomena. *American Journal of Psychiatry, 107*, 764–769.

Tyhurst, J. S. (1957). Psychological and social aspects of civilian disaster. *Canadian Medical Association Journal, 76*, 385–393.

U.S. Department of Commerce, National Bureau of Standards. (1974). *Design, siting, and construction of low-cost housing and community buildings to better withstand earthquakes and windstorms.* Washington, DC: U.S. Government Printing Office.

Valent, P. (1983). A conceptual framework for understanding the impact of disasters. *Australian Clinical Psychologist, 15*(2), 12–25.

Valent, P. (1984). The Ash Wednesday bushfires in Victoria. *Medical Journal of Australia, 141*, 291–300.

Vayda, Andrew, & McCay, Bonnie. (1975). New directions in ecology and ecological anthropology. In *Annual Review of Anthropology, 4*, 293–306.

Verney, Peter. (1979). *The earthquake handbook.* New York: Paddington Press.

Vinso, Joseph. (1977). Financial implications of natural disasters: Some preliminary indications. *Mass Emergencies, 2*, 205–217.

Waddell, Eric. (1975). How the Enga cope with frost: Responses to climatic perturbations in the central highlands of New Guinea. *Human Ecology, 3*(4), 249–273.

Waddell, Eric. (1983). Coping with frost, governments and disaster experts: Some reflections based on a New Guinea experience and a perusal of the relevant literature. In Kenneth Hewitt (Ed.), *Interpretations of calamity: From the viewpoint of human ecology* (pp. 33–43). London: Allen & Unwin.

Wallace, Anthony. (1956). *Tornado in Worcester.* National Academy of Sciences/National Research Council Disaster Study #3. Washington, DC: National Academy of Sciences.

Ward, Peter, & Page, R. (1990). *The Loma Prieta earthquake of October 17, 1989.* United States Geological Survey. Washington, DC: U.S. Government Printing Office.

Warheit, George. (1985). A prepositional paradigm for estimating impact of disasters on mental health. *Mass Emergencies and Disasters, 3*, 29–48.

Watts, Michael. (1979). The etiology of hunger: The evolution of famine in a Sudano-Sahelian region. *Mass Emergencies, 4*, 95–104.

Weber, Max. (1968). *Economy and society: An outline of interpretive sociology.* Guenther Roth & Claus Wittich (Eds.), 3 Vols. New York: Bedminster Press.

Weisaeth, L. (1983). *The study of a factory fire* (Doctoral dissertation, University of Oslo). Ann Arbor, MI: University Microfilms.

Wells, Melissa. (1984, November–December). We can improve relief efforts—If we try. *Ekistics, 309*, 501–506.

Wenger, Dennis. (1980). The nature of panic behavior. In B. M. Levin & R. L. Paulsen (Eds.), *Second international seminar on human behavior in fire emergencies* (pp. 214–219). Washington, DC: National Bureau of Standards.

Wenger, Dennis, James, Thomas, & Faupel, Charles. (1985). *Disaster beliefs and emergency planning.* New York: Irvington. Werner, E., & Smith, R. (1982). *Vulnerable but invincible: A longitudinal study of resilient children and youth.* New York: McGraw-Hill.

Westgate, Kenneth. (1978). Hurricane response and hurricane perception in the Commonwealth of the Bahamas (1). *Mass Emergencies, 3,* 251–265.

Wettenhall, R. L. (1979a). Disaster and social structure in Australia. *Disasters, 2*(4), 241–245.

Wettenhall, R. L. (1979b). Organization and disaster: The 1967 bushfires in southern Tasmania. In B. L. Heathcote & B. G. Thom (Eds.), *Natural hazards in Australia* (pp. 431–435). Canberra: Australian Academy of Science.

White, Gilbert. (1945). *Human adjustment to floods.* Department of Geography Research Paper No. 29. Chicago: University of Chicago.

White, Gilbert. (1974). *Natural hazards: Local, national, global.* New York: Oxford University Press.

Whyte, Anne. (1980). *Survey of households evacuated during the Mississauga chlorine gas emergency November 10–16, 1979.* Toronto: Emergency Planning Project, Institute for Environmental Studies, University of Toronto.

Wijkman, Anders, & Timberlake, Lloyd. (1988). *Natural disasters: Acts of God or acts of man?* Philadelphia, PA: New Society Publishers.

Wilkenson, C. B. (1985). Introduction: The psychological consequences of disasters. *Psychiatric Annals, 153*(3), 135–139.

Wilkenson, C. B., & Vera, E. (1985). The management and treatment of disaster victims. *Psychiatric Annals, 15*(3), 174–184.

Wilkins, L. (1987). *Shared vulnerability: Media coverage and public memory of the Bhopal disaster.* Westport, CT: Greenwood Press.

Wisner, Ben. (1978). An appeal for a significantly comparative method in disaster research. *Disasters, 2*(1), 80–82.

Wisner, Ben. (1979). Flood prevention and mitigation in the People's Republic of Mozambique. *Disasters, 3,* 293–306.

Wisner, Ben, O'Keefe, Phil, & Westgate, Ken. (1977). Global systems and local disasters: The untapped power of people's science. *Disasters, 1*(1), 47–57.

Worth, Marti, & McLuckie, Benjamin. (1977). *Get to the high ground! The warning process in the Colorado floods June 1965.* Disaster Research Center Historical and Comparative Disaster Series, Columbus: Disaster Research Center, Ohio State University.

Wortman, C. B. (1983). Coping with victimization: Conclusions and implications for research. *Journal of Social Issues, 39*(2), 195–221.

Wright, James, & Rossi, Peter (Eds.). (1981). *Social science and natural hazards*. Cambridge, MA: Abt Books.

Wright, James, Rossi, Peter, Wright, Sonia, & Weber-Burdin, Eleanor. (1979). *After the clean-up: Long range effects of natural disasters*. Beverly Hills, CA: Sage.

Yamamoto, Yasumasa, & Quarantelli, E. L. (1982). *Inventory of the Japanese disaster research literature in the social and behavioral sciences*. Columbus: Disaster Research Center, Ohio State University.

Yates, Suzane, Anson, Danny, Bickman, Leonard, & Howe, George. (1989). Factors influencing help seeking for mental health services after disasters. In Richard Gist & Bernard Lubin (Eds.) *Psychosocial aspects of disaster* (pp. 163–189). New York: John Wiley.

Yin, Robert, & Moore, Gwendolyn. (1985). *The utilization of research: Lessons learned from the natural hazards field*. Washington, DC: Cosmos Corporation.

Index

196